Expertise, Authority and Control

THE AUSTRALIAN ARMY MEDICAL CORPS IN
THE FIRST WORLD WAR

Expertise, Authority and Control charts the development of Australian military medicine in the First World War in the first major study of the Australian Army Medical Corps in more than seventy years and reveals that it is about much more than one man and his donkey. It begins with an examination of the provision of medical care to Australian soldiers during the Gallipoli campaign and analyses the imperial and medical–military hierarchies that were blended and challenged during the campaign. It then investigates the work of the AAMC on the Western Front and in England, which was conducted in Gallipoli's shadow. By the end of 1918, the AAMC, transformed by its experiences in battle and behind the lines, was a radically different organisation from that of 1915.

The history of the AAMC in the war is a story of the renegotiation of authority over and responsibility for wartime medicine. Drawing on army orders, unit war diaries and memoranda, Alexia Moncrieff maps the provision of medical care through casualty clearance and evacuation, rehabilitation, and the prevention and treatment of venereal disease. In doing so, she reassesses Australian military medicine during the First World War and charts the development of Australian medical–military practice in the field, especially in response to conflicts between traditional imperial, military and medical authorities.

Alexia Moncrieff is a Postdoctoral Research Fellow in the School of History at the University of Leeds.

OTHER TITLES IN THE AUSTRALIAN ARMY HISTORY SERIES

Series editor: Peter Stanley

EXPERTISE, AUTHORITY AND CONTROL

THE AUSTRALIAN ARMY MEDICAL CORPS IN THE FIRST WORLD WAR

ALEXIA MONCRIEFF

CAMBRIDGE
UNIVERSITY PRESS

CAMBRIDGE
UNIVERSITY PRESS

University Printing House, Cambridge CB2 8BS, United Kingdom

One Liberty Plaza, 20th Floor, New York, NY 10006, USA

477 Williamstown Road, Port Melbourne, VIC 3207, Australia

314–321, 3rd Floor, Plot 3, Splendor Forum, Jasola District Centre, New Delhi – 110025, India

79 Anson Road, #06–04/06, Singapore 079906

Cambridge University Press is part of the University of Cambridge.

It furthers the University's mission by disseminating knowledge in the pursuit of
education, learning and research at the highest international levels of excellence.

www.cambridge.org
Information on this title: www.cambridge.org/9781108478151

First published 2020

Cover designed by Anne-Marie Reeves
Typeset by SPi Global
Printed in Singapore by Markono Print Media Pte Ltd, December 2019

A catalogue record for this publication is available from the British Library

A catalogue record for this book is available from the National Library of Australia

ISBN 978-1-108-47815-1 Hardback

CONTENTS

FIGURES, MAPS AND TABLES

PREFACE

The Australian Army has a long and admirable record in fostering serious research and publication about its history. From its outset 'Military History' was part of the formal education of officers at RMC Duntroon, and for a time officers' promotion depended upon candidates being able to give a coherent analysis of Stonewall Jackson's Shenandoah Valley campaigns in promotion exams. An understanding of the Army's history and traditions remains central to its *esprit de corps* in its most literal meaning.

From the 1970s (as a consequence of educating officers at university level), the Army has produced several generations of educated soldiers, several of whom became historians of note, including John Coates, Robert O'Neill, David Horner, Peter Pedersen, John Mordike, Bob Hall, Jean Bou, Bob Stevenson and Craig Stockings. The creation of an Army History Unit in the late 1990s demonstrated the Army's commitment to encouraging and facilitating serious history.

One of the most impressive demonstrations of the Army's commitment to history has been its long association with several major publishers, and notably with Cambridge University Press. This has been a productive relationship brokered by Dr Roger Lee and my predecessor as General Editor, Professor David Horner.

The Cambridge Army History Series brings to an academic and popular readership historical work of importance across the range of the Army's interests and across the span of its history. The series seeks to publish research and writing of the highest quality relating not only to the Army's operational experience but also to its existence as an organisation and as a part of its contribution to the national narrative.

The Army History Unit has created a community of writers and readers (including soldiers in both roles), the product of whose questions, research, debate and writing informs the Army's understanding of itself and its part in Australia's history. It is a history to be proud of in every sense.

Dr Alexia Moncrieff's study of the Australian Army Medical Corps on Gallipoli and the Western Front represents one of the first and certainly the most substantial academic treatments of the subject in many years, perhaps surprisingly, given the centrality of mass wounding to the history of Australians in that war. Dr Moncrieff's book demonstrates why we can no longer simply rely on Arthur Butler's official medical history, but need to re-examine the experience in the light of new evidence (which she has done) and in the context of international military medical scholarship. The results reflect credit on the AAMC and its members, a finding worth bringing to the attention of their successors a century on.

Professor Peter Stanley
General Editor, Australian Army History Series
UNSW Canberra

ACKNOWLEDGEMENTS

This book, and the research on which it is based, would not have been possible without the knowledge, expertise and skill of librarians, archivists and museum professionals at a range of institutions. I am grateful to the staff of the Australian War Memorial, The National Archives (UK), National Library of Scotland, Wellcome Library, Imperial War Museum, Museums Victoria, Libraries Tasmania, State Library of Queensland, State Library of South Australia, National Library of Australia and the National Archives of Australia. Additionally, the staff at the Liddell Hart Centre for Military Archives at King's College London, went above and beyond in their efforts to help me. Furthermore I thank the trustees of these archives and libraries for permission to quote from their collections. Margaret Hosking's ability to hunt down any obscure source, her intimate knowledge of the Barr Smith Library's collections and her enthusiasm for my project added immeasurably to both the outcome of my research and the experience of conducting it.

This book started its life as a PhD thesis. Accordingly, my thanks go to my supervisors, Dr Paul Sendziuk and Professor Robin Prior, for their advice, support and feedback. My examiners, Professor Mark Harrison and Dr John Connor, provided insightful comments and suggestions for developing my thesis for publication, and I am grateful to them and my reviewers for helping shape my ideas. My thanks go to the trustees of the Hugh Martin Weir Prize, administered through the Barr Smith Library, for their financial assistance towards the end of my candidature, and particularly to Glen and Robina Weir, whose enthusiasm for my work has extended beyond my time as a student. I am also thankful for the camaraderie and friendship of my contemporaries at the University of Adelaide: Dr Christopher Bridge, Dr Jodie Martin, Dr Elsa Reuter, Dr Fidelma Breen, Dr Jill MacKenzie and Dr Clare Parker.

Cambridge University Press and I thank Michael Walsh and Andrekos Vaarnava for permission to reuse text from the proceedings of *The British Empire and the Great War: Colonial Societies/Cultural Responses* in

February 2014, publicised as Alexia Moncrieff, 'Establishing Australian Medical–Military Expertise: The Gallipoli Landings' in Michael Walsh and Andrekos Varnava (eds), *Australia and the Great War: Identity, Memory and Mythology*, Melbourne University Press, Melbourne, 2016, pp. 40–53, in Chapter 1 of this book.

The Australian Army History Unit provided significant support at key moments in the development of this book. Through its Research Grants Scheme, it provided the financial assistance that enabled me to undertake archival research for my doctorate, both interstate and overseas. Furthermore, I am grateful for the unit's generosity in funding this series with Cambridge University Press, for which I thank the head of the unit, Tim Gellal, as well as Dr Andrew Richardson and Nick Anderson for all they have done to produce this book. Additionally, I thank the Series Editor, Professor Peter Stanley, for his advice and assistance, as well as Siobhan Privitera, Michael Spurr, Alison Dean, Olivia Tolich and everyone at CUP for their efforts, particularly their help navigating the publishing process for the first time. My thanks also go to Cathryn Game for her meticulous editing of the manuscript.

Since arriving at the University of Leeds in 2016, I have had the good fortune to work alongside some wonderful people in the School of History and as part of the Legacies of War project. My particular thanks go to Dr Will Jackson, who has been a source of encouragement, solidarity and guidance, and to Dr Jessica Meyer and Professor Alison Fell, whose insights and feedback have shaped my work in important ways. The friendship and support of Dr Jessica Hammett, Dr Claire Eldridge, Dr Alan MacLeod, Dr Marie-Louise Leonard, Dr Sara Barker and Dr Tom Smith have kept me sane while being a long way from home. Thank you.

I am indebted to some incredible women who work in military history. The Chicks of War support, encourage and assist each other with wit and humour, and their capacity for generosity might well be infinite. I am particularly grateful to Dr Meleah Hampton, who taught me how to do archival research, as well as Dr Aimée Fox and Miesje de Vogel, who photographed sources in London and Canberra when I could not get to them. My deepest gratitude goes to Dr Effie Karageorgos and Dr Kate Ariotti. I cannot thank them enough for their constant support and friendship, their enthusiasm for this project and their scholarly generosity in reading drafts and discussing ideas and sources.

The academic collegiality of numerous First World War scholars has been beneficial in the writing of this book. I am grateful to the scholars – too many to name individually – I have met at conferences around the world, who discussed my ideas and helped test out my arguments. I have benefited enormously from the kindness and insights of Dr Bart Ziino, who also provided reassurance and guidance in moments of doubt. I owe a debt of gratitude to Dr Matthew Haultain-Gall, who read almost every word of this book and provided thoughtful feedback. His interest in and enthusiasm for my research came at a critical time, and I am incredibly thankful for his generosity and encouragement.

I would like to express my sincere gratitude to those who supported this research in other ways. Charlotte Marshall and Dr Alison George have been sources of wisdom and sanity. Lisa Jarrett provided expert assistance at a key moment. Additionally, many people in Australia and the UK provided me with spare rooms to sleep in, home-cooked meals and social sustenance in the many months spent travelling for research and conferences. I thank you all.

Finally, and most importantly, I thank my husband, James Moncrieff. He willingly enlisted as research assistant, technical support and barista-in-chief while I was writing my thesis, and then he lived with the process a second time while I turned my thesis into a book. I could not have done this without his patience, humour, love and care.

NOTE ON STYLE

Throughout this book, both Anzac and ANZAC are used. ANZAC signifies the acronym of Australian and New Zealand Army Corps and refers to the military unit(s), whereas Anzac is used in discussions of the Anzac spirit or Anzac legend.

As much as possible, the original wording, grammar and spelling have been retained when quoting from sources. In a number of instances, the punctuation in the original text significantly detracts from its readability and so the punctuation has been altered and an indication given in the endnotes. None of these grammatical interventions alters the meaning of the quotes.

When referring to an individual's rank and position, I have used their rank at the time the source was produced; hence, some individuals are referred to in multiple ways.

ABBREVIATIONS

1AD	1st Australian Division
2AD	2nd Australian Division
3AD	3rd Australian Division
4AD	4th Australian Division
5AD	5th Australian Division
AAH	Australian auxiliary hospital
AAMC	Australian Army Medical Corps
AAMS	Australian Army Medical Services
AANS	Australian Army Nursing Service
AA&QMG	Assistant Adjutant and Quartermaster General
ACCS	Australian Casualty Clearing Station
ACD	Australian command depot
ADH	Australian Dermatological Hospital
ADMS	Assistant Director of Medical Services
ADS	advanced dressing station
AFA	Australian Field Ambulance
AGH	Australian General Hospital
AIF	Australian Imperial Force
AMC	Army Medical Corps
ANMEF	Australian Naval and Military Expeditionary Force
ANZAC	Australian and New Zealand Army Corps
ASH	Australian Stationary Hospital
AWM	Australian War Memorial
BEF	British Expeditionary Force
CCS	casualty clearing station

CGS	Chief of the General Staff
CO	Commanding Officer
DADMS	Deputy Assistant Director of Medical Services
DAG	Deputy Adjutant General
DAQMG	Deputy Adjutant and Quartermaster General
DC	Dardanelles Commission
DDMS	Deputy Director of Medical Services
DGAMS	Director General, Army Medical Services
DGMS	Director General, Medical Services
DMS	Director of Medical Services
GHQ	General Headquarters
GOC	General Officer Commanding
GP	general practitioner
LHCMA	Liddell Hart Centre for Military Archives (at King's College London)
MDS	main dressing station
MEF	Mediterranean Expeditionary Force
MO	Medical Officer
NAA	National Archives of Australia
NCCVD	National Council for the Combating of Venereal Disease
NCO	non-commissioned officer
NLS	National Library of Scotland
NZEF	New Zealand Expeditionary Force
OC	Officer Commanding
PDMS	Principal Director of Medical Services
PHTO	Principal Hospital Transport Officer
PUO	Pyrexia of Unknown Origin
QMG	Quartermaster General
RAMC	Royal Army Medical Corps
RAP	regimental aid post
RDS	reserve dressing station
RMO	Regimental Medical Officer
RSPCA	Royal Society for the Prevention of Cruelty to Animals

SMO	Senior Medical Officer
TNA	The National Archives (UK)
UK	United Kingdom
VAD	Voluntary Aid Detachment
VC	Victoria Cross
VD	venereal disease
WAAC	Women's Auxiliary Army Corps
WL	Wellcome Library
YMCA	Young Men's Christian Association

INTRODUCTION
MORE THAN A MAN AND HIS DONKEY

On 25 April 1915, when John Simpson Kirkpatrick set foot on the Gallipoli peninsula as part of the Australian Imperial Force (AIF), it is unlikely that he had an inkling of the frequency with which his story would be told, retold and mistold to generations of Australians. Nor is it likely he had any idea of the extent to which that story would grow, distort and become part of Australia's national creation myth. The idea that the Australian nation was 'born on the shores of Gallipoli' through the sacrifice, endurance, initiative, resourcefulness, mateship and larrikinism of the Anzacs codified the First World War as a moment of national significance in the formation of an Australian identity. Kirkpatrick's story is entirely enmeshed in this myth-making; as 'Australia's most famous stretcher-bearer', he has come to embody both the 'Anzac spirit' and the work of the Australian Army Medical Corps (AAMC) in the First World War.[1]

Born in South Shields, County Durham, in 1892, Kirkpatrick joined the British merchant navy in 1909 and deserted his ship in Newcastle, New South Wales, in 1910. He worked as a labourer in Australia until the outbreak of the First World War when, in an attempt to get free passage home to England, Kirkpatrick enlisted in the AIF as John Simpson, dropping his surname in what appears to have been an attempt to hide his previous desertion. He became a private in the 3rd Australian Field Ambulance, a unit of the AAMC, and embarked for war only to find that the Australians were not destined for England but for North Africa. Diverted to Egypt, the Australians trained and prepared for battle in and around Cairo before setting off for Gallipoli as part of the Mediterranean Expeditionary Force (MEF).

Landing with the rest of his unit as part of the 1st Australian Division, Kirkpatrick was among the first ashore on the morning of 25 April. Along with his fellow stretcher-bearers, he was tasked with providing first aid to wounded soldiers and carrying those who could not walk to the relative safety of medical aid posts. Kirkpatrick commandeered a donkey – reports differ as to whether he annexed, found or stole it or even smuggled it ashore – and began to use it to ferry wounded soldiers through difficult terrain down from the front lines that ran across the cliffs of Gallipoli.[2] He soon became known as 'the man with the donkey' and, until his death during the fighting at Anzac Cove in May, he and his beasts of burden (he used more than one) worked to bring in the wounded.

Figure 0.1 Not Simpson and his donkey. Private Richard Alexander Henderson, a stretcher-bearer in the New Zealand Expeditionary Force, with donkey and patient. The bearer in this photograph was mistakenly identified as Simpson, and a number of paintings of Simpson's famous escapades were based on this image. (AWM P03136.001)

Kirkpatrick was not the only stretcher-bearer to undertake this work, but, having been singled out for heroic deeds in *Glorious Deeds of Australasians in the Great War*, a piece of wartime propaganda, he is the one who has been remembered.[3] He was Mentioned in Despatches for his work and went about casualty retrieval in this manner with the permission of his commanding officer. Yet the prevailing narrative of this man is of a rogue operator, heroic in his efforts but unrewarded by Australia. Tales of him saving the lives of three hundred men and routinely putting himself in greater danger than other bearers are overblown.[4] Rather than warranting the award of a Victoria Cross, his efforts have been rewarded with a similar degree of recognition as other stretcher-bearers. 'Having peeled back layer after layer of half-truth, mistruth, falsehood and fabrication' when researching this enigmatic character, Graham Wilson 'came to two conclusions: first, that John Simpson Kirkpatrick was an extremely likeable but otherwise wholly unremarkable young man; second, that just about every statement ever uttered or written about Simpson is false'.[5]

Despite their story having been untethered from reality, Simpson and his donkey(s) have become the iconic images of Australian medical care in the First World War. They are synonymous with the Anzac legend, which has 'extraordinary currency' in Australian society.[6] Their likenesses have been cast in bronze and placed at the entrance to the Australian War Memorial in Canberra and on the banks of the River Torrens in Adelaide. In 1997, the Australian chapter of the Royal Society for the Prevention of Cruelty to Animals (RSPCA) awarded one of his donkeys, Murphy, 'and all the donkeys used by John Simpson Kirkpatrick' a Purple Cross for 'the exceptional work they performed on behalf of humans while under continual fire at Gallipoli'.[7] Their efforts are the subjects of numerous histories and children's picture books.[8] They are the stuff of legend, but there is, of course, much more to the story of Australian medicine at Gallipoli, and in the First World War after 1915, than the exploits of one man and his four-legged friend(s).

The Australian Army Medical Services (AAMS) were integral to the work of the AIF in the First World War. As one of its constituent parts, the AAMC served from the beginning of Australia's involvement until the discharge of the final servicemen. Its efforts extended across a broad geographical area, with units working in Australia, the Pacific, the Middle East, the Mediterranean, Egypt, Europe and the United Kingdom and on the ships that transported men between theatres. In addition, the AAMC demonstrated breadth in the range of medical concerns for which it had responsibility. It was involved in the medical assessment of recruits, the maintenance of soldiers' health and fitness, the prevention of disease, soldiers' treatment when wounded, and their rehabilitation and return to duty. Also, members of the AAMC were involved in decisions about the extent of an individual's degree of disability on discharge from the armed services.

In delivering this range of medical care, the AAMC occupied an unusual place in the Australian war effort. The First World War is often discussed in terms of two separate, although interacting, spheres: war and home. However, combat support units, like the AAMC, disrupt this idea and suggest something more akin to a continuum. The AAMC linked these two spheres and bridged the divide between the front line and the war effort at home, working at every stage in between. From collecting casualties from No Man's Land, right through to treatment and discharge in Australia, the AAMC provided care and relief from war injury in service of the war effort.

While the geographical, temporal and therapeutic range of the AAMC's work in the First World War all suggest that it was significant in the Australian war effort, it was the sheer scale of the problem it faced that made the AAMC's contribution integral to the AIF. Colonel Arthur Graham Butler, who was initially Commanding Officer of the 3rd Australian Field Ambulance before he became the official historian of the Australian Army Medical Services, suggests that 60 per cent of the Australian force in the lines in 1918 were men who had recovered from previous illness or injury.[9] More recently, David Noonan's statistical analysis of the AIF exposed flaws in Butler's history.[10] He found that Australia's 318 100 effective embarkations – that is, men who made it to a theatre of war – were admitted to hospital as a result of wounds, injuries and illnesses on more than 737 000 occasions.[11] If hospitalisations for venereal disease are included, the number is well over 750 000. In his official account, Butler suggests that wounded soldiers were hospitalised on only 155 000 occasions, so Noonan's number is around five times higher than Butler's.[12] Noonan's revised statistics suggest that, on average, each effective embarkation was admitted to hospital 2.3 times. This reassessment of the extent of wounding, illness and injury in the AIF goes a long way towards explaining why the medical services were under sustained pressure throughout war, but Noonan does not provide an analysis of how the medical services coped with the scale of the casualties. Therefore Butler's assessment of broader problems over the course of the war warrants revisiting.

Figure 0.2 Arthur Graham Butler, CO 3AFA. He became Official Historian of the AAMS in the First World War. (AWM H18932)

This book investigates how medical care was provided to Australian soldiers in the First World War and where sites of medical–military authority were located. It examines the work of the AAMC across three critical types of care: casualty clearance and evacuation, rehabilitation, and the prevention and treatment of venereal disease (VD). The investigation of these three forms of medical care enables an analysis of three important points of contact between doctors, patients and the army. Each significant in its own right, these were three areas where the AAMC had direct responsibility for sick and wounded Australian soldiers. Previous medical histories discuss these areas in isolation, obscuring the underlying principles that shaped the provision of medical care. What this book reveals is that the AAMC demonstrated consistency in its practice across these three distinct types of care – despite differences in the purpose of that care, the distance from the front lines and the involvement of different actors.

Much more than a history of military administration, this book exposes the ways in which traditional hierarchies – imperial, military, medical and gender – came into conflict in war. At different times, those hierarchies were quietly subverted, openly transgressed, subtly reinforced and strictly upheld. As a result of the conflict between the competing forms of authority, those hierarches were ultimately blended as the Australian medical men of the AAMC sought to establish their expertise, assert their authority, and consolidate and extend their control over sick and wounded Australian soldiers.[13]

STRUCTURES OF MEDICINE IN WAR

The AAMS had a number of constituent parts during the First World War, including the Australian Army Dental Service, Pharmaceutical Service, Nursing Service and Massage Service. The largest was the AAMC. While many doctors had some experience in the militia, the peacetime medical corps had only four officers. Its rapid expansion once war began meant that almost all the doctors in the AAMC were civilians, a factor that distinguished it from its British counterpart, the Royal Army Medical Corps (RAMC). Commissioned as officers, doctors commanded the other ranks of the AAMC, who, like Simpson of donkey fame, worked as stretcher-bearers and orderlies.[14] These members of the AAMC were most often deployed as part of either the Australian Field Ambulance (AFA) or a hospital unit. AFAs were paired with a combat brigade and, as a general rule, they provided casualty clearance and evacuation when their respective unit was directly involved in the fighting.[15] There were also stretcher-bearers within the brigade, known as 'regimental stretcher-bearers', who had responsibility for clearing the wounded back to the regimental aid post (RAP). Staffed by the Regimental Medical Officer (RMO), this was the first unit in the medical evacuation chain. The RMO was a member of the AAMC but was under the command of the combat brigade Commanding Officer (CO). When his brigade was not engaged in combat, the RMO served in a similar way to a general practitioner serving a community. He provided medical assessments and care for ailments as well as monitoring general health and morale in the unit.

AFAs were divided into bearer and tent subdivisions; bearer subdivisions transported and carried the wounded, and tent subdivisions staffed medical posts. If a soldier could not be immediately patched up and sent back to fight, he was evacuated from the RAP to an advanced dressing station (ADS) and then to a main dressing station (MDS). If a soldier's wounds needed surgical intervention, the AFA evacuated him to a casualty clearing station (CCS). These hospitals were staffed by dedicated teams and, over the course of the war, they developed into large and complex units.[16] As well as marking the point at which the AFA's area of responsibility ended, the CCS was also the point at which Australian control of Australian casualties ceased. CCSs were largely stationary and served the area ahead of them in the evacuation chain, irrespective of which nation of the British Expeditionary Force was deployed there. Consequently, Australian soldiers were frequently evacuated to British CCSs, and Australian CCSs often received casualties from British and dominion forces. From here, casualties were transported back to base hospitals, including 1st Australian General Hospital (1AGH). If further medical treatment was required, Australian casualties were transported to England for treatment in British military hospitals before being sent to an Australian auxiliary hospital (AAH) for rehabilitation. Once recovered, Australian soldiers proceeded to an Australian command depot (ACD) or, if they were unfit for further service, they sailed back to Australia for further treatment and discharge from service. Clearly, the system of medical care for sick and wounded soldiers was a complex and multinational one, which required coordination and communication between units.[17]

While the degree of cooperation between units and across national boundaries varied between theatres of war and the stage of the war, in theory it was possible because the imperial forces were designed to work together. The British army went through a series of major reforms in the aftermath of the South African War of 1899–1902. Including contingents from the pre-Federation Australian colonies and (after 1901) the Commonwealth of Australia, the force Britain assembled 'was not so much an army as it was an "aggregate of battalions" from across the empire – disparate, disorganized, and depressingly ad hoc'. Douglas E. Delaney suggests that 'it compared most unfavourably with continental armies that had standard military organizations and procedures, peacetime formations that were the same as those they would use in war, and general staffs to guide them in both their training and their fighting'.[18]

By 1911, a new system was in place. An imperial standard existed for infantry and cavalry divisions, the dominions organised and equipped their military forces in line with British standards, and the War Office disseminated the *Field Service Regulations*. Furthermore, officers from Britain travelled to the dominions to help consolidate these 'adjustments'.[19] This standardisation of military units applied to medical as well as combat forces, and the structure of the AAMC at the beginning of the First World War was virtually the same as that of the RAMC, with only minor alterations owing to their relative size. After the First World War, Delaney suggests that the dominions were less dependent on Britain and 'more confident in their ability to manage their own military and diplomatic affairs'.[20] A study of the AAMC in the First World War provides the opportunity to assess whether Britain managed to maintain a standardised imperial force in the face of the nascent nationalism of the dominion soldiers.

Assessing the relationships between the AAMC and its officers with other units, groups and individuals highlights the different forms of authority with which they had to contend. The AAMC contested the role of the Mother Country in the care provided for Australian soldiers, and questions of national identity emerged from discussions of responsibility for care. Military hierarchies subordinated civilian expertise, so the reliance of the AAMC on civilian doctors with limited military experience required them to establish their expertise in a military context. Medical hierarchies privileged those with medical training over those without, and gender hierarchies differentiated between competing masculinities as well as promoting men over women. None of these forms of authority can be completely disentangled from the others, and in many ways they seamlessly overlapped. In figure 0.3, military and medical hierarchies blend, with the most senior person in the medical hierarchy also occupying the

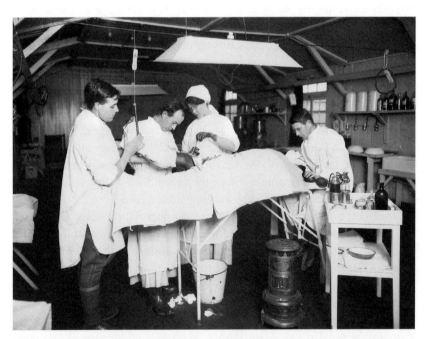

Figure 0.3 The operating theatre at 1ACCS in 1917 demonstrating both harmony and conflict in the blending of military, medical and gender hierarchies. Left to right: Sergeant Haswell, Lieutenant Colonel McClure, Sister Murphy, Major Featonby. (AWM E01304)

highest military rank of those in the room, in this instance the surgeon, Lieutenant Colonel Fay McClure. On the next rung down the ladder in both medical and military terms is the anaesthetist, Major Featonby. After him, things get messy. Sergeant Haswell was ranked lower than Sister Murphy, as nurses held the rank of honorary officers, yet her authority extended only as far as her medical expertise, and she could not exercise any authority beyond nursing matters.[21] These limits on authority and the inversion of the gender hierarchy caused some consternation among the members of the AAMS. The AAMC continually renegotiated its relationships during the war, and this saw the emergence of Australian medical men as the primary decision-makers in the provision of medical care to Australian soldiers.

HISTORIES OF MEDICINE IN WAR

Butler's Official History of the AAMS was the first to examine the provision of care to Australian soldiers in the First World War. Published in three volumes in 1930 (with a second edition in 1938), 1940 and 1943, it has remained largely unchallenged as the definitive account of medical care provided to Australian soldiers during the war. However, it is not without its problems. Its scope leaves many questions unanswered, the statistics collated have recently been scrutinised and found wanting, and it has been implicated in the development of Australia's national creation myth.[22] This was, in part, because it was overseen by Charles Bean, author of the general Official History of Australia's involvement in the war and an advocate of the 'Australian Ideal'.[23] The official account was intended to communicate developments in medical treatments to a wider audience yet, under Bean's influence, it also assumed a tone similar to his official history and attempted to convey to the reader the heroism, innovation and determination of the members of the AAMC.

Despite covering a broad range of issues and theatres of war on three continents, Butler acknowledges from the outset that an Australian medical history of the war must be limited in its scope, as the only theatre in which Australia had full responsibility for medical care was the work of the Australian Naval and Military Expeditionary Force (ANMEF) in the Pacific.[24] In the medical sphere, Australian authority did not extend outside Australian personnel so Butler's work does not venture far into the relationships between British and Australian medical units, asserting that the 'study of what may be termed the medical strategy of the war belongs, therefore, properly to the Imperial history, and therein has been admirably presented'.[25] However, AAMC officers did attempt to influence plans made by their British counterparts, and discussion of these examples feature in the official account. Butler acknowledges that there was conflict in this relationship. He writes that 'the carrying out in a dominion army of certain principles laid down by the medical authorities of the British army opens up the whole field of the relations of the dominion service to that of the Mother Country'. He continues by suggesting that the problems in that relationship and 'the experience of the medical service in their gradual solution, are matters which, so far from possessing a merely academic interest, come white-hot from the furnace in which have been moulded the latest changes in the British Commonwealth of Nations'.[26] Furthermore, Butler suggests that conflict between the Australian medical services and the British General Staff is one reason the AAMC pushed for greater independence.[27]

Given the national creation myth that surrounds Australia's participation in the First World War, the relationship between Australia and Britain and its effects upon medical care warrants further investigation. Butler routinely places the blame for problems within the Australian medical services on the British command, the RAMC and occasionally Australian government officials, while presenting the members of the AAMC, and the AIF generally, as valiant heroes doing the best they could in spite of the conditions in which they found themselves.[28] In a discussion of the merits of the Australian and British official medical histories' analyses of the Gallipoli campaign, Mark Harrison concluded that 'while it is rather too accepting of Australian versions of events, Butler's account stands the test of time rather better, having identified some of the key structural weaknesses which dogged medical aspects of operations on the peninsula'.[29] This conclusion can be carried through to other theatres of war where Butler also identifies key weaknesses and successes, with the caveat that the weaknesses are invariably British and the successes Australian.

Aside from a few notable examples, since the publication of Butler's official history, little has been written about the work of the AAMC in the First World War. Michael Tyquin's analysis of the medical services at Gallipoli in 1915 provides a critique of the work of the Australian medical services that is more nuanced than Butler's official account.[30] Tyquin argues that the system, rather than individuals, was responsible for the medical problems faced at Gallipoli and concludes that there was a distinct disadvantage for Australia in being dependent on Britain for medical and logistical provisions. His assessment that Australia was disadvantaged by its deference to Britain is sound, although neither Australian nor British officials attempted to demarcate explicitly where one's responsibility ended and the other's began. Moreover, the suggestion that the system and structure of the MEF was the cause of the failure also does not adequately represent the way the MEF functioned during the campaign. That the system failed is without doubt; however, individuals in positions of command created and perpetuated this system, even when faced with disaster and the prospect of failure.

Further histories of the AAMC in the First World War have been influenced by Australia's national founding myth, which was itself a response to discomfort with the imperial hierarchy that gave precedence to British endeavours and agency. These histories have largely focused on individuals within the campaign, creating heroic figures of national pride like Simpson, with his indefatigable ass, and others such as Sir Neville Howse, who eventually became Director of Medical Services (DMS) for the AIF.[31] This narrow scope does not adequately present the wide-ranging work of the AAMC.

Figure 0.4 Sir Neville Reginald Howse. Awarded a VC for gallantry in the South African War, he became Director of Medical Services for the AIF in the First World War. (AWM A01189A)

Placing a greater emphasis on military over imperial hierarchies than Butler or Tyquin, Mark Harrison examined the work of the British medical services of the First World War. Harrison argues that 'the breakdown of medical arrangements in Gallipoli was symptomatic of the Army's difficulties in coming to terms with the realities of modern warfare' and suggests that the 'command structure of the Gallipoli campaign resembled that of a small colonial expedition in which traditional hierarchies worked to the detriment of professional expertise'.[32] Moreover, Harrison demonstrates that a more consultative command structure had existed on the Western Front, before the commencement of the campaign in the Mediterranean, highlighting that it was possible for the medical services to be integrated into the planning and execution of combat operations. Therefore a greater emphasis on the personnel involved is warranted. It also suggests that it is worth investigating how the AAMC worked under these two different cultures of command. Accordingly, this book locates Australia's participation in the Dardanelles campaign within the broader context of the First World War and directly relates it to action on the Western Front, the most decisive theatre of war. In doing so, it provides a clearer picture of how the Dardanelles campaign informed the way the AAMC interacted with the British medical services on the Western Front from 1916.

The involvement of civilians in providing care to Australian soldiers disrupted military dominance and altered the nature of the medical–military units in which the AAMC cared for sick and wounded men. Not only did the AAMC rely on civilian doctors in military uniform but, additionally, it was dependent on civilian women in paid and voluntary roles in Australian hospitals in Britain. The British public was invested in the medical care of its soldiers during the First World War, and the involvement of civilians in wartime caregiving was linked to soldiers' rights. Harrison argues that those rights posed a significant political problem in Britain, suggesting that the general public's growing acknowledgement that soldiers were fighting on their behalf resulted in a push for better recognition for those returned from duty.[33] The voluntary involvement of British civilians in Australian military hospitals caring for men a vast distance from their kith and kin extended this humanitarian effort across the imperial network.

The idea of a social contract between the State and the soldier gained momentum after the South African War and was important in the First World War. By the end of the nineteenth century, British 'servicemen were beginning to demand health care as a right, and to regard it as a kind of "social wage" earned in the service of their country'. In this, servicemen 'appealed not only to the paternalistic and humanitarian inclinations of certain sections of the community but also to modern concepts of citizenship and social justice'.[34] This 'social wage' was earned by Australian soldiers not just in service to their country but also in service to empire. I argue that, while British involvement in Australian medical care was reduced and sometimes resented, the antagonism did not trickle down from the institutional or organisational level. Instead, the efforts of civilian British women in Australian auxiliary hospitals extended beyond their professional capacities to the personal, and the resulting relationships between people in these hospitals suggest that there were limits to Australians' distrust of British interventions.

Viewing medicine and the military more as competing priorities, rather than as hierarchies that act on each other, previous histories of medicine in war have attempted to reconcile military and medical concerns. Roger Cooter and Steve Sturdy argue that the First World War marked a new phase in the development of military medicine. They describe it as 'a crucial site for the development of new kinds of medical organization and division of labour. Medicine was no longer simply an ancillary discipline to warfare, concerned merely with patching up the bodies of the injured.' They suggest that medicine became integral to warfare, given that '[b]y the war's end it had become a key site for pursuing the kinds of technical and administrative innovations that were now increasingly seen as crucial for the prosecution of modern warfare'.[35]

The integration of medical care as central to warfare placed the State in control of men's bodies and introduced a third party to the doctor–patient relationship. The medical profession had to confront this issue as the war 'threw into relief the deep ethical conflicts which doctoring under the aegis of an all-powerful third party entailed. Participants in the Great War required that doctors determine whether they could simultaneously heal the patient and serve the State.'[36] Ana Carden-Coyne explored these ideas further. Mainly focusing on British men, with reference to dominion and American soldiers, Carden-Coyne prioritises patients' perspectives and locates the wounded citizen soldier's personal experience and articulation of pain in the 'political realm'.[37] Carden-Coyne discusses the introduction of a third set of priorities, that of the State, and suggests that through a political network of the State, the military and medical practice, '[t]he military subordinated individual will with its hierarchical structures, through its training techniques and its disciplinary regime'.[38] Military patients viewed medical practitioners (including doctors, nurses and physiotherapists) as part of the 'war machine' and party to patients' 'brutalisation' and disempowerment.[39] Medical officers did exert power and authority over soldiers' bodies but, owing to the differing priorities of the various actors at each site of care, this authority was distinctly expressed in each form of medical care. As this authority manifested differently in the various types of medical care, the disempowerment of which Carden-Coyne writes was also inconsistent. I argue that the education and active involvement of soldiers became an essential factor in the AAMC's attempts to combat the effects of venereal disease on the AIF.

The effects of the war on the male body prompted gender historians to examine medical care in the First World War. Joanna Bourke's pioneering work, *Dismembering the Male: Men's Bodies, Britain and the Great War*, examined the effects of the war on masculinity and the male body, including discussions of wounding and bodily inspection. Bourke links the wounded male body with shifting understandings of masculinity and the effects on the men, their families and their communities. Emphasising continuity over change in the increasing importance of heterosexual domesticity to masculine maturity during and after the war, Bourke does not differentiate between scholarly examination of the male body and the study of masculinity. She argues that the war acted as a catalyst for the nascent moves towards disciplining bodies. The routine scrutiny, categorisation and regulation of male bodies suggests that medical–military authorities (i.e. the State) would have inspected and assessed almost all young adult and middle-aged men in Britain during the war.[40] Despite the different context in Australia, where attempts to introduce conscription failed, the equivalent authorities also would have inspected the bodies of the majority of men of fighting age. The men at the younger end of this age spectrum were the same men who, as boys, were subject to inspection by the State while at school.[41] The inspection of bodies had become routine, and the normality of bodily surveillance by the State was one of the factors that enabled the AAMC (in its attempts to limit the effects of VD) to conduct routine genital inspections, with little opposition, in the AIF.

Locating the military patient in a 'web of intimate social encounters and institutionalised relationships', Carden-Coyne focused on the way power operates 'in the fraught negotiations that occur around wounded men's bodies'.[42] She suggests that the gender hierarchy was inverted in some instances, with women, in the roles of nurse or physiotherapist, able to inflict pain on men's bodies. Combined with the crisis in masculinity, as a consequence of the emasculating effects of wounding, she argues that men were required to regain their manhood by transitioning through a feminised state. Suggesting that therapies 'were framed on gendered lines', she explains that '[b]efore regaining the masculine grip of bayonets or guns, the patients learned to hand-stitch delicate material and knit woollen items, practices that were associated with women'.[43] While agreeing that therapies were framed on gendered lines, I am not convinced that men were required to pass through a transitory, rehabilitative feminised state in the gender hierarchy between the infantilised wounded individual and the masculine warrior. Rather, I argue that the rehabilitation activities available to men in Australian auxiliary hospitals were expressions of the gendered nature of the work and workers rather than the patients. Furthermore, I argue that gender norms were actively harnessed in the attempts to combat venereal disease.

Drawing on the wealth of the collections at the Australian War Memorial (AWM), this book uses army orders, unit war diaries and memoranda written to disseminate information within the AIF and between British and Australian officers. It also draws on the statistical records kept by medical officers, especially in the analysis of the response to venereal disease. The war diaries of Australian units are particularly useful. While they were written to record events after they had occurred, and therefore had the potential to be used to justify decisions made or to diminish mistakes, they were subject to review by John Treloar, Officer-in-Charge of the Australia War Records Service. He provided feedback to unit commanders on the quality of their reports and insisted upon the correct naming of units, precise references to dates, locations, units and times, and the accurate use of map references.[44] He also introduced standardised stationery to encourage uniformity in reporting and, according to Anne-Marie Condé, he made officers aware that their words 'were not placed in some "dusty corner" at Base and promptly forgotten [but] would form an "accurate record" on which the history of the war would be written'.[45] As a result, the Australian unit war diaries provide detailed descriptions of events and numerous useful appendices that illustrate the work of the AIF. Private papers, such as those of Sir Neville Howse, Sir Ian Hamilton and Douglas Haig, supplement these official records in order to provide necessary contextual information and demonstrate the unofficial work done by military men in the course of their duties. These personal papers demonstrate commanders' decision-making and the ideas that underpinned their approaches to medicine in war, but were expressed outside bureaucratic processes.

Also in the collection of the AWM is the full catalogue of the *Harefield Park Boomerang*, the magazine of the 1st Australian Auxiliary Hospital, Harefield Park (1AAH Harefield).[46] Hospital magazines were a form of mental and physical care practised in hospitals and are one genre of non-canonical wartime literature.[47] In his advocacy for the use of hospital magazines as sources of patient resistance, Jeffrey Reznick writes: 'As this official literature helped authorities to sharpen their own vision of the hospital it was intended to – and did – allow recovering soldiers to express their frustration with the institution.'[48] Ana Carden-Coyne highlights the cultural life within medical spaces, explaining that 'patients used wit, irony, and gallows humour to negotiate power relations, as a mode of resistance, and to manage systemic tensions'.[49] The *Harefield Park Boomerang* was published from late 1916 through to the victory edition in December 1918, and is used in chapter 4 to illuminate the interaction between staff and patients. It also furthers the discussion of rehabilitative medical care and the context in which it was practised. The magazine is not just a vehicle for understanding patient voices; as a sanctioned form of care, it was another method of rehabilitating the soldier.

Further British archives were used to demonstrate the relationships between British and Australian institutions and organisations. The papers of the British Social Hygiene Council, including sample lectures and information that was disseminated to British servicemen, highlight the transfer of ideas between British and Australian groups grappling with the problem of VD and provide context for the AIF's attempts to curtail the rate of this disease among its soldiers stationed in the United Kingdom. My discussion of the problems at Gallipoli makes significant use of the Dardanelles Commission files from the National Archives. The transcripts of evidence and the submissions to the commission show the politics involved in the imperial hierarchy as many in command sought to shift blame for the failures of the Allied forces in the Dardanelles.

EXPERTISE, AUTHORITY AND CONTROL

This book charts the development of Australian military medicine in the First World War. It begins with an examination of the provision of medical care to Australian soldiers during the Dardanelles campaign and explicitly examines the imperial and medical–military hierarchies that were blended and challenged during the campaign. While the Dardanelles campaign has been overstated in terms of its significance to Australian history and to the outcome of the war, it is vitally important in the development of the Australian medical services in the First World War. The chapter argues that the failure of the medical arrangements made by Britain was a significant factor in the AAMC's push to gain control of the medical arrangements for Australian casualties. Gallipoli had lasting consequences for the medical services, and the AAMC's work on the Western Front was conducted in Gallipoli's shadow.

In explicitly linking the Dardanelles campaign to the campaigns on the Somme and in Flanders, this book highlights the fact that the AAMC was working on the Western Front while the political machinations after and fallout from the Dardanelles campaign were continuing. Chapter 2 is the first of two successive chapters that trace the work of the AAMC on the Western Front and continue to investigate the challenge to imperial, military and medical hierarchies. It focuses on significant battles in which Australian units fought in relatively stationary warfare: Fromelles, Pozières and Mouquet Farm in 1916, and Messines and First Passchendaele in 1917. By examining the refinements made to casualty evacuation procedures between the front and the casualty clearing station, this chapter demonstrates the increasing Australian control of medical care and the AAMC's departures from British plans and processes.

Chapter 3 examines what happened to those plans once the type of warfare changed to one that was comparatively mobile. The chapter assesses the provision of medical care to Australian soldiers in 1918 in retreat (during the German Spring Offensive) and on the advance, during the Hundred Days Offensive. It demonstrates that, while some of the innovations made to medical arrangements the previous year had to be unwound, the return to a system more reminiscent of the one used by the RAMC was not accompanied by a return to RAMC control.

Chapter 4 marks a departure from the chronology of the first three chapters to examine the purpose, place and practice of auxiliary hospitals in the Australian medical services. It suggests that the location of auxiliary hospitals between the home and the front combined with the increased presence of women to change the nature of these medical spaces. Yet, despite this change, the shift towards medical control was maintained.

Chapter 5 evaluates the AAMC's approach to soldiers' sexual health through an analysis of the Australian response to venereal disease. It examines the ways medical approaches to the disease were combined with the exploitation of the military's authority over the individual and the harnessing of prevalent ideas of gender, sex and sexuality. The chapter argues that the AAMC was able to implement a relatively pragmatic response to the problems created by VD because of the willingness of

soldiers to be proactive about their sexual health, through the maintenance of military authority, and because the policies that were enacted
reinforced dominant gender norms.

In bringing together casualty clearance and evacuation with rehabilitation and the prevention and treatment of VD, the chapters present a
broad discussion of the AAMC and its provision of medical care to
Australian soldiers. The AAMC's efforts were integral to the ability of
the AIF to wage war over the course of the First World War, and uniting
these three types of care enables a discussion of the complexity of the
work undertaken. The history of the AAMC in the First World War is a
complex story of the renegotiation of authority over, responsibility for
and control of a medical–military context with imperial ties and gendered
roles. It is about much more than one man and his donkey.

CHAPTER 1

GALLIPOLI

A CASE OF CRIMINAL NEGLIGENCE?

Under oath at the Dardanelles Commission, convened in 1917 to investigate the Gallipoli campaign, Surgeon General Sir Neville Howse, Director of Medical Services (DMS) for the Australian Imperial Force (AIF), stated that 'as far as the Australian troops were concerned' medical arrangements for the Gallipoli campaign 'were so inadequate that they amounted to criminal negligence'.[1] He squarely laid the blame for this 'negligence' on the shoulders of the British General Staff and informed the commissioners that he intended to share his concerns with Australia's leaders. A palpably frustrated Howse stated: 'I personally will recommend my Government when this war is over, that under no conceivable conditions ought they ever to trust to the medical arrangements that may be made by Imperial authorities for the care of their sick and wounded.'[2] His scathing critique not only called into question the British General Staff's ability to plan and execute a comprehensive strategy but also revealed his doubt regarding the benefits of Australian deference to Britain in medical–military matters.

Australia fought in the Dardanelles campaign of 1915 as a relatively minor contributor to the British-led MEF. The participating Australian units served alongside troops from Britain, France, India, Newfoundland and New Zealand against the Ottomans. The MEF was tasked with securing the Dardanelles and the Gallipoli peninsula, which, it was believed, would lead eventually to the capture of Constantinople and the opening up of a sea route to Russia through the Sea of Marmara and the Black Sea.

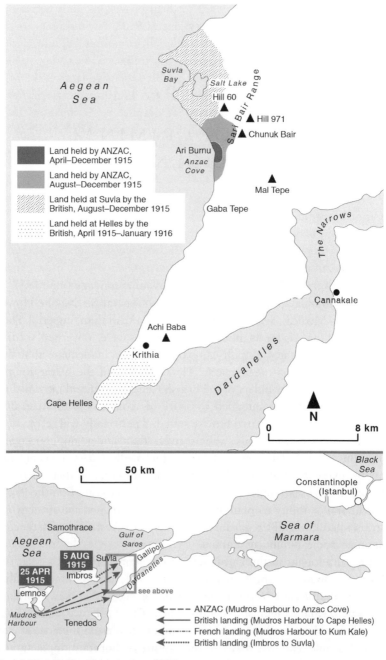

Map 1 The Gallipoli campaign, 1915

Authority over the planning for medical provisions and the medical evacuation of casualties lay with the General Staff. The medical services, including those from Britain, were excluded from strategic and tactical preparations and had limited control or influence over the medical arrangements for the invasion or the August Offensive later in the same year. As a result, the senior members of the AAMC were far removed from the decision-making process and, despite perceiving substantial problems with the medical arrangements, were unable to remedy them. The AAMC was subordinate to its British equivalent, and Australian medical men had little influence over decisions that shaped the provision of medical care to Australian soldiers. While the military significance of the Dardanelles campaign is often overstated, and claims that the Australian nation was born on the beaches of Gallipoli are overblown, the medical aspects of the campaign did spark a change in the way the AAMC saw its role, its responsibilities and the scope of its authority. The disastrous campaign necessitated the development of an independent, self-governing AAMC – one able to draw on its own personnel and resources for expertise and material – that could control medical matters for the AIF.

Organising the Force

Australia's involvement in the army medical services of the British and dominion forces was poorly defined at the beginning of the First World War. Initially, Australia provided the divisional-level medical services required to support AIF troops but did not supply line-of-communication or base units to treat evacuated casualties or units to train recovered soldiers before returning them to the front. Instead, Australian casualties were supposed to filter through the British lines to British bases. When Australia was asked to provide some units for these purposes, there was no clear delineation of British and Australian responsibilities. In his official history, Butler described the nebulous nature of this relationship, writing: 'The position apparently was that anything that the Commonwealth contributed was welcome – Great Britain would make good the rest.'[3] He suggested that this was cause for concern, continuing: 'This absence of definition of the obligations of Australia in the matter of medical arrangements was unfortunate, for sentiment, however generous and reciprocal, cannot take the place of a clear, business-like understanding.'[4] The failure to delineate responsibilities created problems for the Director of Medical Services for the Australian Imperial Force.

Surgeon General William 'Mo' Williams was limited in his capacity to act by the ill-defined nature of responsibility for medical care. Originally based in the War Office in London under the British Director General of Army Medical Services, Sir Alfred Keogh, Williams also liaised with the Australian High Commissioner to London, former Australian Prime Minister Sir George Reid. Despite being the main architect of the AAMC and one of only four regular officers in the corps, Williams struggled to define his role and responsibilities. He left Australia as part of the first convoy of the AIF in late 1914 and continued on to England, where he spent time requisitioning official and Red Cross medical equipment and supplies, as well as organising and equipping a system of convalescence and rehabilitation for Australian soldiers evacuated to England. Once it became clear that Australian forces would be deployed from Egypt to the Mediterranean, Williams went to Egypt to make arrangements for the AAMC units at all levels of command. However, he soon found that he lacked the authority to command the medical forces. A British Director of Medical Services (DMS) was already in position in Egypt, which would function as the base, and another officer took charge of the MEF, and was responsible for medical arrangements on the peninsula and along the lines of communication. Neither of these men recognised Williams as having authority over the Australian troops, who had already been placed under British command, leaving him in the unenviable position of having rank and position without authority.

The British General Staff of the MEF drew up the medical arrangements for the Gallipoli landings and excluded the medical services from this process. 'Force Order No. 1' was issued for the MEF on 13 April 1915; the complete instructions under the heading 'Medical' read: 'Casualty Clearing stations will be located on Beaches "W" and "Z" by the afternoon of the first day. Men and animals unfit for duty on the day of disembarkation will remain on their transports.'[5] These arrangements were expanded and elaborated upon over the following days.

Sir Ian Hamilton, General Officer Commanding (GOC) the MEF, originally estimated 3000 casualties for the entire peninsula during the landing phase of the campaign.[6] As of 18 April, there were two hospital ships, *Sicilia* and *Gascon*, available for use, which could accommodate a total of 700 serious cases for evacuation. Brigadier General E.W. Woodward, British Deputy Adjutant General (DAG) for the MEF, wrote to General

W. Braithwaite, the Chief of the General Staff (CGS), and the Quartermaster General (QMG), with concerns about these arrangements, telling them that if there was serious fighting, those two ships would not be sufficient to accommodate the number of wounded. He believed the arrangements to be so inadequate that he asked permission to requisition nine more ships for casualty evacuation.[7] As DAG, Woodward was responsible for drafts and reinforcements so he needed to know the expected number of casualties and the proposed method of evacuation in order to plan for their replacement with new troops. The following day Woodward again wrote to Braithwaite and outlined the medical arrangements made so far, reiterating the inadequacy of the provision of hospital ships as well as the insufficient number of launches to get casualties from the beach to the ships.[8] At this point the intended date for the commencement of the landings was four days away – no one from either the British or the Australian medical services had been involved in the planning of medical arrangements.

Meanwhile, the British DMS MEF, Surgeon General W.G. Birrell, was still in Alexandria and unable to participate in the planning.[9] His deputy, Lieutenant Colonel Alfred Ernest Conquer Keble of the RAMC, the highest ranking medical officer in the vicinity of the General Staff, attempted to discover what plans were being made but was rebuffed and prevented from voicing his dissent regarding the medical arrangements. Through unofficial channels he had unearthed the plans mentioned above; he felt that they were inadequate and that they should be the responsibility of the medical services rather than the General Staff. When later questioned about his actions at this time, Keble told the Dardanelles Commission that he had written to Surgeon General Birrell in Egypt and 'informed him of my inability to get into touch with the General Staff and suggested that he should come up as quickly as possible'. He went to see numerous junior officers on the General Staff before 'finally one of them – I think Colonel Ward – informed me that he had drawn up a scheme for the medical arrangements. I told him that was no business of his and I refused to have anything to do with that scheme.' Ward then asked Keble to design his own scheme for the medical evacuation of casualties; Keble agreed to do so if Ward would provide an estimate of the number of casualties. Ward later told him that the estimated casualty number was 3000. Keble's response to Ward suggested that he thought the number was farcical. He told the commission: 'I laughed at this and said that as I had to make the scheme I would prepare for 10,000, and my preparations for 10,000 would probably cover

20,000 because the ships would have time to return from Egypt and so would be able to cope with the casualties.'[10]

Having realised how unprepared the General Staff was for the impending battle, Keble drew up his own plan. It was the first to consider the possibility of outright defeat, but it did not contain contingency plans for how to manage partial success, including a scenario in which the invading armies might be able to gain a foothold on the beach without proceeding inland to meet their objectives. Once Birrell arrived, he approved Keble's plans, which were subsequently approved by Woodward, then Hamilton, without further alteration. Still, this was too late for many of the resources and personnel to be available before 25 April and, consequently, the medical services were not at full strength for the landing.[11]

Given the RAMC's limited involvement in the medical arrangements up to this point, it is not surprising that their AAMC counterparts were also restless and concerned. Not satisfied with the state of the medical arrangements, the Assistant Director of Medical Services (ADMS) for the 1st Australian Division, Colonel Neville Howse, implied to the GOC 1st Australian Division, General W.T. Bridges, that Bridges might have responsibilities beyond those that his rank and position conferred upon him, and suggested that Australia would hold Bridges responsible for the medical arrangements for the Australian troops he was commanding during the landings. When Bridges responded by saying, 'That has nothing to do with the Officer Commanding a Division', Howse pushed him further, asking, 'Do you give that as an official reply?'[12]

As a result of this conversation, Howse and Bridges went to see General Sir William Birdwood, GOC of the Australian and New Zealand Army Corps (ANZAC), to find out what medical arrangements had been made for Australian troops at the corps level. Birdwood responded: 'As Corps Commander I have nothing whatever to do with the medical arrangements for landing my troops, but I see it is absolutely essential that we should have some information.'[13] With these conversations occurring as late as 20 April, only days before the landings, it appears as though the official historian of the Australian medical services was correct when he mused that 'the medical problems of the Australian force were not the recognised business of anyone in particular'.[14]

Clearly, confusion reigned in the medical services before the campaign commenced. One of the problems was that, as Australia was not a fully independent state, 'it was not clear at what point British authority overrode Dominion jurisdiction'.[15] A further example of this can be seen in the events at 1st Australian General Hospital (1AGH) in Egypt. On the outbreak of war, Bridges was appointed to two commands: commander of the AIF and commander of the 1st Australian Division. Because he wanted to lead the unit into battle, he focused on his responsibilities as commander of the division and neglected his role as AIF commander, which had responsibility for AAMC units. As a result there was a breakdown in command at 1AGH, which resulted in the Commanding Officer of the hospital, Colonel W. Ramsay Smith, and the Principal Matron, Jane Bell, being returned to Australia. The hospital Registrar, Major J.W. Barrett, was allowed to stay in Egypt but was forced to resign from the AAMC. He joined the RAMC instead.[16] This episode also showed Surgeon General Williams to be 'ineffectual' as a commander and was part of the reason for his later being 'moved sideways'.[17]

On 22 April, Howse received orders that all Australian men unable to proceed to the peninsula because they were medically unfit for battle must be returned to the 1st Australian Stationary Hospital on the island of Lemnos (1ASH Lemnos). Howse duly instructed medical officers to send all their cases from the transports; however, the Officer Commanding 1ASH Lemnos returned the men as he had instructions from the DMS MEF that he was not to take any further cases. That same day Howse visited Birrell to discuss medical arrangements for Australian troops on the Gallipoli peninsula. They discussed the insufficient provision of ships and transports to evacuate Australian casualties as well as the problem of keeping infectious cases, especially measles, on board transports before the landing. Birrell responded to Howse that the infectious cases should be isolated on board their current ships, that no further cases could be sent to 1ASH Lemnos as it was full and could not be expanded further, and that instructions for the evacuation of wounded had been sent to the ANZAC headquarters.[18]

The following day, 23 April, Howse asked General Carruthers, Deputy Adjutant and Quartermaster General (DAQMG) ANZAC, about these arrangements. According to Howse, Carruthers said that 'no further news had been received'. Howse continued: 'I strongly urged upon him the absolute necessity of getting definite instructions before we landed against the enemy [...] He stated that I would receive definite instructions before we landed.'[19] That evening Howse was transported onto HMS *Prince of Wales*, where he remained until the invading force landed. He sailed from Lemnos to the area that would become known as Anzac Cove, arriving early on 24 April, and landed on the beach at 7.22am on 25 April 1915.[20] There is no record in Howse's war diary that he ever received the 'definite instructions' Carruthers assured him would be forthcoming before the landings commenced.

THE APRIL LANDINGS AND AUGUST OFFENSIVE

In the early hours of 25 April 1915, ANZAC forces landed and went ashore at Anzac Cove. While some units were able to reach their objectives, many were not, and the gains that were made were not consolidated.[21] The Ottoman army counterattacked that afternoon and, by the end of the day, the ANZAC troops had established a beachhead but were unable to advance further inland, owing to both the terrain and the fierce opposition of the defenders.[22] The ANZAC forces dug in and formed a series of trenches leading back to the beach. Although the fighting continued on subsequent days, the ANZACs' foothold on the peninsula was not substantially increased.[23]

The lack of foresight in the medical arrangements had dire consequences once the plans were put into action and the invading force set foot on the Gallipoli peninsula. If the MEF had been able to meet its objectives and advance inland, there would have been better outcomes for the casualties. The plans that had been made required significant medical infrastructure on the peninsula, and casualties were supposed to be sorted before being loaded into ships for evacuation to the base. This would have meant that soldiers with minor injuries, who would have been ready to return to service within three or four days, would not have left the area. But the failure to advance inland meant that the full complement of medical services was unable to land on the peninsula, and medical arrangements then had to be improvised.

The inability to land was not confined to the medical services; not all of the troops were able to go ashore as planned, resulting in ships that were already full of soldiers trying to take on board and provide medical care to casualties. The medical services that were established on the beach were also insufficient to manage the casualties. The 1st Australian Casualty Clearing Station (1ACCS) and staff were landed a few hours after the first wave of troops and set up on the beach. This required cutting into the cliff face to create enough space to erect the tents.[24] As there was no shelter from the cliffs above, the casualty clearing station was visible and susceptible to shrapnel; however, the Ottoman army respected the Red Cross markings and did not fire directly on the medical services.

Figure 1.1 1ACCS, Anzac Cove, 1915. Australian troops had to cut into the cliffs in order to have enough flat ground to erect the medical tents. (NLA PIC 413/15793/17)

Figure 1.2 Medical tents, Anzac Cove, 1915. The AAMC had to contend with difficult terrain during the Gallipoli campaign. (SLSA PRG 280/1/12/231)

Given that this was an amphibious landing, a great deal of coordination was needed between the army and the navy in order to move casualties from the beach to the hospital ships. The RAMC was responsible for casualties on land until such time as they were placed on a transport. These transports were under the jurisdiction of the navy, which had responsibility for casualties from the water's edge until the casualty was loaded onto a hospital ship. The hospital ships, as well as the transports used from this point on (known as 'black ships'), were often staffed by the RAMC and AAMC but operated by the Royal Navy. The failure to advance inland also meant that there was a greater demand upon the already limited number of hospital ships. As some of the hospital ships had not arrived at the commencement of the landings, and communication was limited, the disposal of wounded soldiers onto ships was haphazard.

The problems created by the changes in responsibility for casualty transportation between army and navy were exacerbated by the poor communication between branches of the armed forces and between individual ships. The navy reported that, once soldiers were embarked on barges, it had problems finding ships that were able to take on casualties. Some of these barges worked their way around many of the ships waiting offshore, being rejected by one after another. Some ships sailed before they were full and without notifying headquarters. Howse was wary of the poor communication between branches of the military, explaining in evidence to the Dardanelles Commission: 'I do not think the arrangements were adequate and I do not think that there was any cohesion between the Army and the Navy.' He continued: 'I repeatedly made inquiries whether any consultation with the Medical Staff and the Navy and Army took place before our landing, as I had no record of such having taken place.' Finally, he told the commissioners that the unprecedented nature of the landings meant that 'we were in the unfortunate position of having no history to guide us of a previous landing on such a big scale'.[25]

The line of questioning followed by Lord Nicholson, chairing the Dardanelles Commission, suggests that he too was suspicious of the level of communication between the medical services and the Royal Navy. In a discussion of the inadequate number of ships allocated to clear the beach of wounded casualties, Nicholson asked Lieutenant Colonel John Corbin, an AAMC officer from 1ACCS, 'But Colonel Keeble [sic] does not communicate with the Navy, does he?' Corbin, somewhat diplomatically, responded that Keble 'would make a report on the inadequacy if he considered it inadequate', suggesting that he would have communicated

Figure 1.3 A barge loaded with casualties from the fighting on Gallipoli pulling up alongside a hospital ship. The casualties are on stretchers ready to be carried, and some, standing at the front of the barge, are walking wounded. (AWM 02740)

with the navy, but that would require him to recognise the inadequacy of the provisions.[26] Given the interconnected nature of the campaign, it is surprising that there was not better communication between the various services. While the General Staff was on board *Queen Elizabeth*, Birrell, Director of Medical Services, and the rest of the Administrative Staff were located on *Arcadian* and were unable to communicate with GHQ during the landings.[27] This effectively cut off the medical services from handling the medical evacuation of casualties.

With many casualties accommodated on ships that were not properly fitted out for the seriously wounded, and there being a significant period of time between wounding and treatment, many soldiers suffered increased pain and unnecessary difficulty. Some ships initially carried animals such as horses and donkeys to the peninsula. These ships then had to take on

Figure 1.4 Transferring a casualty to a hospital ship. The amphibious nature of the landings meant that the evacuation of casualties was particularly complex. (NLA PIC/15793/17)

casualties without adequate time to equip or clean them sufficiently. In at least one instance, the horses remained on the ship along with the casualties. In his evidence to the commission, Lieutenant Colonel Charles Ryan, Consulting Surgeon to the Australian and New Zealand forces at Anzac, suggested that the horses caused problems for patients. He said that, on *Luxoor*, 'I think there had been about 200 horses on board her for six weeks, and the result was that they were kicking and screaming, and making a great noise all night, with the consequent result that a lot of the poor unfortunate fellows were driven distracted with the noise.' He then invited the commissioners to put themselves in the position of the wounded men and suggested they 'imagine what it is to be in a considerable amount of pain, and to hear horses screaming and kicking'.[28]

Exposure to infection was a significant problem for casualties with open wounds. Ryan continued with his evidence, stating: 'But you see the trouble was that we had to do very serious operations under great difficulties.

A man, say, was shot through the abdomen, and his bowels were perforated, and the only chance of his recovering was an immediate operation.' He outlined the necessary provisions for successful operations: a short period between wounding and surgery, and the ability to take 'every possible antiseptic precaution'. There was, however, no way to sterilise medical instruments or procure proper dressings on board the ships, which Ryan pointed out was particularly bad for men with head wounds.[29] Along with this evidence, Ryan gave the commission examples of ships being ill-equipped for casualties; one ship, *Luxoor*, carrying 700 wounded soldiers for a voyage of more than three days, did not have a single bed pan. In addition, no ships were staffed with nurses, and there were only three medical officers and a surgeon for a ship with 800 casualties.[30]

In response to the failure of the medical services to manage the casualties from the April landings, the British military made significant structural and personnel changes to alter the way the medical services functioned and better delineate lines of responsibility and reporting. The changes were made from June 1915, once it became clear that a new strategy would be needed in order to salvage the campaign and enable the MEF to meet its objectives. Unfortunately, these changes only ended up further muddying the waters rather than providing clarity to the division of medical responsibility.

Figure 1.5 Medical officers and a quartermaster in a quiet moment during the Gallipoli campaign, 11 December 1915. Left to right: Arthur Tebbutt, Claude Tozer, Sir Neville Howse and Andrew Aspinall. (AWM C00694B)

In an attempt to remedy the problems caused by the army and navy both having responsibilities in this context, and acknowledging that the number, organisation and loading of hospital ships were weaknesses in the plans for the landings, Sir James Porter was made Principal Hospital Transport Officer (PHTO) by the Royal Navy. The RAMC then appointed Surgeon General William Babtie to the newly created position of Principal Director of Medical Services (PDMS) for the MEF. The scope and responsibilities of the roles of these men were not satisfactorily outlined, and they were found to be very much replicating the same role. Despite the overlap in their responsibilities, the Dardanelles Commission found that they generally worked well together.[31]

The medical services were once again unaware of impending operations in the lead-up to the August Offensive.[32] A sudden influx of troops at Imbros on 11 July was the first clue that there might be a major campaign in the near future.[33] After initiating contact with Braithwaite, the Chief of the General Staff, in order to find out what medical planning was needed, Keble was told to make arrangements for a major offensive, which might occur any time after 1 August.[34] The medical services were not the only ones not to have been told of the plans. When Keble spoke to Woodward, the Deputy Adjutant-General, regarding reinforcements on 12 July, it was the first the DAG had heard of the forthcoming offensive.[35] Keble's plans for land and sea evacuation were then passed up the chain of command only to be amended and complicated by Porter, the PHTO.[36]

The General Staff seemed determined to avoid direct contact with the Director of Medical Services despite the importance of the belated input from the medical services into the medical arrangements for the April landings. In his war diary on 29 July, Birrell stated that 'the G[eneral] S[taff] did not confer with other staffs, so that Directors did not know what other Directors were doing and much additional work resulted'. He continued, writing: 'The GS did not deal direct with the DMS but through A[djutant], resulting in delay.'[37] With only limited British medical involvement at this stage of the plans, the Australians were not yet privy to the medical arrangements for this new offensive. Imperial hierarchies were maintained, to the detriment of military and medical concerns.

Some lessons learnt from the April landings resulted in different procedures in the August Offensive. The initial casualty estimate, a more realistic 30 000, was made by Keble, an officer of the RAMC (although the estimate was required before he was informed of the location, date or methods to be used in the new operation). Hamilton revised this number down to 20 000. With reports of the final number of casualties for August ranging from 23 000 to 30 000, Keble's estimate had the capacity to handle another military failure. The problem of not having a trained staff officer monitoring casualty evacuation at the corps level for ANZAC was rectified for the August Offensive, with Hamilton appointing Keble to the post. This gave a Briton responsibility for ANZAC troops rather than promoting Howse, who was the logical AAMC officer to take on the role.[38]

Despite these structural improvements in the medical arrangements for ANZAC, the lack of communication between the medical services and the General Staff continued to cause problems, and the failure of the army once again to reach its objectives had continued consequences for the medical services. Once Keble arrived at Anzac Cove for the August Offensive, he set about ensuring that adequate arrangements were in place for the forthcoming military action. He asked the Beachmaster, Lieutenant Carter of the Royal Navy, whether any instructions had been forthcoming from Porter, the PHTO. Carter advised that they had been received and went to retrieve them but was killed before he could pass on the details. Carter's replacement, Lieutenant Drummond, could find no record of the orders in Carter's office. There was also an attack planned of which Keble was entirely unaware, and for which there were no casualty evacuation plans. He was informed of the attack only the day before it took place, leaving him with insufficient time to assemble a makeshift evacuation scheme.[39]

The problem of the availability of personnel in August mirrored that of April, with some of the medical establishments failing to arrive on the peninsula before the offensive began. However, in his statement to the Dardanelles Commission, Keble questioned the significance of this failing to the outcome of the campaign. Of the area in which the casualty clearing station was intended to be pitched, he wrote that it 'was found to be absolutely untenable'. As he noted in his submission to the Dardanelles Commission, 'Our offensive did not succeed and consequently the ground which the Casualty Clearing Station destined for No. 2 Post were to occupy was never able to be occupied; it was swept by machine gun fire, and it was certain death for anybody to go on it.'[40] If the CCS had been established, it would have been in a location that placed patients and staff in danger. This bears a remarkable similarity to the problems of the location of the 1st Australian Casualty Clearing Station during the April landings.

Just like the initial phase of the land-based offensive in April, the lack of hospital ships created problems for the AAMC on the beach during the August operations. During the Dardanelles Commission, Lord Nicholson asked Lieutenant Colonel John Corbin, medical officer of the 1ACCS: '[S]urely the business of improving those arrangements rested with the corps, that is to say with General Birdwood and the staff under his orders and so on, would it not?'[41] After some clarification, Corbin responded that 'chaos existed on the beach because [. . .] there were no means of clearing the beach; that is to say there was no transport'. Corbin described the limited space available to shelter and protect the casualties. Once those 300 very tightly packed spaces were full, the medical services had to put casualties where they would be in danger, where they were susceptible to shrapnel and were unprotected, and the wounded kept coming. Corbin told the commission: 'We had our 300 on the beach, and they were still coming in, from 40 to 50 an hour and likely to be very much increased in numbers when other fighting commenced.'[42]

The similarity to the experience of the landings suggests that the MEF had failed to learn from the problems it encountered in April. In both cases this meant that casualties accumulated on the beach, which needed to be cleared not only of serious cases but also those deemed to be 'less serious' or 'slight'. Then the problems encountered loading casualties onto transports, and from there on board ships, further encumbered the ability of the medical services to provide adequate care to wounded soldiers on the beach.

After the failure of the August Offensive, the British Government made changes to the command of the MEF. The most obvious personnel changes with respect to the medical services were that Birrell was replaced in September and, in October 1915, Hamilton was sacked as Commander-in-Chief of the MEF and recalled to London. Birrell had been found wanting in the incredibly complex role he occupied, and Hamilton, as the GOC MEF and the man responsible for the campaign as a whole, was roundly chastised for its failure. Within the AIF, Neville Howse was promoted to the position of Deputy Director of Medical Services (DDMS) for ANZAC and became responsible for medical services at corps level, a position he had declined at the commencement of the campaign. He initially declined the opportunity once again, but was persuaded to take on the role once Birrell and Hamilton were no longer in charge of the medical services and the MEF.

Persistent voices within higher command continued to push for further attacks. After growing criticism of the campaign, however, it took Hamilton's replacement, Sir Charles Monro, only one day on the peninsula to recommend that the Allied forces withdraw. The British War Cabinet made the decision to evacuate on 7 December, and Anzac Cove and Suvla

were evacuated on 19/20 December, followed on 8/9 January by the
forces at Cape Helles.[43] The medical services were, by necessity, more
involved in the arrangements for the evacuation as part of the process
entailed removing from Gallipoli the medical infrastructure that had been
erected, including regimental aid posts and casualty clearing stations
(along with the wounded men they were treating), as well as medical
stores. Had serious fighting been encountered, the arrangements were to
leave some medical personnel, supplies and patients behind to be collected
later. This was planned under the assumption that the Ottoman army
would continue to respect the Red Cross insignia and the Geneva Convention. The plan was, however, not enacted as there was no significant
opposition from the defenders, who did not prevent the remainder of the
invading force from retreating and withdrawing.

AFTERMATH

The initial post-campaign responses to the work of the Australian Army
Medical Services as part of the MEF and the force in Egypt were swift. The
Director of Medical Services for the AIF, Surgeon General Sir William
'Mo' Williams, had been shown to be past his prime and no longer capable
of performing competently in the role. His poorly defined responsibilities
were decreased, and he was made Director of Medical Services for the AIF
in the United Kingdom, a role with diminished responsibilities mostly
centred on the rehabilitation of convalescing Australian soldiers in the
UK. Taking his place as Director of Medical Services for the AIF was his
former staff officer, Neville Howse, whose promotion to Knight Commander of the Order of the Bath had been conferred as a result of his
service as medical officer to the 1st Australian Division in the Dardanelles
campaign and his later service as DDMS for ANZAC. This separation of
roles caused further problems, as the chain of command and the spheres of
responsibility for Williams and Howse were not clear. Once Howse began
to assert his authority, and Williams became aware of the constrained
scope of his role, Williams returned to Australia and soon retired.

Williams had failed to impress other Australian officers despite being
well qualified and sufficiently experienced to take on the role. Major
General Sir William Bridges, GOC 1st Australian Division, believed that
Williams was a relic of a former time whose behaviour left much to be
desired. Official historian Charles Bean wrote that Williams treated his
time on board the ship sailing from Australia like 'a month at one of his
clubs'.[44] There is no doubt that personality was a major factor in Williams

being sidelined; however, he was also 58 years old and in poor health. Michael Tyquin suggests that Williams' heavy drinking had taken its toll and was not well regarded by his colleagues, many of whom were teetotallers.[45] The biggest factor in his professional demise was, however, not age, personality, health or relations with his superiors but the fact that no one was really sure where the AAMC fitted within the AIF, the wider British dominion forces or the Allies more generally. Given that the Australian medical services were the particular responsibility of nobody in particular, Williams was in a precarious position. As the man in charge, he was responsible for the actions of the AAMC but had no recourse when decisions affected the ability of the AAMC to function. The AAMC variously fell under the command of Williams, Birrell and Ford (DMS for the AIF in Egypt) depending on where each unit was located, with the DMS AIF and Surgeon General in the AAMC having no authority to command AAMC units or personnel in Egypt or the MEF. This all changed after 1915. Australia could no longer afford to take a passive role in medical arrangements and rely on British plans; the man promoted to bring about this change, Neville Howse, was a strong advocate for Australian medical expertise and the importance of efficiency in wartime medical care.

The Dardanelles Commission was convened in order to investigate the failure of the campaign. It was the solution to a political problem for the British Government; a number of those in positions of authority, especially Winston Churchill and Ian Hamilton, advocated for a commission in the belief that an airing of the evidence would vindicate their actions and restore their standing in public opinion.[46] Officially, though, the commission's stated purpose was to inquire into 'the origin, inception, and conduct of operations of war in the Dardanelles and Gallipoli'. This was to include the provision of men, ammunition and equipment to both the army and naval units, as well as the arrangements for the sick and wounded and 'the responsibility of those departments of Government whose duty it has been to minister to the wants of the forces employed in that theatre of war'.[47] It is clear from this statement of purpose that the medical services were only one part of the larger whole under review. The commission had the full powers of a Royal Commission to compel testimony and make recommendations. It sat from August 1916 to September 1917, issuing interim reports in February and December 1917 and a final report after the end of the First World War in 1919.

Despite its stated purpose, the Dardanelles Commission became preoccupied with medical care, for two main reasons. First, by focusing on the provision of medical care and the very serious problems faced in terms of medical evacuation of wounded and sick soldiers, it was possible for those who would benefit from a cursory examination of their involvement to present a compelling case where events did not run smoothly but could be shown to be outside their own realm of control or expertise. Second, the standard of medical care provided for soldiers had become a political issue since the South African War. Mark Harrison has argued that, in Britain, governments ignored the health of the soldier at their peril – that a covenant had come to be understood as existing between the soldier and the State regarding health care – and the failure to provide adequate medical services to soldiers was regarded unfavourably by the public.[48] This public concern was not new; it could be traced back to the work of Florence Nightingale in the Crimea and the typhoid epidemics of the South African War. Fears about the transformation of public concern for the medical care of sick and wounded soldiers into political action on their behalf worried authorities. This political expediency enabled the Dardanelles Commission to emphasise the issues in the medical arrangements on par with, if not over, some of the military concerns.

As with all source material, there are problems inherent in using the submissions, testimonies and reports that constitute the evidence given to the Dardanelles Commission to write the history of this campaign. Without acknowledging the context in which they were created, one risks failing to take into account the intrinsic inconsistencies in the evidence presented. The commission itself was aware of these inconsistencies and made statements as to which version of events was taken as being true.[49] The level of collusion between witnesses suggests that the outcome of the commission was susceptible to influence from those it was scrutinising. General Sir Ian Hamilton, GOC MEF, was one of the men whose actions were to come under the microscope. Even a cursory reading of his personal papers demonstrates just how much he attempted to manipulate the commission in order to have his own actions painted in a more favourable light. In her analysis of Hamilton's involvement with the Dardanelles Commission, Jenny Macleod stated that reading the commission evidence in context with personal papers and military orders and reports shows that Hamilton was 'a clever and guileful political operator'.[50] Owing to the problematic nature of the source material, the evidence of the Dardanelles Commission must be read in conjunction with unit diaries, orders and reports from the campaign and the personal papers of those who gave testimony.

Hamilton's approach to command was hands off.[51] Having ignored members of the medical services in the planning stages of the Dardanelles campaign, he was eager to remember them while giving evidence at the Dardanelles Commission and called on them to furnish him with information about medical matters.[52] Once the commission was underway, Hamilton wrote to Keogh, who had been the Director General of Army Medical Services, to request the addresses of Birrell and Keble.[53] Keogh supplied this information, and then Hamilton wrote to Birrell, Keble, Keogh and Woodward regarding their evidence to the Dardanelles Commission.[54] Through these letters Hamilton attempted to influence the evidence presented to the commission. Keble wrote to Hamilton: 'I wrote very much on the lines you suggested, indeed I practically adopted the whole of your suggestion.'[55] Woodward wrote along similar lines, stating: 'I have noted the four points you mention in your letter and will do all I can to produce a good case for you.'[56] Hamilton was not particularly discreet in attempting to influence others' testimony, writing to Birrell:

> Be sure you remember to bring in (drag it in by the heels if necessary) the fact that you never heard anything about General Woodward's supposed request to Braithwaite or myself that the operations should be delayed two days. I put in myself, as you know, a very strong paragraph on this very point, but by Mears' advice I struck it out as he thought it would come so much better from you.[57]

To do his best to ensure that everyone concerned got their stories straight, Hamilton then included Braithwaite's assessment of the situation, having already ascertained from him what he would write in his statement to the commission. It is also worth noting that 'Mears', referred to in the excerpt above, who coached Hamilton on what to include in his evidence and what to get others to discuss for him, was Secretary to the Dardanelles Commission.

In his letters to his colleagues during the Dardanelles Commission, Hamilton demonstrated how little he knew of the medical arrangements for the campaign; he was not even aware who the author of the scheme was. He wrote to Keogh:

> The Dardanelles Commission (if it has served no other purpose) has at least revealed to this ex-CinC of an ill-fated enterprise the strong and weak elements in his old Staff. Only quite lately have I realised to the full (I always knew to some extent) the value of LtCol Keble to our enterprise. And now that I do realise the truth I realise also that he has been very much under rewarded. For over two years General Woodward my late DAG has claimed and thriven upon the credit due

to the admirable scheme for the evacuation of the wounded at the first landing. Largely on this false credit I have got him mentions, a CB, and a Major Generalship. Now it turns out that the whole of this work was Keebles' [*sic*] who has gained nothing of value through me. Well, it is never too late to put straight an injustice and I hope very much you will, at the next opportunity, remember that Keble has arrears of honours due to him.[58]

Hamilton's lack of knowledge of the medical services' work during the Dardanelles campaign demonstrates, at best, a lack of interest in wartime medical matters and, at worst, incompetence as the Commander-in-Chief of a complicated, multinational, multiservice campaign. The subsequent scramble to gain an understanding of the issues suggests that Hamilton knew this was a weak point in his command of the campaign. This 'old' way of thinking about the role of medical services in war, reminiscent of the South African War where he had last served, will be contrasted in the following chapters with the integration of the medical services into strategic preparations that occurred on the Western Front.

Australian medical–military expertise

During the campaign, Howse attracted attention because he left his transport to command the medical services and manage casualty evacuation from the beach. Howse's decision to land with his troops was considered questionable by other medical officers as it left ANZAC without an officer to direct the evacuation of casualties. As the Assistant Director of Medical Services for a division with the 1ACCS under his command, he was supposed to be on the beach. However, there was no designated DDMS for the corps in April. Had this position existed, as it had previously in the RAMC, it should have been a trained staff officer whose responsibilities would have included managing the evacuation of casualties for ANZAC, which included Howse's 1st Australian Division as well as the New Zealand and Australia Division. This was the role Keble was given for the August Offensive.

In Howse's evidence to the Dardanelles Commission, he stated that he foresaw this flaw in the medical arrangements, but when he questioned the arrangements before the landings he was told that 'a corps was not entitled to any senior officer under the Establishment then existing, and it had been refused'.[59] Therefore the lack of a medical officer at corps level was a structural problem within the AIF. Howse perceived the deficiencies in the medical arrangements and was prevented from altering the structure of the medical corps in order to rectify the problems, but was then subject to unfair criticism for his decision to obey orders and remain with his division and casualty clearing station for the landings. Colonel Keble, staff officer to the Director of Medical Services for the MEF, suggested in a statement for the Dardanelles Commission that, despite being ordered not to, Howse missed a chance to step up and fill the role of DDMS for ANZAC. He said that Howse 'lost an opportunity which comes very seldom to anybody, but I do not blame him because he was not a soldier nor was he a trained staff officer. Had he been a trained staff officer he would not have left his ship.' According to Keble, Howse made this mistake because of his limited experience. He continued: 'Previous to the war he was a surgeon in a small country town in Australia, and his only military experience as far as I knew was as medical officer to an Australian unit during the South African War.'[60]

This statement represents a three-pronged critique of Howse. He was a civilian, from the country and, finally, a colonial. To Keble, military training and expertise were more important than medical expertise or experience as a medical officer in a previous war. Although rural living had been equated with a rugged masculinity, the rural doctor was seen as more closely resembling his city counterparts than his local patients, but without the diversity of cases and experience available to those practising in large cities. At the time of the campaign, Howse was not an inexperienced provincial GP, as was sometimes claimed. Howse had served in the South African War in the medical corps and had been awarded a Victoria Cross for gallantry. He had also led the medical contingent in the ANMEF, which captured German New Guinea in the first months of the First World War. He was not a regular member of the AAMC – the peacetime establishment for the corps before the war was four men – but he was not unaccustomed to, or unaware of, the workings of a medical corps in wartime. The reason he was not in a higher position in the AIF was that it was formed while he was commanding the medical contingent of the ANMEF and all the senior positions had been filled before he returned. He departed Australia on the first AIF convoy but as an 'unallotted officer'.[61]

Hamilton did not think that Australia had any men suitable for positions as commanding officers of medical or combat units. When questioned by the Australian Governor-General about the promotion of Australian officers, Hamilton responded: 'The fact is, it takes a long time to manufacture a true military character and frame of mind, although all the actual work he has to do, and decisions he has to take, may appear on paper so simple and so easy.' He went so far as to suggest that the AIF would struggle to find men in its ranks who could step up the military ladder, telling the Governor-General: 'So far I am at present aware the Australians, magnificently as their fighting men have done, have not yet produced many of that peculiar calibre.'[62] The criticism of Howse is harsh. Howse had limited options available to him when Hamilton had refused to grant him the authority and resources to act effectively as the senior medical officer of the corps.

Some historians have seen British and Australian identities as having much more in common than in conflict. The idea of the British World emerged in response to the status of the nation-state as the fundamental unit of historical analysis.[63] It brought together different parts of the empire to examine the 'networks and identities of global Britishness'.[64] Carl Bridge and Kent Fedorowich discuss the 'phenomenon of mass migration' that transported Britons to 'the "neo-Britains" where migrants found they could transfer into societies with familiar cultural values'.[65] Neville Meaney suggests that 'Britishness' was much more important to Australians than it was to the British.[66] However, the 'sentimentally driven desire for making common cause with Britain was frustrated by the fact that Australia and Britain held two different views of the empire'. In Meaney's eyes, these differences were stark: 'Whereas Britain tended to treat the British-settled countries as subordinate colonies and to see them as expendable resources available for the protection of the heart of the empire, Australia thought of the empire as being made up of separate and equal British peoples all of whose interests were entitled to the same degree of security.'[67] These differing attitudes to the relationship between Britons and Australians and the differing understanding of their similarities and differences came into conflict during the Gallipoli campaign and in its aftermath.

In response to the disregard shown by members of the British army for Australian medical–military expertise, a number of Australians attempted to assert that expertise and demonstrate it to the British authorities. One example of this is the interaction of Neville Howse and Andrew Fisher at the Dardanelles Commission. Fisher was the Australian member of the Dardanelles Commission, a former Prime Minister of Australia, and the Australian High Commissioner to the UK at the time. Fisher sat on the commission with the permission of the Australian Government but, as the Australian Government was not consulted in establishing the terms of reference for the commission, he was not considered to be formally

representing or speaking for Australia. His framing of questions to Neville
Howse emphasised Howse's experience and knowledge.

In order to establish Howse's military credentials, Fisher asked: 'And
you fought in Africa, did you not, and won the highest honour a man can
win?'[68] Regarding the medical arrangements for the landings and
whether or not a conference of medical officers had taken place, Fisher
asked Howse: 'You were not consulted in any way, notwithstanding your
knowledge of war work as a medical officer?' Howse responded: 'No,
there was no conference and no consultation of medical officers, with the
exception of that time when I had a discussion with Colonel Kebbell
[sic].'[69] Fisher then established that it was Howse who had initiated that
conference before continuing the examination in a way that allowed
Howse to demonstrate his competence.[70] Fisher said: 'You foresaw the
danger and you pointed it out to the officers you had access to in
language that could not be misunderstood.'[71] This was followed by:
'You did everything a man could do with safety to see that better
arrangements were made.'[72] And finally: 'I, as a layman, think it would
be the duty, whatever ability the command had, to have had a free
consultation on the matters.'[73]

This succession of questions and statements established Howse's
credentials, portrayed him as a man of foresight and enabled him to
demonstrate that he had done what he could to improve the medical
arrangements before the landings. The last of the three statements in
particular presents Howse as a man of sense. By describing himself as a
'layman' who found it obvious that a consultation on medical issues
should take place, Fisher positioned the General Staff as lacking in even
the most basic common sense possessed by a civilian colonial politician.
Having demonstrated that Howse had the appropriate experience and
expertise to critique the medical arrangements, Fisher asked Howse his
final question: 'Was it rather the system do you think or the man which
caused the trouble – was it a case of do as you are told?' This then
enabled Howse to make his assessment of the situation, which he did in
a way that once again demonstrated that he was excluded from the
planning stages. He stated: 'That is assuming there was no consultation;
but I do not know. There may have been perfect coordination between
the Navy and the Army people of which I have no knowledge; but I do
not believe it existed or there could not have been the breakdown which
took place.'[74]

It is significant that it was necessary to use the forum of the
Dardanelles Commission to assert Australian medical–military expertise.

Australian medical officers had their authority undermined and their expertise undervalued during the campaign, and the Dardanelles Commission provided an opportunity to air those grievances. This critique was partly based on the perception of their skills as doctors, although their readiness to assume roles as officers in a wartime army was as important. Given the nature of their medical education, this critique might have surprised many of the Australian doctors in the AAMC. Bryan Egan found that Australian doctors who served in the AAMC were educated in Britain or, if they were educated in Australia, in a system that was based on that of Britain. He particularly noted the influence of the Edinburgh style of medical training and its emphasis on anatomy. These doctors had been the recipients of a 'British education in Australia'.[75] The AAMC had a pre-war full-time staff of four officers, yet many Australian doctors still had some military experience. Michael Tyquin has demonstrated that, in 1910, 700 militia doctors were attached to the AAMC.[76] On the basis of this number, together with statistics from the Commonwealth Statistician, Kate Blackmore has suggested that 25 per cent of doctors who practised medicine in Australia were involved in military activities in 1910, when there was no conflict on the horizon.[77] Tyquin also suggested that, as of September 1914, all but eight members of the AAMC had some level of military experience.[78]

Instead of viewing the similarities between Australians and British people as evidence for the competence and capability of Australians, this idea of Britons in Australia is one of the reasons given for the exclusion of Australians from the planning of medical arrangements. By the time of the Dardanelles Commission, Keble had become aware of the problems caused by the view that Australians were Englishmen living in the antipodes. He wrote to the Dardanelles Commission: 'My opinion . . . is that the Australians felt themselves left out from the higher command.' He appeared surprised by this realisation, writing:

> I, together with the whole of the General Headquarters Staff, and I expect a greater part of England, had an idea that Australians were Englishmen living in Australia; whereas as a matter of fact I have since – and so have others – found that an Australian is not an Englishman but is an Australian, a member of a new Nation secondarily a member of the British Empire.

He then continued, suggesting that had GHQ realised the significance of the nascent national identity and nationalism of the Australians within the AIF, '[A]n Australian officer would have been attached to every branch as liaison officer, and the Australians would have felt that they were taking part in the higher command of the expedition and very few of the complaints which did arise would then have arisen.'[79] It is worth noting that Keble suggested the Australians would have *felt* like they were taking part in the decision-making processes, not that they would have been active agents in discussion and able to influence decisions.

The Australian forces and the AAMC were subordinate to the British army. However, Howse, Bridges and Birdwood all thought that they had a responsibility based not only on their rank and position but also on their roles as commanders of Australian men (this despite none of them spending any of their childhood in Australia, nor identifying as 'Australian'). The rigidity of the British army's command structure was such that there was no regard for the countries that made up a corps. Information was disseminated according to rank and not national affiliation. After he stated that he would recommend to the Australian Government that they never again trust the imperial authorities with medical arrangements for Australian troops, Howse suggested that it would be a difficult thing for him to do. He said: '[I]t is an opinion, unfortunately, which I have had to form because I am an Englishman myself; I am merely an adopted Australian.'[80]

As a result of the Dardanelles campaign, the AAMC sought greater autonomy. After many communications between the Australian Defence Department, the War Office and various members of the AAMC and AIF, Neville Howse was promoted to Surgeon General and made Director of Medical Services for the AIF. Every AIF medical unit serving outside Australia came under his command, and he became medical adviser to the Australian Government. Howse's own views were instrumental in achieving this, and he agitated for an independent AAMC despite significant opposition from the War Office, Defence Department and some members of the AAMC.[81] To the Dardanelles Commission he said: '[I]f I had an opportunity today of advising my Government, I would say we are entitled to some control over the arrangements that are made for our sick and wounded.'[82] The internal structure of the AAMC was altered, and those positions that had been lacking at Gallipoli were incorporated into the new structure. Australian base and line-of-communication units were created, a system of evacuation of Australian soldiers was developed, and Howse established a working relationship with Sir Alfred Keogh, who continued as British Director General of Army Medical Services at the War Office. Under Howse's leadership, Australian responsibility for Australian casualties increased dramatically.

The medicalisation of the military

The deliberate exclusion of medical services from the strategic planning for the Dardanelles campaign demonstrated an outmoded understanding of the medical services' role in the armed forces. Harrison suggests that this would not have happened on the Western Front, 'where medical considerations were central to the planning and conduct of operations'.[83] The cultures differed between the two theatres of war owing, in large part, to the people who conducted the campaigns. The staff at GHQ MEF were not the best the British army had to offer – those soldiers were already occupied on the Western Front. The members of the MEF staff were relics of a bygone era, and some, such as Birrell, were brought out of retirement in order to serve. Sir Ian Hamilton had been Chief of Staff to Kitchener in the South African War and was, according to Robin Prior, 'a man who it can reliably be said knew little of the Dardanelles, the Turkish army or of modern war'.[84] Prior notes that Hamilton 'was 61 and had been plucked from Central Command in England, hardly the most prestigious of posts'. He suggests that Hamilton went ahead with the campaign despite its change from a naval offensive with back-up ground troops to a full-scale amphibious landing because it 'was clearly his last chance to command troops in the field'.[85] In 1914, Kitchener contemplated replacing Sir John French, Commander-in-Chief of the British Expeditionary Force (engaged on the Western Front), with Hamilton; his decision not to make that change appears prescient given Hamilton's approach to the medical services. Hamilton's method of command was to exclude the auxiliary services from strategic planning and have the General Staff control medical planning, which was even more important on the Western Front with its significantly higher casualty rate.

During the Dardanelles campaign, medical officers from both Britain and Australia sought greater authority over medical issues. This included the logistical arrangements for casualty evacuation. Birrell, Keble and Howse were all increasingly vocal in their advocacy for medical control of medical issues. This process has been described by Mark Harrison as the 'medicalisation of the military'. He argues that the incorporation of the medical services into strategic planning was not 'a function of scientific and technological advances (of the emergence of bacteriology, antiseptic surgery and so forth)'.[86] Rather, this phenomenon was an expression of Max Weber's theory of rationalisation, which promoted the quest for efficiency and the maximisation of resources, including manpower, through the prevention of sickness and the efficient return to service of wounded men. Harrison also questions the morality of this process and acknowledges that Weber 'was uneasy about the subjugation of human beings to what he termed a "means-ends" rationality . . . which objectified and depersonalised the individual'.[87] This increasing medicalisation of the military also led, conversely, to the militarisation of medicine.[88]

The medicalisation of the military was evident in the increasing participation of the medical services in the actions of the army. Harrison's definition of medicalisation provides a solid foundation for this analysis. He states that it was 'the gradual extension of medical authority into new areas such as discipline and administration, together with the growing authority of medical men in the planning and conduct of military campaigns'. Acknowledging that this process was 'partial and often highly contested', he notes that the term 'medicalisation' 'nevertheless encompasses a complex of interconnected changes that occurred in the armed forces of most industrialised nations from the middle of the nineteenth century'.[89]

Despite, and partially as a result of, its exclusion from the planning at Gallipoli, during the First World War, the AAMC would exert influence over a wide range of areas in the military. The medical services were involved in the recruitment of soldiers. They undertook physical checks of soldiers' bodies at the point of enlistment, and they provided expert advice on the appropriate diet for soldiers. The medical services became more involved in the planning of military campaigns and were incorporated into the process for making decisions regarding casualty clearance, location of aid posts and the medical duties of RMOs. The medical services also came to be involved in all aspects of soldiers' health and were the primary vehicle through which the State attempted to control soldiers' bodies. They were responsible for sanitation and for educating soldiers in the appropriate methods of waste disposal. Development and implementation of new vaccines were also undertaken by the medical services. They were responsible for campaigns based on health and moral issues, including those regarding venereal disease. All of this medical decision-making took place in addition to the treatment and rehabilitation of sick and wounded soldiers, and demonstrates that the medical services in the First World War developed into a very different force from the providers of care and comfort they were seen as in earlier conflicts.

The increasing militarisation of medicine is a less easily defined phenomenon, but Harrison, along with Steve Sturdy and Roger Cooter, has argued for its existence.[90] Harrison suggests that Britain was a far less militarised state than Germany, for example, which is routinely held up as the example of a militaristic society in the late nineteenth and early twentieth centuries. While he argues that British militarism was less overt and more like a form of 'liberal militarism', Harrison states that 'it was militarism nonetheless'.[91] Citing such examples as the quasi-military style of organisations like the Boy Scouts and the increasing popularity of 'muscular Christianity', Harrison argues that British society was more militaristic than has been previously considered and suggests that the process of militarisation of medicine is demonstrated in nursing. The use of military-style uniforms and the introduction of hierarchies reminiscent of military ranks can be considered examples of this phenomenon. Harrison also makes clear that the discourse of disease became militarised as well. Doctors fought disease (and they still do), those who harbour disease were the enemy, and titles of the literature published in this period reflected this.[92] This changing discourse, which portrayed medicine as sublimation of war, can be read as an attempt by the medical services to legitimise their place in the increasingly rationalised military.

Although a discernible medicalisation of the military was evident in the British army, the AAMC was not satisfied with its level of control over medical issues. This dissatisfaction was complicated by the desire not just for medical control of medical issues but also for Australian medical control of Australian medical issues. As a result, the AAMC lobbied both the AIF and the Australian Government for greater responsibility for sick and wounded Australian soldiers. Given the outcome of the ill-fated expedition in the Mediterranean, it was not difficult for them to make the case that Australian soldiers were disadvantaged by Australia's subservience to Britain. As a consequence, and as will be seen in subsequent chapters, the AAMC was granted greater autonomy and responsibility for Australian casualties once the AIF shifted its focus to the Western Front. The Dardanelles campaign made evident the dire consequences of failing to integrate medical services into strategic planning in modern warfare, and the Dardanelles Commission enabled medical officers to articulate their foresight and expertise. As a result, the medical services established themselves as competent custodians of medical care and were then able to assert greater influence over medical matters on the Western Front.

Much has been written about the significance of the Dardanelles campaign to Australian nationhood. Although I reject the idea put forward by the then Prime Minister of Australia, Billy Hughes, that the Australian nation was 'born on the shores of Gallipoli', Australia's participation in the Dardanelles campaign did result in a divergence of British and Australian interests. The medical services are an example of a small, tangible, practical way in which, as a result of action on the beaches of Gallipoli, Australia stepped away from its colonial past towards a self-sufficient independence. Additionally, it was not inevitable that Australia's first major battle would result in this divergence. As we will see in subsequent chapters, there is sufficient evidence to suggest that had Australia's first engagement occurred in different circumstances, such as the more consultative command structure that Mark Harrison has argued already existed on the Western Front, then the drive towards medical–military independence might not have been so strong. The move towards self-sufficiency for the AAMC was a reaction to the inadequacy of the medical arrangements, the lack of Australian control of Australian casualties and the lack of recognition for Australian medical–military expertise in the Dardanelles campaign. Gallipoli, and its aftermath, fundamentally changed the way the AAMC provided medical care during the First World War.

CHAPTER | 2

MEDICINE IN THE LINES

STATIONARY WARFARE ON THE WESTERN FRONT, 1916–17

'In the very elaborate medical arrangements for "Messines" every possible factor in the problem of collecting, clearing, treating and evacuating casualties, was foreseen and exactly provided for,' wrote Butler in the official history. He continued: 'As it turned out, "events" were in so close accord with "arrangements" that, as an exposition of military medical technique, an account of the medical features of the battle may be based on either.'[1] This glowing description of the medical provisions at Messines stands in stark contrast to the medical care provided to wounded and sick soldiers at Gallipoli.

In roughly eighteen months, from the conclusion of the Dardanelles campaign in January 1916 to the Battle of Messines in June 1917, the AAMC underwent a series of beneficial changes both to its internal structure and to the way it worked with external organisations, particularly the RAMC. These changes enabled the AAMC to take increasing responsibility for planning the evacuation and treatment of Australian casualties. Consequently, medical arrangements for Australian soldiers at the Battle of Messines were entrusted to Australian medical personnel.

After the conclusion of the Dardanelles campaign, most of the AAMC was relocated to the Western Front along with most of the AIF. Once in France, Australian forces remained a small cog in the much larger British war machine attempting, in cooperation with its allies, to wage a cohesive war along a protracted front. The medical services and their plans for casualty evacuation and treatment were placed under the greatest strain during periods of intense fighting, so this chapter focuses on the major campaigns. In examining the work of the AAMC on the Western Front in 1916 and 1917, this chapter traces the development of casualty clearance and evacuation during this period of relatively stationary warfare. It considers the Battle of the Somme in 1916, specifically the three subsidiary battles that involved the AIF: Fromelles, Pozières and Mouquet Farm, when four of the five Australian divisions were involved in the fighting.[2] It then analyses Australian efforts in 1917, focusing on the Battle of Messines before assessing the medical events of the AIF's final major battle of the Third Ypres offensive, First Passchendaele.

The lack of integration of auxiliary services, like the medical corps, during the Dardanelles campaign was not indicative of the way the British army functioned on the Western Front.[3] The more consultative and inclusive approach to medical planning in the European theatre developed as a result of coordination, flexibility, good staff work and excellent communication.[4] This was led by senior commanders, who, unlike their equivalents on Gallipoli, actively encouraged trust and mutual respect between different branches of the army.[5] These changes, and the development of the medical services, were integral factors in making the BEF an effective force, capable of victory on the bloody battlefields of Europe.[6]

THE SOMME: AUSTRALIANS ON THE BATTLEFIELD IN 1916

The original Australian and New Zealand Army Corps (ANZAC), which included the 1st Australian Division and the New Zealand and Australian Division, was restructured in Egypt in February 1916 as part of the response to the failure at Gallipoli and the impending move to the Western Front. The 1st and 2nd Australian Divisions and the New Zealand Division combined to form I ANZAC, and the new 4th and 5th Australian Divisions, together with the British 25th Division, formed II ANZAC. In March 1916, I ANZAC was shipped to France under the command of General Sir William Birdwood, who had commanded ANZAC at Gallipoli and had been made commander of the AIF in 1915. That corps was attached to the British Second Army under General Sir Hubert Plumer. In July 1916, I ANZAC was transferred to General Sir Hubert Gough's Fifth Army and took its place in the force to attack Pozières. At this time further changes were made to the organisation of the two ANZAC corps as General Alexander Godley, commander of the New Zealand Expeditionary Force (NZEF), was appointed commander of II ANZAC. In order to consolidate commands, the New Zealand Division from I ANZAC and the 4th Australian Division from II ANZAC traded places. As a result of this change, Godley was responsible for New Zealand's troops as both commander of the NZEF and commander of the corps containing the New Zealand Division. The Battle of the Somme did not involve II ANZAC Corps in a significant way; however, the 5th Australian Division was attached to the British XI Corps for the Battle of Fromelles.

BATTLE OF FROMELLES

The Battle of Fromelles was not an integral part of the Battle of the Somme. Rather, it was a feint, an attempt by British forces to draw German troops and firepower away from the main battlefront and secure an advantageous position around the village of Fromelles in northern France. The 5th Australian Division was attached to the British XI Corps, First Army, for the battle, in the so-called nursery sector, which was used to train inexperienced troops before their move to the main part of the line. The 5th Australian Division was there as it had never before been involved in combat and was in the line at Fromelles in order to acclimatise the troops to trench conditions and to participate in small-scale raids of the German lines. The Battle of Fromelles commenced in the evening of 19 July 1916 and ended the following morning with the 5th Australian Division having incurred 5533 casualties, a number that still places it as the worst twenty-four hours in Australian military history.[7]

Colonel Charles Henry William Hardy, Assistant Director of Medical Services for the 5th Australian Division, was responsible for the evacuation of casualties at divisional level. It is unclear from his war diary when exactly he was first made aware of the intention to use his division in the attack on Fromelles, but it appears to be soon after planning commenced. On 8 July 1916, Lieutenant General Sir Richard Haking, commander of the British XI Corps, was ordered by General Sir Charles Monro, First Army commander, to prepare plans for an attack against the German line at the boundary between the First and Second Armies.[8] The following day, the 4th Australian Division was moved to Pozières, and the 5th moved in to take over the various posts.

There was some confusion over which posts the division was to occupy. Orders from the Deputy Director of Medical Services (DDMS) for the corps not to take over particular posts were immediately countermanded by the Director of Medical Services (DMS).[9] In the week following the orders, Hardy spent considerable time ensuring that the 5th Australian Division was ready for battle. He inspected the sanitation and hygiene provisions at divisional medical posts and intervened to fix them when necessary, and sought an adequate supply of stretchers, dressings and motor ambulances.[10] On 15 July 1916, Hardy recorded in his war diary that, acting on instructions from the DDMS, II ANZAC, he spoke to the DMS for the British Second Army and 'reported on steps [he] had taken with reference to operation orders'.[11] This suggests that, at some point between 8 and 15 July, Hardy had been ordered to prepare for battle. Specific orders for the Battle of Fromelles were issued to the First Army on 15 July 1916, and it was on this date that Hardy received orders to plan for the evacuation of casualties from the impending attack on what was known as the Sugarloaf Salient.[12] This was a significant improvement on the treatment of medical services at Gallipoli. Hardy had been given sufficient warning of an attack to improve sanitation and hygiene, settle into new positions and ensure adequate provisions of medical stores. On the same day that specific orders were given regarding the assault, the medical units were informed of the details, and Hardy was commanded to make casualty evacuation plans. Whether this was an example of Gary Sheffield's 'learning process', Mark Harrison's explanation that a more consultative approach existed on the Western Front or some combination of the two, the medical services were included in the planning stages for Fromelles much earlier than they were for Gallipoli.[13]

The early involvement of the medical services did not necessarily ensure that events went smoothly, as the command structure was still muddled. Hardy was initially instructed, by the DMS Second Army, to prepare plans to evacuate casualties to Estaires. When he reported this to the General Officer Commanding (GOC) the 5th Australian Division, the GOC disagreed and ordered Hardy to draft a plan of operations to evacuate to Bailleul.[14] On 15 July, after a conference of officers, Hardy prepared a plan to evacuate casualties to Bailleul, taking into account the GOC's intention to close the routes through Le Nouveau Monde and Sailly. This plan required him to establish another main dressing station, and the only suitable place was a 'manufactory' that was already partly occupied by the artillery. Hardy wrote that he 'took up the large vacant machinery rooms & Colonel Kershaw OC Artillery & Captain Carter RMO kindly gave up portions of the building and shared the Dressing Station'.[15]

The following day, 16 July 1916, Hardy issued '5th Australian Divisional Medical Order No. 1', which informed recipients that arrangements were being made for an attack 'on the enemy's front line system', then detailed the location and staffing arrangements for the divisional and Field Ambulance units.[16] Ominously, Hardy indicated to his medical officers that 'preparations are to be made for heavy casualties'.[17] The statement regarding the levels of cooperation between the artillery and battalion and brigade-level medical services supports Mark Harrison's findings of a more integrated force on the Western Front when compared to the command of the Gallipoli campaign. The willingness of the artillery commander and the RMO to give up space and share facilities suggests a cooperative approach to battle preparations between units; however, these were both Australian units so the example cannot be used to draw conclusions about international or imperial cooperation.

Not having to contend with an amphibious landing simplified matters immensely for the AAMC. The three field ambulance units of the 5th Australian Division, the 8th, 14th and 15th (8AFA, 14AFA, 15AFA), were prepared and ready to start receiving casualties before the battle commenced. On 18 July 1916, the Commanding Officer (CO) of 8AFA, Colonel A.E. Shepherd, issued orders to AAMC members under his command and wrote to Colonel Hardy: 'All other arrangements mentioned in Operation Order No. 1 have been completed.'[18] The commanding officers of 14AFA and 15AFA also recorded in their war diaries that they were in position and prepared to receive casualties the day before the attack commenced.[19] The CO 15AFA reported that Colonel Hardy had inspected all medical posts, and on his recommendation a few minor alterations were made to the deployment of medical personnel. The length of the evacuation route appears to have caused some consternation as Captain Bullen, OC 15AFA, recorded in his war diary: 'A much shorter motor route was arranged with the additional advantage of passing along unfrequented roads – this greatly facilitated the subsequent work of collecting.'[20] This change would have helped to avoid congestion on the roads; when they had to be used for both resupplying combat units and for the evacuation of casualties, it was almost always the resupply of combat units that took precedence. This change was also possible owing to the presence of significant infrastructure in western France. The road and rail networks facilitated the movement of people to and from the front line and differed from the largely non-existent infrastructure in the areas occupied by the Entente powers on Gallipoli.

The three field ambulance units and the divisional medical units provided medical care to 3277 soldiers between noon on 19 July and 8pm on 21 July 1916. If the total casualty number of 5533 is correct, then 2256 officers and men of the 5th Australian Division died or went missing before they reached a field ambulance unit. The cases evacuated by the 8th, 14th and 15th AFAs are shown in figure 2.1 and figure 2.2.

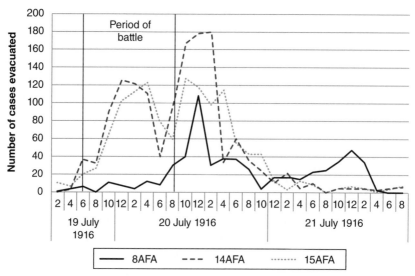

Figure 2.1 Cases through Australian Field Ambulance units from 12 noon, 19 July to 8pm, 21 July 1916
Source: compiled from 'Number of cases passed through field ambulances', war diary, July 1916, Appendix 34, ADMS 5th Aust. Div. (AWM4 26/22/6 Part 1)

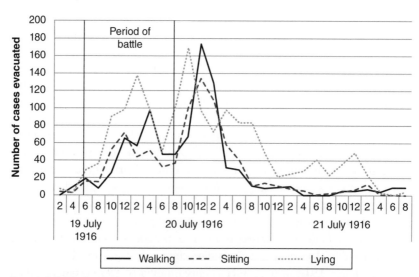

Figure 2.2 Method of carry through Australian field ambulance units from 12 noon, 19 July to 8pm, 21 July 1916
Source: compiled from 'Number of cases passed through field ambulances', war diary, July 1916, Appendix 34, ADMS 5th Aust. Div. (AWM4 26/22/6 Part 1)

The evacuation statistics for the 5th Australian Division show that the majority of casualties were evacuated from the centre and right parts of the line, where the 14th (43 per cent) and 15th (39 per cent) AFAs were positioned, whereas 8AFA on the left of the line evacuated 18 per cent of the casualties. Colonel Shepherd, Officer Commanding 8AFA, was keen to highlight that, despite the comparatively low number of casualties evacuated through the field ambulance, it was still under strain. He recorded in his war diary that, while their portion of the line did not have many casualties, the men of 8AFA worked along the entire front occupied by 5th Australian Division. He wrote: 'Although the casualties admitted do not appear large it must be borne in mind that every officer & man were distributed in every ADS and RAP over the whole front and thus the work done was much greater than appears from the records.' He continued: 'Officers & men of the Unit in my opinion carried out their duties magnificently. Nothing was to [sic] big for them to tackle & every available man including transport detail, batmen, dental detail & office staff were in the field and struggled on although completely exhausted, till the area was clear of wounded.'[21]

The scale of the task that confronted the stretcher-bearers is indicated by the time it took to retrieve all of the casualties. Hostilities commenced at 6pm and concluded at 8am; however, it took a further thirty-six hours to bring in the casualties from the front lines. The method of carry used to move soldiers to the medical posts can be read as an indicator of the severity of the soldier's injury. A wounded soldier with a femur fracture, an abdominal wound or a major head injury would be a lying case, whereas a less severe head contusion, a broken arm or a lower leg fracture could sit on a transport. The least severe injuries still required medical treatment, but the soldier would make his own way to medical assistance on foot so as to enable medical personnel to assist soldiers with more significant injuries. Figure 2.2 shows a large number of lying cases being brought in by the field ambulance units eighteen to thirty-six hours after the cessation of hostilities. Reading the graphs in concert suggests that the 8AFA stretcher-bearers were scouring No Man's Land for soldiers who were still alive well after the fighting stopped. These men would have been unreachable by medical units until that point and unable to make their own way to medical assistance. As shown in figure 2.3, almost 80 per cent of the wounds sustained in the battle were injuries to the upper and lower limbs and head injuries. This is borne out by the proportion of soldiers brought in using each method of carry. Lying cases made up 47 per cent of wounds, sitting accounted for 26 per cent and walking cases made up

27 per cent of casualties for the Battle of Fromelles.[22] With almost three-quarters of casualties requiring some form of assisted evacuation, it is not surprising that the AAMC was stretched to its limit and that the men doing the physical work of evacuation were exhausted.

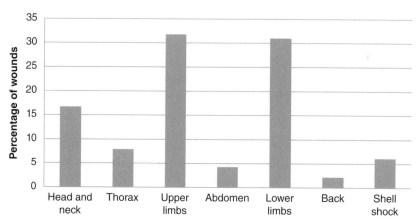

Figure 2.3 Wound type admitted to Australian field ambulances, 19–20 July 1916 (as a percentage of total)
Source: compiled from 'Percentage table showing location of wounds of casualties admitted to field ambulances in action 19th/20th July', war diary, July 1916, Appendix 35, ADMS 5th Aust. Div. (AWM4 26/22/6 Part 1)

That some injured soldiers were able to walk to medical assistance did not always mean that they arrived at a medical unit with minor medical problems. Of the walking cases Captain Bullen wrote: 'These present a difficult problem for satisfactory handling in that although often slightly wounded there is usually a certain amount of shock and many collapse at the ADS.'[23] The distance that the men had to walk to reach the advanced dressing station (ADS) was substantial and, while the provision of hot soup and coffee helped to reduce the number of men collapsing, Bullen suggested that alterations be made to the standard medical arrangements for future battles. He advised that establishing a depot around 2000 yards behind the trenches on the main evacuation lines would assist. Slightly wounded men could then walk to this depot, receive rudimentary treatment and sustenance, then be transported to the main dressing station in motorised vehicles, thereby substantially cutting the distance wounded men had to walk.

It was common at Fromelles for non-medical corps officers and men to be drawn into casualty clearance and evacuation and to be used for work that was not their responsibility. As mentioned above, the 8AFA deployed transport, batmen, dental and office personnel in order to clear the wounded from the front to medical posts. Similarly, in the 15AFA area of operations, men in the artillery helped in the physical work of the medical corps providing 'valuable assistance' in unloading waggons and assisting the bearers.[24] The evacuation of casualties was hard physical work. Close to the front, wounded soldiers were carried by stretcher-bearers on stretchers or, occasionally, a bearer would simply pick up a soldier and carry him. Once in an area where motorised transport was used to cross the terrain, the stretcher-bearers were still required to lift and shift patients on and off transports and into position in the medical units. As noted above, Colonel Shepherd reported that those clearing casualties worked until completely exhausted. This battle, although one with a high casualty rate, was over in less than a day, with all casualties being collected in fifty hours from initial bombardment to the clearing of No Man's Land. The ability of the field ambulance units to manage the workload of the men would become more significant in future battles once multiple divisions were used in military operations over extended periods of time.

Despite the medical services being prepared in advance of the commencement of hostilities, they were still stretched once the battle started. This was most evident in the problems with evacuation from the trenches. The scale of the casualties was unprecedented for such a short period of time and, while Captain Bullen acknowledged the success of casualty evacuation from the ADS onward, he was more critical of the system from the trenches working back to the ADS. The men from the 2/4 Battalion of the Oxfordshire and Buckinghamshire Light Infantry Regiment (Oxford Bucks), the 5th Sanitary Section and the New Zealand Army Medical Corps all helped to reinforce the men of 15AFA. By the time the last of these started working in the area, some bearers in 15AFA had been working continuously for twenty-two hours. Bullen described them as 'completely knocked out'.[25] In the period from the commencement of battle to 5.30am on 20 July, around 800 casualties had been evacuated through Bullen's ADS by three officers, seven non-commissioned officers (NCOs) and seventy-five men from 15AFA and the Oxford Bucks. Bullen thought that the job was made more difficult because of problems at the regimental level, suggesting that the provision at that level 'proved quite inadequate and soon broke down completely'. He continued:

> The fact that plenty of work was found for the large number eventually engaged at this one Station shows the advisability of providing for such a rush of cases either by:

1. Increase of strength of Bearer Subdivision of Ambulances
2. Increase in strength of AMC details of Fighting Units
3. Obtaining details in advance from Reserve fighting units to stand by until required.[26]

There were eventually 8 officers, 16 NCOs and 143 men evacuating casualties from the regimental aid posts to the advanced dressing station. This breakdown of casualty evacuation at the regimental level is supported by the war diaries of 8AFA and 14AFA, which show that field ambulance bearers were working right up to and in the trenches to clear injured soldiers. The breakdown at this level of the clearance chain is different from that found in the campaign at Gallipoli. In that instance evacuation to regimental aid posts was relatively smooth, but the breakdown occurred owing to the inability of the AAMC to land its full complement of medical units on 25 April 1915. At Fromelles the evacuation from the ADS was relatively smooth, owing in large part to good roads and motorised transport, but the work in the trenches failed.

The assessments by members of the AAMC of the medical arrangements for Fromelles provide insight into their priorities and problems in battle. They noted the significance of cooperation from non-medical units, both in sharing facilities and in the form of manpower, to alleviate some of the physical strain casualty evacuation placed on the men of the Australian Field Ambulance. They also highlighted the problems associated with locating the medical units a long way behind the lines, especially for the walking wounded and the stretcher-bearers clearing casualties from the front to advanced dressing stations and regimental aid posts. At Fromelles it is also possible to see the difference in procedure from the campaign at Gallipoli. The early and active inclusion of the medical corps in planning and the ability of the medical corps to prepare and refine procedure were vastly different from the lack of autonomy granted to Australian medical units in the Dardanelles campaign. Gary Sheffield argues that, owing to the casualty rate in a newly constituted division in its first major engagement, the attack damaged British–Australian relations. However, as far as the medical services were concerned, the Battle of Fromelles was a step forward from their recent experience in Gallipoli.[27]

Battle of Pozières

As the events at Fromelles were unfolding, preparations were being made for an attack on the tactically significant village of Pozières. It was situated on top of the ridgeline that ran from Thiepval to Ginchy. Capturing it, and the nearby land around Mouquet Farm, would enable British forces to observe the German positions around Thiepval from the rear. If the Fifth Army was able to capture Pozières, it would be in a position to attack the German second line, and it would also provide protection, in the case of a major British advance, to the flank of the Fourth Army.[28] The initial attack was undertaken by the 1st Australian Division on 23 July 1916. It secured the town of Pozières, incurring 5286 casualties, before the 2nd Australian Division relieved it on 27 July. The 2nd Australian Division then expanded the territory held to include the land surrounding the village, sustaining 6800 casualties in the process, before being relieved by the 4th Australian Division on 6 August. This division remained in the line until the battle ended the following day after a final attack by the German army.[29]

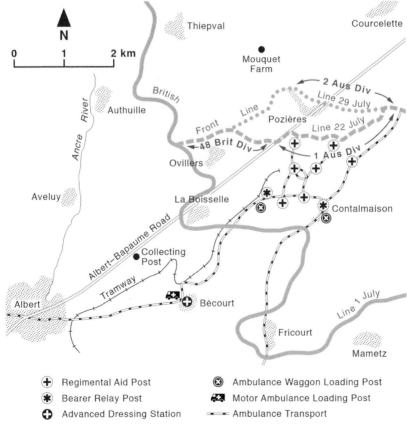

Map 2 The Battle of Pozières – Casualty Evacuation Scheme, 1916

The planning for the Battle of Pozières was generally methodical and sound. Despite urgency being advocated by Fifth Army commander General Hubert Gough and Sir Douglas Haig, commander of the British Expeditionary Force, the 1st Australian Division Commanding Officer, Major General Harold Walker, planned thoroughly and delayed its beginning by one day in order to ensure that his troops were prepared for battle.[30] The same cannot be said for the initial attack by the 2nd Australian Division. The first operation by this division, on 29 July, was described by Robin Prior and Trevor Wilson as a 'fiasco', although one the divisional staff learned from in order to plan for and execute a successful second attack on 4 August.[31]

When I ANZAC Corps moved into the area around Pozières, much of the medical infrastructure was already in place, which, combined with the landscape around Pozières, dictated the location of medical posts. However, unlike at Fromelles, the cooperative use of buildings and the handing over of premises did not occur at Pozières, at least not in the case of the 1st Australian Division. The Assistant Director of Medical Services for the 1st Australian Division, Colonel Alfred Hobart Sturdee, wrote in an appendix to his war diary: 'In drawing up the original scheme for evacuation of the wounded much difficulty was encountered as none of the Main Dressing Stations, formerly used for the Area in which our troops were operating were handed over to us.' He also pointed out that the advanced dressing station at Bécourt Château, 'which from the lay of the ground and the formation of the roads was our natural clearing spot was outside our area'. He reported: 'It was at first refused to us and then when we had occupied it we were instructed to vacate it upon the evening of July 22nd.' Vacating that position on that evening would have thrown the medical arrangements into disarray so Sturdee 'reported the matter to the AA&QMG and received instructions from him and the AA&QMG of the Corps to continue its use'.[32]

In this instance, the landscape was not sufficiently taken into account when drawing up areas of operation. Sturdee had to choose between two difficult options. He could have hoped the soldiers under his care ignored the logical path to medical assistance and would find their way to his unit, or he could intervene to alter the arrangements. He chose the latter, which was a deliberate subversion of the military hierarchy in place. When the flaws in the plan became obvious to Sturdee and he occupied the advanced dressing station even though he had been ordered not to, he did so late enough before the commencement of the battle that to order him to move his unit would have created too high a risk for the AAMC and to the soldiers it served. As a result, the Assistant Adjutant and Quartermaster General (AA&QMG) had little choice but to accept the violation of military doctrine. There is no indication in his records of Sturdee facing disciplinary proceedings as a result of these actions; his concern that the logical place for the ADS was Bécourt Château was validated by the clearance statistics.[33] Those statistics show that two-thirds of the casualties for the 1st Australian Division passed through his ADS at Bécourt Château.[34]

Much like at Fromelles, distance was a factor in the casualty evacuation process at Pozières. Sturdee wrote: 'Our evacuations again were made difficult owing to the Main Dressing Stations being so far removed from the scene of operations.'[35] While this problem was largely resolved by the use of motorised transport, the co-opted transport units were not from the 1st Australian Division. The DDMS of the corps gave the 1st Division use of the 2nd and 4th Australian Divisions' motor ambulances, as well as the motor lorries and buses of the 1st Australian Division Supply Company along with four lorries from the British 19th Division. This sharing of resources was beneficial for the purposes of casualty evacuation, but it was not just vehicles that were used from other units. Over the course of 1st Australian Division's time in the line, officers and other ranks from 13AFA, 5AFA and 12AFA were added to the 1st Division's usual complement of field ambulances (1AFA, 2AFA and 3AFA). These units were ordinarily attached to the 2nd and 4th Australian Divisions, which then meant that medical units were on active duty more often than their corresponding fighting units.

Sturdee broke with military doctrine again in the way he organised the personnel of the field ambulances. Ordinarily each field ambulance had a tent subdivision and a bearer subdivision that worked together under one commanding officer to take care of one section of the evacuation chain. At Pozières, the tent subdivisions of 1AFA and 2AFA established two main dressing stations, one for stretcher and severe cases and one for slight and walking cases. The three bearer subdivisions as well as 3AFA's tent subdivision were placed under the command of Lieutenant Colonel Harry Nairn Butler of the 3AFA. Under Butler, ADSs were established at North Chimney Albert and Bécourt Château. The availability of motorised transport and decent roads meant that bearers were more useful closer to the front and, as at Fromelles, the AAMC bearers worked forward to reinforce the regimental bearers to facilitate casualty clearance from the trenches. This level of adaptability and flexibility in the deployment of medical personnel demonstrates that significant decision-making responsibility had been handed over to Australian officers. While the RAMC was learning that the keys to success were coordination and flexibility, the AAMC was particularly adaptable.[36] In his report, Colonel Sturdee wrote: 'In conclusion I would like to add that owing to the good and willing work performed by all, the evacuation of the wounded surpassed my most sanguine expectation.'[37] The relative success of casualty evacuation with this new model of deployment for the field ambulance subdivisions would form the basis of further departures from established doctrine once the Australian forces were engaged at Messines in July 1917.

Once the 2nd Australian Division (2AD) relieved 1st Australian Division, it laid the groundwork for another innovation that would come later, in the Battle of Messines. Colonel Alfred Sutton, ADMS 2nd Australian Division, took pains to ensure that wounded soldiers were not being unnecessarily attended to. Sutton wrote to all RMOs: 'In the event of heavy casualties RMOs and Medical Officers of Advanced Dressing Stations and Posts are reminded that the urgent necessity is to clear casualties to Main Dressing Station as rapidly as possible.' He added: 'A wound covered by a First Field Dressing and not bleeding will not be touched.'[38] In order to avoid congestion, all cases that could tolerate a delay in further medical intervention were to be evacuated further back from the front, thereby preventing the wounded from accumulating in areas exposed to enemy fire or blocking communication networks.[39] This was a lesson learned from Gallipoli where soldiers awaiting treatment accumulated on the beach around the 1st Australian Casualty Clearing Station and were thus vulnerable, with some of those on the beach subsequently being wounded or killed by shrapnel. The decisions not to redress stable wounds before evacuation and to push wounded men away from the front as quickly as possible were both ideas that were utilised to greater effect at Messines.

After the attack of 4 August, Colonel Sutton again reported that AAMC bearers also assisted regimental bearers to clear casualties from the trenches during both the late July and early August operations. Echoing his counterparts from other divisions and previous battles, Sturdee wrote: 'The experience has shown the need for increase in number of Regimental Stretcher Bearers. Over and above the 16 men on the establishment another 16 men per Battalion should be available as a reinforcement.' Continuing his point, he emphasised the significance of the problem by pointing out that 'Stretcher Bearers cannot be provided from the Field Ambulances without materially delaying evacuation of the wounded further down the Line'.[40] This problem of overwork for an insufficient number of bearers would continue beyond Pozières.

BATTLE OF MOUQUET FARM

Unlike at Pozières, where each division of I ANZAC was used in successive phases, at Mouquet Farm the three divisions were used simultaneously. From this battle there were 8600 casualties with the majority (some 4650) from the 4th Australian Division.[41] The three battalions of 4th Division used in the attack were ordered to capture Mouquet Farm on 14 August. All three were much depleted already, and the results were disastrous. Prior and Wilson's damning assessment of the attack is telling, arguing 'the melancholy fact is that the three battalions which were in no

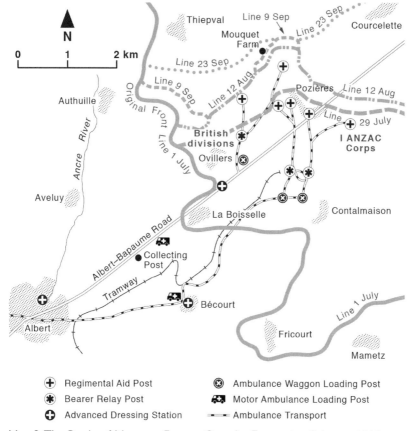

Map 3 The Battle of Mouquet Farm – Casualty Evacuation Scheme, 1916

shape to attack at all suffered some 1,100 casualties for precisely no gain of ground'. They continued: 'The husks of the three battalions had been reduced to a state of rebellion by the incompetence of their superiors. In truth the operation should never have taken place.'[42] The Australian divisions were pulled out of the line, much reduced in size from when they began the Battles of Pozières and Mouquet Farm, and the Canadian Corps was brought in to capture the objectives.

With the Battles of Pozières and Mouquet Farm effectively forming one longer Battle of Pozières Ridge, it is not surprising that the same factors that were problematic for the AAMC at Pozières were encountered again at Mouquet Farm. Distance was a particular problem. Despite the front moving forward from attacking Pozières to Mouquet Farm, a distance of around 1.7 kilometres, the advanced dressing station was maintained at Bécourt Château. The problems associated with having an advanced dressing station well behind the front were then exacerbated by the front moving further forward. Colonel Sturdee, ADMS 1AD, decided against moving the ADS closer as it would endanger the motor ambulances that were evacuating soldiers from that point. As a result, the seriously wounded still had to be carried long distances, thereby placing greater strain on the stretcher-bearers. In this instance, not only did the bearers work right up to the trenches but also, in at least one case, a soldier was brought in from No Man's Land by divisional bearers under the protection of a white flag.[43]

The issue of walking wounded not finding their way to aid posts, identified at Pozières, was noted again by the medical men at Mouquet Farm. The logical path to evacuate from an area owing to the lay of the land was not always the path required to reach the soldiers' respective medical units. The artificial boundaries of divisional command did not adequately take into account the specifics of the landscape. Most – but not all – wounded soldiers successfully negotiated the terrain to find the correct collecting post. As Sturdee reported, 'A few found their way into a British Field Ambulance by taking a turn to the right at Pozières and so wending their way to Ovillers a natural but, owing to the division of the area, a wrong course.'[44] Solving this problem would require cooperation between divisions within a corps, as well as between corps and, at the extreme flanks of the front, potentially between the armies of the British Expeditionary Force and its allies. As will be seen in chapter 3, the work of the various medical services in 1918 went some way towards achieving this objective.

At Mouquet Farm the AAMC improvised some of the medical arrangements in an attempt to limit the impact of the extended evacuation on casualties. In the 1st Australian Division, Colonel Sturdee reported that during periods when casualties were light, Colonel Shaw, Officer Commanding 1AFA, evacuated slightly wounded cases using ambulance waggons. This sped up the process and increased the level of comfort experienced by wounded soldiers. It would also have limited the number of cases who went into shock, as had been the case for many at Pozières. Once casualty numbers increased again, the usual process of evacuation resumed. Sturdee pointed out, yet again, that the number of stretcher-bearers was insufficient to cope with the demand. At the end of his report he concluded that 'the number of bearers attached to a Division is at times too small to cope with the large number of casualties which occur in modern warfare'. Because of this, he continued, 'the various bearer divisions had to be grouped together and controlled more or less by the Corps, with the result that when the Divisions went into rest the bearers were still left at the front nominally in reserve but actually more or less at work'.[45] This separation of bearer and tent subdivisions and placing the bearers under one command continued the practice established during the Battle of Pozières and would continue at Messines.

In Flanders Fields: The AIF in 1917

I ANZAC was withdrawn from the line in early September 1916. The Australian units were then rebuilt and underwent further training before being used in the Battle of Bullecourt in April 1917. Australian units fought in a series of battles between April and October 1917; however, the most significant battles, in terms of the AAMC's evolving model of casualty evacuation, were at Messines and Passchendaele in Belgium.[46] For the AAMC, these battles consolidated Australian control of medical care for Australian soldiers, then challenged the idea of military primacy in decision-making, with doctors working in a manner more reminiscent of their civilian work than their military role.

Battle of Messines

Preparations commenced well before the fighting in the Battle of Messines, which started in June 1917.[47] In the eighteen months before the battle, the Royal Engineers led a significant effort to place mines underneath the German Fourth Army lines. Once objectives were identified, the BEF began to put in place plans that required considerable preparation. The commanders were able to do so because the front had not moved substantially for the best part of two years, and there was no indication of that changing. This led to significant tactical successes in pursuit of limited objectives for combat operations, including the innovative use of a creeping barrage, mined explosives under the German lines, and extensive artillery bombardment. Despite coming at a significant cost in terms of casualties, this battle was a turning point for both combat and medical operations. The institutional learning that occurred after Messines was by no means immediate or evenly distributed across the military – old mistakes would be repeated – but the successes and innovations would be harnessed, eventually, to win the war on the Western Front.[48]

In a report written after the war, Lieutenant Colonel John Hubback Anderson,[49] who had been Deputy Assistant Director of Medical Services for the 3rd Australian Division, identified what were, to his knowledge, a number of 'distinctive characteristics' of the Australian medical arrangements for Messines.[50] These characteristics were varied and included innovative treatments, revising the structure of the medical services along the evacuation route, and altering the deployment of personnel within that structure.

The first innovation discussed by Anderson was the use of Thomas splints. These splints, the invention of Welshman Hugh Owen Thomas, came into widespread use in military medicine in 1916, owing to the advocacy of Thomas's nephew, Robert Jones, and over the protestations of London-trained doctors.[51] The splint's ability to stabilise a limb was a significant factor in the dramatic reduction of the mortality rate for femur fractures in the British army and of the need for leg amputations.[52] At a meeting of the Second Army Medical Society, Major Sinclair of the RAMC argued for the use of Thomas splints in forward areas. Anderson, however, was sceptical about their use. He thought they would be too cumbersome to be effective in the trenches, on the basis of his experience of using them during 1916 at Pozières, where the splints were used as far forward as advanced dressing stations. From the summer of 1916, medical staff were ordered to use the splints when appropriate, and the application of the splint was taught in the RAMC School of Instruction from October 1917, by which time splinting was routine in dressing stations.[53] It was, however, not yet commonly performed forward of dressing stations.

In order to overcome his objections to using Thomas splints in forward areas, Anderson carried out what he described as 'experiments' in the trenches using dummies. During these experiments the splints performed well, which Anderson attributed to the quality of the trenches around

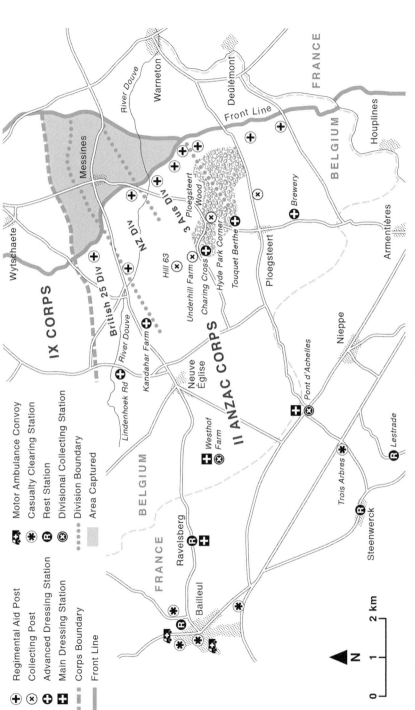

Map 4 The Battle of Messines – medical arrangements of II ANZAC Corps, 1917

Symbol	Description	Symbol	Description
✚	Regimental Aid Post	🚑	Motor Ambulance Convoy
✖	Collecting Post	✳	Casualty Clearing Station
✚	Advanced Dressing Station	Ⓡ	Rest Station
✚	Main Dressing Station	✖	Divisional Collecting Station
	Corps Boundary	●●●	Division Boundary
	Front Line		Area Captured

IX CORPS

II ANZAC CORPS

Wytschaete

Messines

River Douve

Warneton

Dedÿlémont

FRANCE

BELGIUM

Houplines

Front Line

British 25 Div

NZ DIV

3 AUS DIV

Ploegsteert Wood

Brewery

Armentières

Hill 63

Underhill Farm

Charing Cross

Hyde Park Corner

Touquet Berthe

Ploegsteert

Kandahar Farm

Lindenhoek Rd

River Douve

Neuve Église

Westhof Farm

Pont d'Achelles

Nieppe

Lestrade

Trois Arbres

Steenwerck

Ravelsberg

Bailleul

FRANCE

BELGIUM

N

0   1   2 km

Messines. Having overcome his initial objection, Anderson set about finding a way around his second objection: the difficulty of getting adequate supplies. In order to get sufficient supplies Anderson visited as many advanced depots of medical stores as he could and collected a few splints from each in order not to drain one completely. These were then sent up to regimental aid posts at the last minute with both advanced and main dressing stations carrying supplies as well. Each car that travelled to an ADS from a main dressing station carried a couple of splints to resupply the regimental aid post. This system worked well, and Anderson proudly boasted that the splints 'proved a great boon and one, if not more, was actually applied in [a] firing trench by an RMO taking it up from RAP to patient. Some time after, I heard personally from a visiting Surgeon that fract. femurs got down extra well.'[54] This innovation was the result of the industry and ingenuity of the doctors involved. From the participation of the Second Army Medical Society to the experimentation and eventual implementation of the use of splints, this is an example of civilian medical training influencing military medical practice.

Part of the success of Thomas splints in Messines was a consequence of the well-planned and sound structure of casualty evacuation. The plans for casualty evacuation at Messines were laid down by Colonel White, ADMS of the 3rd Australian Division, on 21 May 1917, seventeen days before the battle commenced.[55] This contrasts with Gallipoli where Howse had virtually no ability to make plans himself, and improved upon events at Pozières.

As part of Colonel White's arrangements, the three field ambulance units were used in an integrated fashion rather than as three discrete units. The area they worked was divided into three sections, each under an ambulance commanding officer, as can be seen in figure 2.4. There was one commanding officer for the regimental aid post through to, but not including, the advanced dressing station, and another CO for the advanced dressing station up to the main dressing station. The third CO was in charge of the main dressing station and the collecting point, which was the place the walking wounded made their way to and were able to rest and receive treatment.

A field ambulance consisted of tent and bearer subdivisions, distinctions that were still relevant under White's plan. The subdivisions were allotted with bearer divisions to forward areas and tent subdivisions towards the rear. This was a logical distinction that allowed for stretcher-bearers with extra training in carrying and manoeuvring casualties and applying first aid to be closer to the front, and those whose training was focused on assessment of injuries, redressing and the stopping of bleeding located further back. Under this system – an extension of

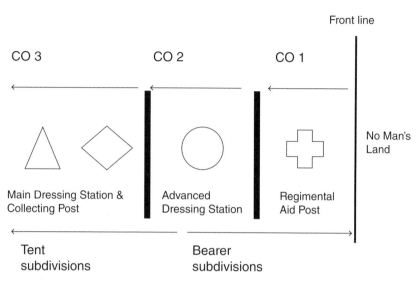

Figure 2.4 Diagram of Australia Field Ambulance areas of responsibility for the Battle of Messines, 1917

the system used at Pozières and Mouquet Farm – each CO had part of each of the three field ambulance units under him. Normally one unit would be allocated a section of the line; Anderson wrote that this change was possible because of the method of training the field ambulances had received where they were trained together as a single body. Anderson explained that the experiment had been partially tried at Pozières, 'but it was more fully exploited at Messines'.[56] In these examples, officers of the AAMC were willing to depart from standard procedures when they saw an opportunity to function in a more efficient manner.

There were, however, instances where the AAMC changed its structure out of necessity rather than perceived opportunity to increase efficiency. Much like Sturdee's 1st Australian Division at Pozières, the 3rd Australian Division at Messines was functioning along a narrow front, making it impossible to provide eight regimental aid posts with sufficient protection from enemy fire, as was the ideal (see figure 2.5). Having learnt from the problems at Pozières, where there were lots of regimental aid posts feeding the vast majority of cases through one advanced dressing station and creating a bottleneck (as in figure 2.6), White placed two RMOs at each of four regimental aid posts. As Anderson commented: 'the possibilities of the scheme were then seen and fully exploited as it was considered a good idea' (see figure 2.7).[57]

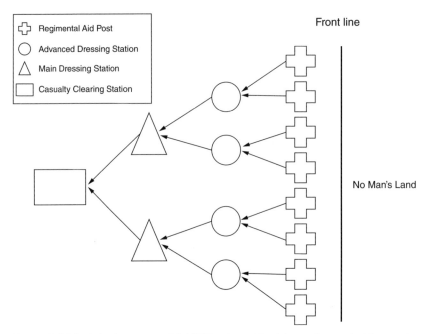

Figure 2.5 Ideal deployment of AAMC units with eight regimental aid posts in early 1916

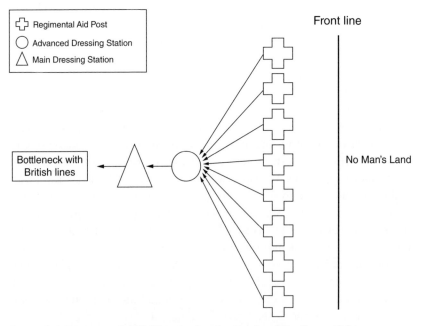

Figure 2.6 Diagram of AAMC units for the Battle of Pozières, 1916

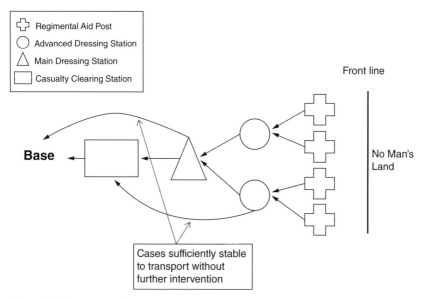

Figure 2.7 Diagram of medical arrangements for the Battle of Messines, 1917

This system, at Messines, had some significant benefits. First, the RMOs could work in shifts. This enabled them to get some rest but, during busy periods, it was possible to limit the waiting time for the wounded by having both RMOs at work. Second, when the line advanced, one RMO could establish a forward regimental aid post that then evacuated casualties to the existing RAP, a well-known spot, rather than leaving it unattended in the advance. Third, when there was an emergency in the trenches that required the attendance of a medical officer, such as a major abdominal wound or severe injury to a senior officer, the RAP was not left unattended. Finally, in the event that one of the RMOs was injured, this move to halve the number of RAPs – and therefore double the number of staff at each – would enable the RAP to keep functioning under the command of the second RMO.

In his assessment of the medical arrangements for the Battle of Messines, Lieutenant Colonel Anderson noted a significant problem with this model: it created the possibility that the army could lose two medical officers if the RAP was hit with a large shell. This was not out of the realm of possibility, although it did not happen in this instance. Presumably, if this had occurred, the nearest RAP would have been split in two, with one half remaining in its original location and the second half forming a new RAP, in much the same way as was laid out above in the case of an advance. In the Dardanelles campaign, the structure of the medical evacuation process was changed out of necessity, owing to the failure of the combat units to reach their objectives and secure enough ground inland for the medical services to be fully deployed. In that instance, the plan had to be abandoned because the system laid down by the General Staff and the RAMC broke down completely. In the case of Messines, Colonel White knew before the commencement of hostilities that he would have to contend with a limited area and so modified the structure to fit the specific circumstance faced by his division.

Another change in the way Australian casualty evacuation functioned at Messines was, in Anderson's opinion, due to the proximity of the casualty clearing station to the forward medical units, although in his report he adds 'an Australian one at that', seemingly happy with the opportunities this afforded the 3rd Australian Division.[58] Anderson, together with the Commanding Officer of the main dressing station, went to see the Commanding Officer of the casualty clearing station, Colonel Ramsay Webb. There they organised for cases appropriately marked at the advanced dressing station to bypass the main dressing station and be cleared directly to the casualty clearing station. They also put in place a similar procedure to evacuate casualties from the main dressing station directly to the base without needing to be seen at the casualty clearing station. This would not have been possible if the casualty clearing station was positioned a significant distance behind the MDS. Anderson wrote that he 'got the idea from the Jap. arrangements as described in some book I read about the Russo-Jap war'.[59] This builds on the idea put forward at Pozières by Sutton, then ADMS for the 2nd Australian Division, when he ordered that casualties who were not bleeding and were adequately bandaged not be redressed at advanced dressing stations in order to prevent congestion. By skipping stages in the casualty evacuation chain, these medical men decreased the chances of congestion at the various medical stations and improved the care of wounded soldiers.

Lieutenant Colonel Anderson did not give an explicit reason for his enthusiasm for the casualty clearing station in the evacuation chain being an Australian one. He did suggest that it was easy to make changes to procedure within divisional medical services (from the advanced dressing station to the main dressing station) and wrote that 'having an Australian at the CCS made it possible for us'.[60] It is also possible that Anderson and Ramsay Webb knew each other in their civilian lives, given that both were practising medicine in Melbourne immediately before the war. I suggest he suspected that an Australian Commanding Officer of an Australian casualty clearing station would be more willing to depart from military doctrine in consultation with an Australian Deputy Assistant Director of Medical Services (DADMS) than a British officer would have been. Whatever his reasoning, it is significant that this was not a top-down order. Rather, it was an idea from a divisional medical officer shared with his immediate colleagues, then passed up the chain of command.

These changes had implications for the routes taken by the transports as they evacuated casualties and brought up supplies. At Pozières the same road was taken by the supplies being brought up to the front and the casualties being evacuated out. This added to the congestion and frequently meant that either supplies or casualties had to be prioritised, as it was often impossible for both to happen simultaneously. At Messines the transports worked in circles and no roads overlapped. As a motor ambulance full of casualties arrived at the main dressing station, another one would set out from the other side of the station so that there were always multiple ambulances moving to take up medical supplies such as splints and carry casualties back from the front. There was also a motor ambulance always on standby at the advanced dressing station as a contingency.

The work of the AAMC at Messines once again reinforces Mark Harrison's argument that a more consultative and inclusive culture existed on the Western Front than in the Dardanelles campaign. Four days before the intended commencement of the Gallipoli landings, no one from the medical services had been officially informed of, or involved in, the planning of medical arrangements. In contrast to this, Colonel White had enough information at his disposal to publish thorough plans for the medical evacuation of casualties two and a half weeks before the beginning of the Battle of Messines. Decisions about the evacuation of casualties on the Western Front were increasingly made on medical grounds, and likewise the medical services were involved earlier in the preparation for battle.

While it made sense for the efficiency of transport to send casualties through each stage in the clearance chain, it had poor outcomes for the patients being evacuated. By skipping steps in the casualty evacuation chain and providing soldiers with a more direct route to medical assistance for complex issues, the medical services reduced the number of times the soldier needed to be transferred onto or off a transport. This minimised the pain and trauma of being lifted and shifted, and decreased the amount of time it took to reach the destination as there was no need to stop at each stage of evacuation and have casualties re-sorted for transport to the next medical unit. The use of Thomas splints in forward areas was seen as being in the best interest of the patient so Anderson found a way to include them in casualty evacuation from Messines, and the experience at Pozières gave the AAMC plenty of scope to reform the evacuation process in order to get patients to appropriate medical care in a timely fashion.

Assessing Gallipoli, the Somme and Messines in this way, it becomes evident that British involvement in Australian medical care in the First World War was gradually pushed further and further away from the front. The Dardanelles campaign took place in 1915, but its consequences influenced the rest of the First World War. As discussed in chapter 1, Surgeon General Sir Neville Howse gave evidence to the Dardanelles Commission and declared that the medical arrangements 'amounted to criminal negligence'. He made that statement on 10 July 1917; that is, between the Battles of Messines and Passchendaele.[61] Howse told the commission that he thought the AAMC should be responsible for Australian casualties. He could do so with confidence because the AAMC had just proved itself to be an appropriate provider of medical care for its soldiers in the Battle of Messines.

A STRANGE INTERLUDE: FURTHER ATTEMPTS AT CONTROL

In what appears to be a strange choice in timing, during this period between the Battles of Messines and Third Ypres, discussions were held between Britain and the dominions regarding the future of the imperial medical services. This occurred despite the fact that it was still 'fighting season' and plans were already in progress for Third Ypres. The apparent shift towards Australian control of Australian casualties was extended to include some level of Australian control of imperial medical services.

On 4 September 1917, in the lead-up to the Australians' main involve-ment in the Battle of Passchendaele, Major General Sir Alfred Keogh, Director General Army Medical Services, wrote to the administrative heads of the dominion medical services to advocate for a more integrated approach to medical care administration.[62] Butler, the official historian, states that this was a result of a suggestion by Sir Neville Howse to Keogh.[63] Keogh drew upon the shared heritage of the medical services, with those of Australia, Canada and New Zealand having been modelled on the RAMC, and noted that once the dominion medical services had begun arriving for the First World War it had become clear that they expected to maintain some level of autonomy. He lamented this in writing: 'My own instincts were against this separatist tendency but it was obvious that any attempt on my part to weld all the Medical Services together for the common good would have been misunderstood and misinterpreted.' Keogh argued that the empire did not receive the 'full benefit' of its resources as they were not being used in an efficient manner during the war. He wrote that, as a general rule, the medical administrations of the dominion armies 'so far as they are individually concerned ... are of the opinion that the medical resources of the Empire should be pooled for the common object. It is, however, not probable that the political heads of their respective Governments would concur.' The proposed structure of this 'Empire Medical Service' advocated by Keogh acknowledged that the dominions would not agree to their medical corps merging with and being subsumed by the RAMC. Instead, Keogh suggested the dominion medical services have 'a share in the control and management' of an 'Imperial Medical Administration'. His proposal would have entailed the medical corps remaining separate but combining their administrations, thereby filling scientific, clinical and administrative posts based on merit without regard for the service to which the individual belonged. There would be one supply department and one medical headquarters to avoid unnecessary duplication of roles and minimise waste. Finally, Keogh wrote that the plan would allow for a greater degree of flexibility as 'while the personnel of the several Medical Corps would as a matter of good administration be kept at work with the Fighting Troops of their respective Armies', he suggested that 'they could in fact be available for all and every service which might be thought necessary'.[64]

These administrative changes were to be overseen by a medical council with the dominion medical administrators being attached to the War Office and equivalent to the Director General Army Medical Services. Keogh, clearly uncomfortable with his own proposal, wrote: 'So far as I am personally concerned I have no objection, but as a firm believer in personal responsibility and a convinced opponent of Government by Committees, I consider this to be the weak point in the whole conception.' He continued: 'I am not in the least anxious to evade my responsibilities, and would prefer to stand or fall by my own work, but the conclusion that the Dominions Medical Administrators must be equal to the DG, AMS is logical.'[65] His final point in the proposed plan was to suggest that the Army Council should have the right to appoint representatives rather than leaving that issue in the hands of the respective dominion governments. He wrote:

> It should be remembered also that my impression as to the possible
> success of the scheme outlined above is derived rather from the
> knowledge I possess of the characters and abilities of the present
> D'sMS [sic] of the Dominions – their successors and my successor
> might not work so amicably – moreover to secure the right men the

appointments of the former could not be allowed to rest with the Dominions, but should be made by the Army Council.[66]

This plan, outlined by Keogh, does not demonstrate much confidence in the governments of the dominions. Keogh thought he would be misunderstood if he advocated for his ideal structure for the medical services and then does not trust those governments to appoint appropriate replacements for their directors of medical services should the need arise. In this way the imperial hierarchy continued. While Keogh had accepted that the individuals working as the directors of medical services for the dominions were worthy of the position as his equal, he was not convinced that the dominion governments could make an appropriate choice a second time.

The Deputy Director of Medical Services and the Commanding Officer of the New Zealand Expeditionary Force, Colonel Parkes and Sir Alexander Godley, both responded to Keogh's memorandum, as did the Director of Medical Services of the AIF, Sir Neville Howse.[67] Parkes and Godley were in agreement with the reasoning in Keogh's plan but disagreed with him on the committee structure. Parkes told Keogh he thought the main difficulty would be the issue of equal representation on the committee. He wrote that it was possible that 'a deadlock might arise in matters where the opinions of the representatives are equally opposed, perhaps on a question not directly concerning the Dominions, and although this may be a remote chance it is a contingency which might occur'.[68]

To remedy this problem, Parkes proposed that the directors of medical services for the dominions take up positions similar to that of staff or executive officers to the Director General and advise him, with the Director General, Sir Alfred Keogh, being the one to make decisions. Although Sir Alexander Godley was not originally included in the correspondence by Keogh, Parkes showed him both the letter from Keogh and his response. Godley wrote to Keogh in support of Parkes' suggestion that the Directors of Medical Services act as an advisory council of staff officers.[69] Sir Neville Howse was opposed to this alteration. Having discussed the issue with the Directors of Medical Services of Canada and New Zealand, he responded to Keogh:

> I have carefully considered the clear and concise principles enunciated by you and assuming that I am correct in thinking a Medical Council would be of assistance to the empire and admitting this presumption, I cannot see any logical solution of the question unless each member of the council had an equal share and responsibility in the administration of the Medical Service of the Empire.[70]

This suggestion is in agreement with Keogh's original plan and would have allowed the Australian medical services to have a more direct say in the administration of the medical care provided to Australian soldiers, but it was in direct opposition to the position advocated by Parkes and Godley – a disagreement that did not bode well for a group contemplating embarking on a mission of management by committee. Howse's reason for opposing the position of Parkes and Godley was that the war was simply too big for one person to hold responsibility for a service of fundamental importance such as the medical corps. He wrote: 'I am a strong believer in personal responsibility, but might I respectfully suggest that the War has become so vast and carried on under such varied conditions that it has become practically impossible for any one man to effectively control the Medical Services.'[71]

Whether as a result of this disagreement between the potential committee members or the opposition of the various governments to give up some level of autonomy, the administrations of the empire medical services were not amalgamated. Although the 'imperial army project' pushed British and dominion armies towards greater interoperability and prompted the creation of forces with interchangeable structures, this episode suggests that there were limits to cooperation. Once it gained control of medical matters for the AIF, the AAMC was unwilling to give it up.

First Battle of Passchendaele

Although the AIF's initial involvement in the Third Battle of Ypres took place in relatively fine weather, heavy rains between the Battles of Broodseinde, on 4 October 1917, and Poelcappelle, on 9 October 1917, turned the ground to mud that was ankle deep in most places but knee or waist deep in others. This caused major problems for the stretcher-bearers, who had to trudge through the mud to evacuate casualties. Duckboards were laid to help mitigate the problem, but they were not initially available, were often only in single file, and were sometimes damaged by the use of animal-drawn and motorised transports.[72] The distance between the regimental aid posts and the advanced dressing station was such that it was unexceptional for it to take six stretcher-bearers five hours to carry one wounded soldier.[73] Frequently this was increased to eight, ten or, in at least one case when it was particularly muddy, twelve stretcher-bearers per wounded soldier.[74] This was a significant use of resources; once the bearers had handed over their casualty, they were to make their way back to the front carrying replacement stretchers and other medical stores with them.[75] The

Assistant Director of Medical Services for every Australian division wrote in his war diary of the long shifts, under-resourcing and utter exhaustion of the stretcher-bearers of the Australian Field Ambulance during the battle.[76] And it came without any substantial gain in territory, with Prior and Wilson stating: 'In all, the campaign probably reduced the strength of the BEF by the equivalent of 10 to 12 divisions out of a total strength of 60. No significant accessions of territory were made as a result.'[77]

The medical arrangements for First Passchendaele extended the changes to military doctrine that had developed after the Battle of Messines. They provided for a process of directly evacuating wounded soldiers from the advanced dressing station to the casualty clearing station, skipping the main dressing station when possible. The arrangements also made changes to the record-keeping, with the abolition of all medical record-keeping other than field medical cards. On 23 September, Major J.B. Metcalfe, on behalf of Colonel Manifold, Deputy Director of Medical Services I ANZAC, wrote to the Director of Medical Services for the Second Army to query the efficacy of the process.[78] The DMS Second Army requested the information from the commanding officers of the various casualty clearing stations and their response was overwhelmingly positive.[79] Lieutenant Colonel R. Blanchard, Officer Commanding the 3rd Canadian Casualty Clearing Station, reported that 'there has been no difficulty in carrying out the new method in the case of the walking wounded with the assistance of the staff supplied by the Field Ambulances'. He continued: 'The lying wounded have, with few exceptions, come with Field Medical Cards as before and this has relieved us of considerable extra work and inconvenience. Both walking and lying wounded have arrived here with wounds practically as well dressed as ever before.'[80]

As well as making some suggestions to refine the procedures for managing influxes of walking wounded, the Officer Commanding the 2nd Canadian Casualty Clearing Station replied: '[S]o far as my observations go the scheme has worked very satisfactorily especially from the standpoint of the welfare of the patients.'[81] Lieutenant Colonel Warmott, CO of the British 10th Casualty Clearing Station, suggested further refinements to the system. He suggested that field medical cards be filled out for all patients at the ADS as the process of not completing them until they reached a CCS created considerable delay as 'every case [had] to be redressed for diagnostic purposes only, whereas many of these cases could go straight on to train without being redressed'.[82] With these developments, the principle of casualty evacuation before the Battles of Pozières and Messines had been largely eroded. The aim had been to keep wounded soldiers as close to the front as possible so they could be returned to their units and resume their place in the fighting force without too much delay. This principle was unrealistic in modern warfare given the unprecedented scale of the casualties. On the Western Front, it soon became apparent that casualties needed to be cleared as quickly as possible away from the lines in order to prevent congestion at medical posts and to avoid placing an unnecessary burden on the AAMC.

EXERCISING AUTHORITY: CHANGING THE SYSTEM

The men of the AAMC challenged the traditional hierarchies in place throughout 1916 and 1917. The imperial hierarchy that fostered Australian deference to Britain had already been disrupted by the end of the Dardanelles campaign, and Neville Howse was clear in his determination to maintain Australian control of Australian medical arrangements as far as was possible. Consequently, other hierarchies were challenged.

Whereas in the British army the medical corps was an important, if subordinate, part of the military, the small number of AAMC officers before the war meant that the AAMC was almost entirely dependent on civilian doctors. These medical men sought each other out and discussed solutions before informing their superiors of substantial changes to military doctrine, as demonstrated by the changes they made to the casualty evacuation systems for the Battles of Pozières and Messines. These changes were built on and extended throughout these two years of stationary warfare. What started as an attempt to prevent the unnecessary redressing of wounds at the Battle of Pozières developed into a sophisticated system of casualty evacuation that allowed for the rapid removal of casualties from the fighting area to the point of treatment, without unnecessary stops at medical posts along the way. Lieutenant Colonel Anderson suggested that having an Australian casualty clearing station at Trois Arbres to receive Australian casualties from the Battle of Messines allowed for the development of this process, yet the move to Flanders enabled the sharing of these ideas with the British and Canadian medical services through their casualty clearing stations at the First Battle of Passchendaele. It is clear from the first two years of the AIF on the Western Front that the civilian medical men who comprised the AAMC increasingly made decisions about the evacuation and treatment of Australian casualties and began to influence the process of evacuation beyond the AAMC.

CHAPTER 3

THE WESTERN FRONT IN 1918

THE AAMC IN MOBILE WARFARE

The European winter of 1917–18 was a time of change for the Australian Imperial Force. In Australia, two plebiscites to introduce conscription had failed, and plans to raise a sixth Australian division were scrapped. Recruits originally destined for this new division were distributed among the existing five divisions, which had suffered significant losses in the fighting in September and October 1917, during the Third Battle of Ypres. In November 1917, having been withdrawn from the line the month before, the five Australian divisions were reorganised into one Australian Corps and attached to the British Fourth Army. The British and New Zealand divisions that had been part of II ANZAC became the British XXII Corps, part of First Army. General Sir William Birdwood, who had been Commanding Officer of I ANZAC, was originally put in charge of the new corps, but in May 1918 he was made Commanding Officer of Fifth Army. As a result, Major General John Monash was promoted to lieutenant general; the Australian Corps was in his command from May onwards, marking the first time an Australian was in command of a fighting unit at corps level on the Western Front.[1]

The conditions of war in 1918 were different from those in 1916 and 1917. Butler argued in the Official History that the changes made in the way casualty evacuation was handled at divisional and corps level in 1918 were 'a natural and simple adjustment' that 'was accomplished with a smoothness which in some measure masks its significance'.[2] The most revolutionary changes to casualty clearance processes used by the AAMC in the First World War were made in the shadow of Gallipoli and before

Messines. However, the changes made in 1918 were important, not because they signalled a major departure from military doctrine or British authority, but because they required the Australian medical services to retreat from some of the procedural innovations made to casualty clearance in 1916 and 1917. Despite the enormous loss of life on both sides in those years, the front line did not move substantially. In 1918, however, the front was much more mobile.

There were distinct phases to the fighting in 1918. The German Spring Offensive of March and April made sweeping gains, especially early in the campaign, but the German army was soon beyond the reach of its supply lines and was then pushed back by Allied forces, now supplemented by the arrival of the American Expeditionary Force. The Battle of Hamel, on 4 July, is often seen as a turning point in the combat history of the war as it was the first all-arms battle with the integrated use of tanks, aircraft, artillery and machine guns. Assessing the battle from the perspective of medical administration highlights the extent to which that integration extended to the incorporation of non-fighting units into the military machine. In subsequent battles, collectively termed the Hundred Days Offensive, the Allies reclaimed much of the territory that had been in German hands since 1914, and had almost cleared the German army from France before the fighting stopped with the Armistice at 11am on 11 November 1918.

The nature of the warfare meant that 'flexibility was the order of the day'.[3] It was imperative that medical services were able to move with the retreating or advancing army. This had been difficult enough in the relatively stationary warfare of the previous two years, but it posed particular difficulties for a medical service that had become a little too accustomed to working behind a stable front line. The Hundred Days Offensive saw the development of new casualty evacuation processes in the final months of the war. With the Allies on the advance, some of the changes that had been made to the AAMC's casualty clearance processes became untenable and necessitated a return to previous systems. Additionally, new medical innovations were incorporated into the medical plans, against the advice of the RAMC. With the creation of the Australian Corps, the vast majority of medical care at divisional and corps level provided to Australian soldiers was given by those enlisted in the AAMC. The structure of medical care for Australian soldiers in 1918 was the practical expression of Surgeon General Sir Neville Howse's desire to see the AAMC have control over the care provided to Australian soldiers.

MAKING OFFICERS COMPETENT: STAFFING AN AUSTRALIAN CORPS

The Director of Medical Services for the AIF, Surgeon General Sir Neville Howse, was one of the advocates for a more self-contained Australian Corps. On 20 July 1917, ten days after Howse gave his controversial evidence at the Dardanelles Commission, he wrote to the influential Major General Cyril Brudenell Bingham White, Chief of Staff to General Birdwood. In the letter Howse first outlined what had transpired during his testimony. He informed White that he had spent two and a half hours testifying to the commission and reported that the commissioners were 'very surprised' to hear that Howse 'considered the medical arrangements so inadequate that the Officers responsible were in my opinion guilty of criminal negligence' and that, in future, he would urge the Australian Government 'under no consideration to accept the assurance of the Imperial Government that adequate arrangements had been made for the care of our sick and wounded'.[4] Clearly, Howse was not trying to hide his opinions of the medical arrangements. He then directly linked the failure of the medical arrangements at Gallipoli to his argument for an Australian Corps, informing White that 'a very strong feeling exists, and is spreading amongst the AIF that we should have an Australian Corps'. He also suggested that it was time to remove British officers from the AIF, suggesting that the Commander-in-Chief 'should be called upon to state the number of Imperial Officers now employed with the AIF who, in his opinion, cannot be replaced by AIF Officers'.[5]

Howse proposed that all but four or five imperial officers could be redeployed by the War Office to provide space for the promotion of AIF officers. He wrote: 'I heard an Officer who is not an aggressive Australian say that beyond General Birdwood, General Napier, and two or three General Staff Officers every Imperial Officer could be replaced without diminishing the efficiency of our Force.'[6] The practical application of Howse's idea within the AAMC meant assessing whether Colonel Courtenay Clarke Manifold, who was at that time the Deputy Director of Medical Services (DDMS) for I ANZAC, should remain in his position or be replaced by an Australian.[7] Howse's description of the officer who was pushing for the change as 'not an aggressive Australian' reveals a concern that an opinion such as the one expressed would be dismissed as an example of unrestrained nationalism and continues Howse's efforts, from his evidence at the Dardanelles Commission, to present his ideas as inherently reasonable.

Howse was conscious of the significance of removing an officer from an important position without cause. Yet the fact Manifold had served the AIF well was not enough to stop Howse advocating his replacement. Howse wrote of the 'very grave discontent' of AIF members who opposed the retention of Colonel Manifold. He reported that this opposition was 'not on personal grounds, but because they feel it is reflective upon the Corps'. Agreeing with this position, he wrote: 'I think the time has arrived when he should be replaced by an AIF officer.' Manifold had been appointed as no Australian was seen as being a sufficiently competent officer to fill the position of DDMS. A lot had happened since Manifold started serving in the AIF, and Howse argued that the Australian medical services were 'now able to stand on our own bottom'. Howse continued: 'I know it looks a rotten thing to even discuss the question of replacing Imperial Officers who have done us well, but we cannot overlook the fact that we are now nearly 3 years at War.' He concluded that 'we should have made our Officers competent during that period'.[8]

Three and a half months after this letter was written, the Australian Corps was created. Colonel Manifold was not removed from the command hierarchy in the new corps; rather he was made DDMS for the Australian Corps, the equivalent position to the one he held in I ANZAC. However, on 9 April 1918, another five months further on, he was replaced by Colonel George Walter Barber, who had emigrated to Australia in 1895 and enlisted in the AIF in 1914.[9] After vacating his position with the Australian Corps, Manifold continued his imperial military career and returned to his previous duties with the Indian Medical Service.

'THE ONLY CORPS': AUSTRALIANS AHEAD OF THE CURVE?

During the war, the doctors of the AAMC were aware that they had put in place systems not used elsewhere in the Allies' medical services. On 18 February 1918, Colonel Manifold recorded in his war diary that he went to a conference at Fourth Army's headquarters along with all Deputy and Assistant Directors of Medical Services (DDsMS, ADsMS) working under the aegis of Fourth Army. It was presided over by the Deputy Adjutant and Quartermaster General (DAQMG) under whose jurisdiction the medical services fell. Manifold recorded three issues that had been discussed: venereal disease, the creation of an army school, and the elimination of main dressing stations. The details of the methods used to prevent and treat venereal disease will be discussed in greater detail in chapter 5; however, it is worth noting at this point that Manifold recorded in his diary that the Australian Corps was 'the only Corps which had regimental arrangements for preventive treatment for men returning from large towns and also arrangements for this in towns near the troops'.[10]

Regarding the second topic of discussion, Manifold wrote: 'An army school for medical officers was discussed and again we were found to be the only Corps which had had a School during the winter.'[11] This army school was intended for medical officers and was approved by the Corps Commander on 10 January 1918.[12] Its purpose was 'to provide to junior officers of the medical service essential knowledge of military organisation and special military medical subjects as will enable them more efficiently to carry out their duties to the service'.[13] The school went for eight days with a written examination on the morning of the ninth day, and it included general military topics such as military law, map-reading and field sketching, and pay duties, as well as medical topics including demonstrations on shock and medical and surgical equipment, and visits to a casualty clearing station (CCS), baths and laundries. It also incorporated lectures on the care of soldiers' health, the evacuation of wounded, water supply and chlorination, as well as sanitation in the field, the duties of a medical officer in active operations, the use of Thomas splints and the treatment of trench foot.[14]

This school was a way of bridging the gap between the civilian medical training and experience of the medical officers and the military context in which they were practising medicine. For many of the RMOs in the AIF at this point in the war, battlefield medicine was their first experience of medical practice. The three medical schools in Australia, at the Universities of Sydney, Melbourne and Adelaide, had, at the request of the army, fast-tracked the medical education of many later-year medical students. This helped meet the needs of both the army at war and the civilian population of Australia, many of whose medical practitioners had enlisted in the AAMC and were serving either overseas or in Australia.[15]

The final issue discussed at the 18 February conference – the elimination of main dressing stations – was of particular relevance to the development of casualty clearance and evacuation processes in the First World War. On this topic Manifold wrote: 'Central registration and elimination of Main Dressing Stations was discussed. Again we were the only Corps who had already instituted a system of registration on the CCS being reached by the patient.'[16] As was demonstrated in chapter 2, by the end of Australian participation in the Third Ypres campaign, the main dressing station, as a medical unit, was well on its way to becoming redundant, given that the AAMC had ended all medical record-keeping other than field medical cards until a casualty reached a CCS and was evacuating casualties directly from advanced dressing stations (ADSs) to CCSs. Large numbers of cases were skipping the MDS entirely. This principle was applied by British units outside the AAMC's direct influence. In early February, Fifth Army's Director of Medical Services wrote a memorandum outlining that in 'ordinary circumstances' all wounded should be sent directly from the ADS to the CCS and that during 'special operations' a walking wounded collecting post should be established to house patients who could soon be returned to duty. Sitting and lying cases were to be evacuated as normal.[17] This suggests that the British Director of Medical Services for Third Army supported the changes the AAMC had made to casualty clearance and evacuation and did not anticipate the problems a mobile front would pose to this system developed in the context of virtually immovable front lines.

PREPARING FOR ATTACK: DEFENSIVE MEDICAL PLANNING

Bombardment by the enemy in early March had led the British army to believe that a German attack was imminent on the Western Front. The expectation of an attack led to the creation of a new form of medical arrangement by the AAMC. A 'defence scheme' was issued by the DDMS for the Australian Corps, Colonel Manifold, on 14 March 1918.[18] It followed much the same principles as had been used in 1917 by the AAMC. The medical plan provided for three sectors – right, left and centre – and stated:

> Each Division may make its own arrangements for the establishment of Divisional Collecting Stations for sick and Battle Casualties which are so slight that they can be returned almost at once to the line, but no arrangement of this sort must be allowed to hamper the speedy evacuation back from Advanced Dressing Stns of all cases suitable for direct transmission to CCS.[19]

Motor ambulances were provided for evacuation from ADS to CCS and the same record-keeping practices were maintained with field medical cards 'when possible … made out at ADS, so long as speedy evacuation is not interfered with', but with the registration of casualties to be undertaken at a central bureau at the casualty clearing station.[20] The emphasis of the medical arrangements was on haste, with all but the most minor injuries and illnesses being evacuated directly to the CCS and skipping the MDS altogether. It is then reasonable that the medical services had, a month earlier, discussed removing main dressing stations from the medical infrastructure – they no longer served the purpose for which they were originally instituted.

Instead of abolishing main dressing stations (MDSs), the AAMC found other uses for them in the casualty clearance and evacuation process. The defence scheme of medical arrangements laid down by Colonel Manifold in March gave three instances in which casualties should be sent to an MDS. He wrote: 'The MDSs will only be used to switch off to if congestion occurs anywhere, for cases of severe shock, and for gassed cases.'[21] By allowing them to be used in the case of congestion at other points in the casualty evacuation chain, Colonel Manifold created a flexible casualty evacuation system that was capable of expansion if either or potentially both the advanced dressing stations and the casualty clearing stations became overcrowded. These changes indicate that Manifold was actively contributing to the AAMC's innovative approach to casualty evacuation and that, despite being British and trained in a different system from the Australians, he showed the same kind of flexibility that distinguished the AAMC from the RAMC. His approach to change provides evidence for why Howse felt it was a 'rotten thing' to recommend Manifold be removed from the AAMC.

The special provision of using MDSs for cases of gas poisoning were necessary as, although not a new problem, it had become more significant.[22] The use of gas as a weapon became more concerning in the early part of 1918, and it was discussed frequently by the medical men, not just in terms of the immediate effects of exposure but the cumulative effects of the gas lingering in the air. In his war diary, on 24 March 1918, Colonel Manifold recorded that he had seen General Walker and 'discussed [the] question with him. He was under the impression that the air in forward area had become so impregnated with gas that it had cumulative effect on the men and he said he had felt this himself.'[23]

As GOC 1st Australian Division, General Walker was speaking on the advice of medical officers working in his division. On 13 March 1918, Captain Keith Stanley Rae, RMO for the AIF's 9th Battalion, wrote to the battalion's adjutant to request that the unit not be sent forward into the line. Writing that he felt 'bound to make the following report on their health', he advised: 'All men who showed signs of gas poisoning have been evacuated, but there still remains a large number, who, while not actually ill, are affected in the nose and throat by breathing a low concentration of gas.' He suggested that it would 'be madness to send these men into the line while they are in this condition, as in the event of a gas attack, they would be unable to wear their respirators for any length of time'. He continued: 'From the men I have seen on daily sick parades I would say that there would be at least 60 who will not be fit for duty in the line within two weeks. In addition to the men who have been attending sick parades, there are still mild cases developing daily.' He then suggested that the 'majority of the Bn is more or less affected by the gas, and would find it extremely difficult, if not impossible, to wear gas respirators for a prolonged period'.[24]

The problem of gas in the 9th Battalion was confirmed by the RMO of the 11th Battalion, which had relieved the 9th of its place in the line on the night of 8/9 March. On 19 March, Major Leonard May, RMO 11th Battalion, wrote to the ADMS 1st Australian Division, Colonel Huxtable, about gas in the area. He described the gas attack that was sustained by the battalion between 15 and 18 March and the satisfactory 'gas discipline' in the unit as demonstrated by there being only one 'definitive case' of gassing. He then described in detail the symptoms suffered by the men and compared them to his previous experience of serving in a gas-drenched sector earlier in the war. Major May reported that the lack of sleep owing to constant coughing (which, aside from being unpleasant for the individual, made him inappropriate for use on a patrol or for duty on an outpost) caused significant problems. He tried to alleviate the problem by 'holding four or five in a shelter for two days or so, but [could not] see that they improve up here, and the evacuation rates from being very low promises [sic] to reach a very high figure'.[25] Major May then recommended that, in a gas-drenched sector, the period of duty in the line should be four, but no more than six, days. In the final sentence of this letter, Major May suggested that this problem, if left alone, could affect the efficiency of the army. He wrote: 'I think it my duty to lay these facts before you and to state that in my opinion the Bn should not be left until the men are seriously affected and require a very long rest to recover.'[26] While the men were not exactly 'sick', the medical officers intervened and suggested a change to military procedure based on the health effects of remaining in the line. This was not a benevolent request for the good of the soldier; rather, it was a suggestion based on the perception of a looming disaster for the manpower economy of the AIF and ensured that there were sufficient men available for military actions.

Planning for the effects of gas was only one of the contingencies worked into plans for the evacuation of casualties in early 1918. The Assistant

Directors of Medical Services (ADsMS) for the 1st, 2nd and 5th Australian Divisions all wrote some form of contingency planning into their schemes for medical arrangements as they prepared to defend the line against a German attack in March 1918. Colonel Huxtable, ADMS 1st Australian Division, devised a medical evacuation plan for his division that incorporated alternative routes to be used if the primary routes were inaccessible owing to shelling.[27] In the 2nd Australian Division, the ADMS, Colonel Shepherd, went further and created plans for medical evacuation in the event of a withdrawal by Australian troops.[28] Similar plans were put in place by Colonel Downey, ADMS for the 5th Australian Division, who drew up plans for relocating advanced dressing stations or main dressing stations if their positions became untenable, as well as providing plans to be enacted if the military situation necessitated the withdrawal of those units.[29]

The inclusion at this point of significant contingency planning suggests that those making the medical plans had learned the lessons of previous battles and had a realistic appreciation of the combat units' ability to hold the line against the German advance. Not only were plans put in place for the potential advance, for high casualties or for no substantial gain in territory but also they were made for a range of other options. In March 1918, in preparation for the impending German attack, there were plans for alternative routes of evacuation if stretcher-bearers were unable to traverse the original routes, for the relocation of ADSs and MDSs if they were rendered unsafe owing to enemy shelling, and to shift all units if a complete withdrawal was required because of a German advance. The Australian medical men involved in the development of these new casualty evacuation procedures had created, during the war, a flexible system that provided high-quality medical care to Australian soldiers involved in combat along a relatively stable front. The problem for the AAMC – and the British medical services more broadly – was that, in 1918, the front line was anything but stationary.

MEDICINE IN RETREAT: THE GERMAN SPRING OFFENSIVE

On 21 March 1918, the Assistant Director of Medical Services for the 3rd Australian Division received word that the enemy had attacked the British Third and Fifth Armies near Saint-Quentin in northern France.[30] Field Marshal Sir Douglas Haig, Commander-in-Chief, British Armies in France, wrote to all ranks of the British army in France and Flanders in a 'Special Order of the Day' on 23 March 1918, declaring:

We are again at a crisis in the War. The enemy has collected on this Front every available Division and is aiming at the destruction of the British Army. We have already inflicted on the enemy in the course of the last two days very heavy loss and the French are sending troops as quickly as possible to our support. I feel that everyone in the Army, fully realizing how much depends on the exertions and steadfastness of each one of us, will do his utmost to prevent the enemy from attaining his object.[31]

The 3rd and 4th Australian Divisions, including their corresponding medical units, were temporarily attached to the armies under attack in order to provide further reinforcement to those sections of the line. The 3rd Australian Division was moved into the area on 23 March and, after an initial mishap with the 9th Australian Field Ambulance (AFA) being left off its train, they were in place, initially in reserve, on 24 March. The division took up its position in the line on 27 March for the Battle of Dernancourt.[32] The 4th Australian Division was in place on 26 March.[33]

The Australian medical officers were unimpressed by the handling of the medical arrangements in late March and early April at the Battle of Dernancourt. Colonel Barber, ADMS 4th Australian Division, found those of the Third Army to be substandard. He wrote: 'Medical Arrangements [sic] in this Army (Third) seem to be totally disorganized – CCSs have been closed down – some apparently without any justification … and in consequence all cases have to be evacuated a very long distance to Doullens and its vicinity.'[34] In the same entry he also complained of a shortage of stretchers and dressings and a lack of communication and coordination. The problems of waging war in these conditions were also apparent to Colonel Maguire. In his war diary he wrote: 'Very little information obtainable as to the situation on Corps Front. Line North of MIRAUMONT reported to be broken and enemy said to be through HEBUTERNE with armoured cars. This was later proved to be wrong.'[35]

Barber and Maguire criticised the coordination of these armies when compared to what they had been accustomed to. It is likely, however, that this disorganisation was more an expression of the shift to providing medical care while the combat units were retreating and not yet having adapted to the new circumstances. In early 1918, the ability of the German army to pierce the British lines and move its troops forward highlighted the deficiencies and inconsistencies in the Allies' communication and casualty evacuation processes.

The British forces, including the Australian divisions, had become accustomed to evacuating casualties along a static and largely impenetrable front. However, from 1918 the nature of the warfare required a different approach to casualty evacuation and created the need to wind back some of the deviations from medical–military doctrine that had been used in the battles of 1916 and 1917. In early April 1918, Lieutenant General Sir Arthur Sloggett, Director General of Medical Services for the British Armies in France, wrote a memorandum to the Director of Medical Services for Third Army, to which the 3rd Australian Division was still attached, for distribution to all deputy directors of medical services of corps and all assistant directors of medical services of divisions. In it, Sloggett articulated the problems with continuing to use the same system of casualty clearance and evacuation from 1916 and 1917, which had been developed with largely static front lines, in 1918, in a situation with vastly greater movement.

According to Sloggett, the events of the last ten days of March demonstrated 'the paramount importance of medical units maintaining their mobility in the field'. He reported that trench warfare and the 'desire to carry on surgical work to the highest degree of perfection has led casualty clearing stations to become large and immobile units, pushed as far forward as possible, thus diminishing the tactical importance of maintaining mobile main dressing stations at intermediate positions'. He articulated the dangers of this, stating: 'The consequence [...] has been that in certain areas, Casualty Clearing Stations have had to abandon valuable equipment in retiring, that in some instances no main dressing stations had been opened in their place for the reception of wounded.' He added that, because field ambulance motor cars were needed to transfer the wounded to the new casualty clearing station positions further back, the cars 'have not been able to arrive in time to remove lying down cases collected at the collecting post by the bearer divisions, and many wounded unable to walk have been abandoned'.[36]

Sloggett's memorandum suggests that the casualty clearance and evacuation system developed by the AAMC throughout 1916 and 1917 was well suited to the type of war being fought at that stage. Sloggett, however, advocated a return to previous policies. Pushing the casualty clearing stations further to the rear reinstated the need to have main dressing stations that were mobile and did more than act as overflow capacity for excess patients from advanced dressing stations. He added that 'the motor ambulance transport of the field ambulances in the front area shall be employed for bringing wounded back only to these Main

Dressing Station points'.[37] Sloggett's plans reduced the area for which field ambulances were responsible. The result was that the motor ambulances that worked between advanced dressing stations and main dressing stations had their travel times reduced significantly as casualty clearing stations were removed from their responsibility. This would then enable them to make more trips more frequently, thereby transporting more casualties away from the front to the main dressing station.

In response to Sloggett's memorandum, the Australian divisions began to develop plans to better suit casualty evacuation in mobile warfare. Instead of combining all the bearer subdivisions of a division's allotted field ambulances under one Commanding Officer, Colonel Barber, who had just replaced Colonel Manifold as DDMS Australian Corps, put forward medical arrangements that began to separate the units again. In his medical instructions, issued on 10 April 1918, his policy allowed for one Australian field ambulance (AFA) to be in charge of the advanced dressing station, as well as evacuation from regimental aid posts to main dressing stations. Attached to this AFA, in order to assist with the move-ment of casualties, was the bearer subdivision of a second AFA whose tent subdivision was in charge of the main dressing station. Finally the third field ambulance of an Australian division was to be held in reserve with one section (roughly a third) of the tent subdivision staffing the divisional collection station for walking wounded. If there was congestion owing to large numbers of walking wounded, this reserve field ambulance was to be used to open a second collecting station near the main dressing station to clear casualties more rapidly.[38]

Not only did the staffing of the various posts in the casualty evacuation chain retreat from the changes made in 1916 and 1917 but also the use of the main dressing station began to revert to that of earlier battles and to regain some of its importance. Despite having discussed eliminating main dressing stations altogether only months before, then finding alternative uses for the units, they once again became integral parts of the casualty evacuation chain during the German Spring Offensive. This was partly owing to the extended distance of the main dressing station from the casualty clearing station. Barber ordered that 'first aid only to be given at Advance Dressing Station and thorough dressing be undertaken at Main Dressing Stns owing to the distance from Cas. Clg Stations'.[39] An officer was then detailed to the main dressing station to sort the casualties for their onward movement to a casualty clearing station, back to a divisional or corps rest station or, in the case of 'stragglers or malingerers', to the military police.[40]

During the same month, in the 2nd Australian Division, plans created in case of a retreat involved the 'leapfrogging' of medical units. For the fighting around Villers-Bretonneux, the ADMS, Colonel Shepherd, wrote in his 'Emergency Measures in Necessity of Quick Evacuation' on 26 April that, if it was necessary to evacuate an advanced dressing station, 'a minimum of personnel and equipment will be left making this only a relay to MDS and a new ADS will be established further back withdrawing the rear party when this new ADS is in working order'.[41] These plans provided for medical care to be continuously available to Australian soldiers even as the army was forced back.

The ongoing issue for the AAMC was the location of main dressing stations and casualty clearing stations, relative to each other and the front-line trenches. This was one area where British medical–military authorities questioned the procedures in the Australian divisions more explicitly. Colonel Downey, ADMS 5th Australian Division, reported on one such incident in his war diary, writing: 'On 29.4.18 the DMS 4th Army inspected MAIN DRESSING STN (14th Aust. Field Ambulance). He believed the station to be too far forward. This question presented itself when the MAIN DRESSING STN was first fixed on.' Downey then recorded the reasoning behind the decision to place the main dressing station there, reporting: 'A site at BUSSY was inspected but rejected, on account of bad roads leading to and from it, this post is however retained for use if necessary.' He then continued: 'All the horse transport of the 14th Australian Field Ambulance and all spare personnel are in BUSSY or at Ambulance Stn ... so that the equipment of the MAIN DRESSING STN and personnel is all that would have to be removed from DAOURS.'[42] Here Downey demonstrated that although he had realised the main dressing station was too far forward, there were few other options once the landscape and existing infrastructure were taken into account. To manage this problem, he modified and minimised what was kept at the main dressing station in order to facilitate a quick retreat if the circumstances of warfare warranted it.

This reversion to a casualty evacuation system more reminiscent of the one from early 1916 than late 1917 was not a result of pressure from the British army to conform to a uniform standard or military doctrine. Sloggett's memorandum provided general principles around which the medical evacuation of casualties should be organised in mobile warfare, and the suggestion by the DMS Fourth Army to move the 5th Australian Division's main dressing station was shown to be a factor already taken into consideration when the MDS was initially set up. These were not instances of overreach by imperial authorities; rather they were examples of the appropriate oversight of medical care by those who were ultimately responsible for it within the imperial command. The internal structure at divisional and corps level was still the responsibility of the AAMC officers who had made the changes that proved so successful at Messines.

As they had done in the battles on the Somme and in Flanders, the Australian medical men made decisions about medical care in response to the situation in which they found themselves. This included considering the principles handed down from higher up the chain of command, as well as taking into account the landscape, the distance between the front and the casualty clearing station, and the nature of the warfare being waged in the particular battle. Once the AAMC had claimed medical control of Australian casualties and demonstrated its competence in handling those casualties, its authority over sick and wounded Australian soldiers at divisional and corps level was never seriously challenged by the RAMC or the British army more generally.

IN RESERVE: MAY AND JUNE ON THE WESTERN FRONT

After the Battle of Villers-Bretonneux in late April, the Australian Corps was placed in reserve and, while there, experienced an outbreak of influenza. The May 1918 outbreak, during the lull between major engagements, was an issue of concern among the medical men developing casualty evacuation protocols. While influenza had been a problem before, a fresh outbreak at this stage was particularly unfortunate. The Allied armies were planning an operation to regain territory claimed by the Germans over the preceding months. Given the need for the prompt evacuation of casualties, large numbers of sick not only depleted the effectiveness of the fighting force but also had the potential to create congestion in the evacuation lines and clog up what had become a remarkably smooth process. In the 2nd Australian Division, the source of this outbreak was traced to the 28th Battalion. Thirty men in the battalion slept in one billet with twenty of those presenting themselves for medical checks at the sick parade the following morning; fourteen of them were then evacuated sick. The rest of those thirty men were then isolated from other units and a further eleven were admitted to medical units, meaning that a total of twenty-five were incapacitated. Influenza also affected the efficiency of the AAMC with two officers and five other ranks of the 5th Australian Field Ambulance, who provided care to the 28th Battalion's sick, also needing to be evacuated to the CCS for care and recovery.

Colonel Shepherd, ADMS 2nd Australian Division, pointed out that 'exactly the same condition of Pyrexia was prevalent among the troops of this Division at the same time last year, which points to a vernal infection to which these men are predisposed'.[43] He suggested that it was easier for the infection to spread when units were behind the lines in billets rather than in trenches, where the men tended to be more spread out. Colonel Shepherd reported that slight or suspicious cases were held in the field ambulances' medical posts, which goes some way to explaining the high rate of infection among the division's field ambulance personnel. Given that the disease first presented as fever, which could indicate multiple illnesses, the soldiers were initially diagnosed with Pyrexia of Unknown Origin (PUO). On 11 May, Colonel Shepherd gave the sick admissions rates for the eight previous days to Colonel Barber, DDMS of the Australian Corps, stating that admissions owing to PUO were 291 of 443 (or 66 per cent of) total admissions owing to sickness, and evacuations owing to PUO were 203 of 282, or 72 per cent of total evacuations owing to sickness from the 2nd Australian Division.[44]

Medical officers discussed influenza and the attempts to limit its effects. On 21 June 1918, Colonel Huxtable, ADMS of the 1st Australian Division, forwarded information from the DDMS of the British XV Corps to the RMOs under his command. This information suggested that the 'influenza-like disease' they were working against appeared to be airborne and warned against overcrowding in billets, impressing upon RMOs the importance of ventilation.[45] Preventive measures were also put in place in the 1st Australian Division that replicated those put forward by the DDMS of the British XV Corps. He suggested that for several days after exposure to infection, soldiers should use a system of nasal douching and gargling with antiseptic solutions daily – if possible twice a day. This system, recommended by the DDMS, cited an issue of the *British Medical Journal* from March 1918 on the prevention of epidemic disease in schools.[46] A few days after these instructions were given regarding influenza, the Director General of Medical Services (DGMS) for the British Armies in France gave further instructions. He repeated the calls to minimise overcrowding of men in tents, billets and mess rooms, and wrote: 'Whenever the military situation permits, it is advisable that troops should sleep in individual blanket-shelters in the open air.'[47] Other precautions suggested included airing all blankets and kits from the billets where infections had occurred and quarantining new arrivals to the area. The DGMS wrote: 'As the infection appears to be spread by the movement of infected individuals, drafts arriving at Reinforcement Depots from England or the Bases should, as far as possible, be accommodated in separate lines for a period of 4 days. Individual shelters should be insisted on in order to avoid the necessity for quarantine if any cases arise.'[48]

This information was passed along to all RMOs and commanding officers of field ambulances in the 5th Australian Division by the ADMS, Colonel Downey.[49] This sharing of information highlights the change in priorities in the medical services between major combat operations. Not surprisingly, during major offensives the focus of the medical men was on casualty evacuation and treatment, yet, when the fighting subsided, the attention of the medical services was drawn to preventive health measures in order to maintain the fighting strength of the army. As a result, the AAMC exerted influence over the AIF soldiers' bodies outside battle.

Along with the outbreak of influenza, the quiet period between major offensives on the Western Front in May and June 1918 was also a time of administrative change in the British medical services. One key difference between the Commander-in-Chief of the Mediterranean Expeditionary Force, Sir Ian Hamilton, and the Commander-in-Chief of British Armies in France, Sir Douglas Haig, was the extent to which they engaged with their respective medical services. At Gallipoli, Hamilton excluded the medical services from preparations for battle. In contrast, Haig's approach demonstrated an awareness of the significance of the medical services. Military historian Gary Sheffield has suggested that Haig had learned the lessons of Gallipoli and the early days of the war in France, writing: 'Typically, Haig took a close interest in medical matters and proved very supportive of his senior medical staff as they carried out radical changes in response to the lessons learned in the first years of the war.'[50]

Haig recognised the problem of Sir Arthur Sloggett, DGMS in France and Flanders, being forced to retire in the middle of a war during what had become the fighting season. On 19 May 1918, Haig noted in his diary that Sloggett was being made to retire at 60 and wrote of his intent to ask the War Office to reconsider its decision.[51] By 22 May, he had received word from the War Office that Lieutenant Colonel C.H. Burtchaell was to replace Sloggett. If Sloggett had to be replaced, Burtchaell was not Haig's preferred candidate. In response, Haig wrote to the Secretary of State for War, Lord Milner, and considered it a certainty that Sloggett would remain in his post as a result of this intervention.[52]

Haig was wrong and, owing to the British army's age restrictions, Sloggett was compelled to retire on 1 June 1918. When documenting in his diary a lunch he had with Sir Anthony Bowlby, Consulting Surgeon to the BEF, Haig wrote that Sloggett's 'great merit is that he has allowed the Civil Surgeons and Medical men to do what they thought necessary without any interference'. He recorded telling Bowlby he 'had written to Milner (S. of S. for War) but he declined to modify the War Office decision because it would be unfair to rising men in the Army Medical Corps to keep Sloggett and others on'. Haig continued: 'I added that I would do my best to see that no interference by the new DGMS took place; and B. is to come and report from time to time on what is being done.'[53]

Haig's statement that Sloggett minimised his interference with the civilians in the medical corps is borne out by Sloggett's previously discussed direction to the medical officers to observe certain principles in the planning of medical evacuation in mobile warfare. As Ana Carden-Coyne writes, Sloggett was an advocate for the use of civilian doctors in the military during the war whereas Burtchaell was uncomfortable with this deployment of resources.[54] Haig, appearing to value the independence afforded civilian surgeons and medical men, undertook to see that it continued and, assuming that the 'B.' in the above quote refers to Bowlby and not Burtchaell, he intended to use Bowlby as an informant to ensure that Burtchaell did not interfere unnecessarily.

This was the context in which the AAMC worked for the remainder of the war – a situation in which civilian medical expertise had come to be valued by one of the highest ranked military officers. Mark Harrison's assessment of the remaining months of the war supports this idea. He argued that 'the last few months of fighting on the Western Front provide ample evidence that the medical services had been fully integrated into operational planning and that the evacuation and treatment of casualties was a matter of high priority'.[55] This acceptance of civilian medical expertise in the RAMC flowed through to the AAMC. The work at divisional and corps level of the AAMC is remarkable for the absence of interference from the British services.

HAMEL AND THE HUNDRED DAYS: MEDICINE ON THE ADVANCE

A conference of medical men in charge of the Australian Corps and the 2nd and 4th Australian Divisions was held on 1 July 1918 to finalise medical arrangements for the Battle of Hamel. The battle commenced on 4 July, after extensive planning by Lieutenant General John Monash, commander of the Australian Corps. The bulk of the attacking force came from the 4th Australian Division, under the command of Major General Ewen Sinclair-Maclagan. Evacuation of casualties was therefore the responsibility of the ADMS of that division, Lieutenant Colonel Roy Stanley McGregor, who was temporarily acting in that role. His responsibilities included the casualties on the 2nd Division's front so the Acting ADMS 2nd Australian Division, Lieutenant Colonel William Crowther, reported to the ADMS 4th Australian Division for the duration of the battle. Action commenced at 3.10am, and Crowther described the evacuation from his area as 'remarkable [*sic*] prompt and successful'.[56] Crowther reported that the shelling of back areas was light and, as a result, the motor ambulances were able to push almost the whole way forward to the regimental aid posts in order to transport casualties back to the ADS. By 10.00am almost all casualties had been evacuated at least to the ADS, and in this the stretcher-bearers were assisted, as had become commonplace, by German prisoners of war who had been pushed into service in casualty clearance.[57] Lieutenant Colonel McGregor reported that in the twelve hours after zero hour (3.10am) more than 800 cases had been evacuated, which equated to more than one per minute over a distance of 7000 yards and included an abnormally high ratio of lying to walking cases (3:4).[58]

The Allied counterattack to the German Spring Offensive, the Hundred Days Offensive, commenced on 8 August with the Battle of Amiens in which the Australian Corps participated. The corps was also involved in the subsequent advance to the Hindenburg Line, including fighting at the Battle of Mont Saint-Quentin (including Péronne) from 31 August to 3 September and the attempts to capture the Hindenburg Line from 18 September, the line breaking on 29 September. After the capture of Montbrehain, on 5 October, the exhausted Australian Corps was withdrawn from active duty for retraining and reorganisation after six months in the line. The Armistice was signed before they returned to active service. The casualty clearance and evacuation systems that had been developed in stationary warfare over the preceding years and tested and refined with a retreating mobile front earlier in 1918 continued to work well when the force was on the advance.

The morning of 8 August 1918 was described by Colonel Shepherd, ADMS 2nd Australian Division, as a '[f]ine morning with a ground mist, most favourable for attack'.[59] From Colonel Shepherd's perspective, the events of the day could not have been much better. He wrote that the attack appeared to be 'a complete surprise to the Germans' and that '[t]he whole of the Medical Arrangements seem to have gone without a hitch'.[60]

This success was due, in part, to good planning and the clarification of command issues before the attack began. A conference was held on 3 August for the assistant directors of medical services of the Australian divisions with the DDMS Australian Corps to discuss the medical arrangements for the impending operations. The following day Colonel Shepherd held a conference with the commanding officers of the field ambulances under his command as well as the ADMS of the neighbouring 5th Australian Division, Colonel Downey. Colonel Shepherd recorded in his war diary: 'The whole of the Medical Arrangements of intended Operations was discussed [...] and the cooperation of all Medical Units of both Divisions was arranged.'[61] The area to the right of the Australian divisions was under the control of the 2nd Canadian Division, and Colonel Shepherd also made arrangements with the ADMS of that division to assist each other if either division encountered any problem with its medical arrangements.

Although it was decided that the field ambulances of both the 2nd and 5th Australian Divisions would work in cooperation at each medical station throughout the action, there was still some confusion as to command.[62] Colonel Shepherd received a report from Lieutenant Colonel Welch, CO 6AFA and Officer Commanding the main dressing station for the divisional sector for the Battle of Amiens, that the plans Welch had made for the battle were in conflict with orders given by Colonel Downey, ADMS 5th Australian Division. Downey had wired the Commanding Officer of 14AFA to say that he should take over command of the main dressing station from Lieutenant Colonel Welch at zero hour (4.20am) plus 44 minutes. In response to the report from Welch, Colonel Shepherd recorded: 'Phoned Colonel DOWNEY and explained that it was not a fair arrangement as Lt Col. WELCH had made all preparations for the battle at MDS and it was unfair to change the command until MDS moved from there.' He concluded: 'Finally arranged that Lt Col. WELCH retains command. Saw all Ambulance Commanders and went over the instructions so that there should be no misunderstanding.'[63] The close working relationship between the two assistant directors of medical services of the 2nd and 5th Australian Divisions enabled this issue to be resolved before the battle commenced.

In much the same way as the 2nd and 5th Australian Divisions worked together during the battle, the 3rd and 4th Australian Divisions were also paired. At zero plus four hours, the command in this divisional sector passed to the GOC 4th Australian Division at which point the personnel of both the 3rd and 4th Australian Divisions came under his control.[64]

The GOC 4th Australian Division held a conference on 1 August at which he outlined his plan of operations. In his report on the medical arrangements for the battle, Colonel Kenneth Smith, ADMS 4th Australian Division, wrote that two possible outcomes were 'immediately evident'. Either the operations would be successful and 'the casualties would be light and provision would have to [be] made for the rapid advance of Dressing Stations in order to ease the strain on Divisional Ambulance Transport', or else, if the divisions were not successful, 'casualties would be heavy and all the resources of both the 3rd and 4th Australian Divisions would be needed for the efficient evacuation and treatment of the casualties'.[65] According to Colonel Smith, 'The obvious solution was, therefore, to pool the Medical Units of both Divisions and place the Ambulances so that both alternatives could be met with equal success.'[66] The result of the evacuation in this divisional sector was similar to that of the 2nd and 5th Australian Divisions, with Colonel Smith reporting that 'all arrangements worked splendidly'.[67]

As seen by the averted problem in the 2nd and 5th Australian divisional sector, the changing command of main dressing stations, necessitated by the change to a more mobile form of warfare, had become a source of confusion for the assistant directors of medical services for the five Australian divisions. On 12 August, after the Battle of Amiens, Colonel Barber, DDMS Australian Corps, wrote to his ADsMS to clarify the procedures for forming, opening and closing main dressing stations. He reinforced the authority of the ADsMS to decide when and where to position and move main and advanced dressing stations but reminded the officers that he and the Officer Commanding the Motor Ambulance Convoy needed to be informed as early as possible of the intent to make changes so as to prevent congestion and maintain satisfactory clearance from those posts. Barber also wrote that each divisional sector was to have only one MDS, which were limited in number because of a shortage of motor ambulances to move the casualties appropriately to a casualty clearing station. Given the success of the attack on 8 August, in which divisions worked in tandem, Barber also used the opportunity to outline the procedure for the deployment of medical personnel in the event of an advance where one division leapfrogged another. Barber wrote: 'In the event of a Division passing through another Division (leapfrogging, as in recent operations) to attack a position beyond, tent division personnel of the attacking Division must double up at Main Dressing Station, Advanced Dressing Station, and all posts of the Division through which the attack Division passes.'[68]

Once the front line had been pushed far enough forward and the area secured, the advancing medical units could, for example, turn the advanced dressing station into a main dressing station, and a regimental aid post into an advanced dressing station, and establish forward regimental aid posts, in the way suggested by Colonel Anderson at Messines.[69] Colonel Downey showed that he was aware of the issue of consolidating the territorial gains before sending forward further medical units at the Battle of Amiens, when he reported: 'I did not form an ADS and W[alking] W[ounded] D[ressing] S[tation] immediately after capture of RED LINE (although Motor Posts were established) because I consider it tactfully [sic] unsound to send forward Tent Division personnel into captured territory before the objective is definitely consolidated.'[70]

Colonel Barber also provided a procedure for closing main dressing stations so that his instruction that only one be open in each divisional sector at any time could be followed. He wrote:

> When a Main Dressing Station opens in a Sector, the station previously acting as Main Dressing Station for that sector must automatically close at the same hour, and become a Reserve Dressing Station. The M[otor] A[mbulance] C[onvoy] will clear remaining patients, and afterwards should it be necessary to send patients to Reserve Dressing Station owing to congestion at Main Dressing Stations on application by C[ommanding] O[fficer] or ADMS to O[fficer] C[ommanding] Motor Ambulance Convoy.[71]

The reserve dressing station (RDS) was then to be used either in the case of congestion at the main dressing station or in the event that the advance was rebuffed and the attacking division had to retreat. For this reason Barber ordered that either a tent subdivision of a field ambulance or 'holding parties' – made up of either divisional collecting station or dental unit personnel – should staff the RDS. Through this personnel deployment the RDS was staffed with medically trained men, but those with the greatest experience treating and evacuating wounded were pushed forward. This clarification of the use of main dressing stations by Colonel Barber provided for a casualty evacuation chain that could push forward or back as required and was the type of scheme that Colonel Smith had reported was necessary for the Battle of Amiens. The scheme outlined the administrative procedures for the assistant directors of medical services to follow in establishing, relocating and closing MDSs but ensured that the authority to select the timing and location of those changes rested with the ADMS of a division.

The Battles of Mont Saint-Quentin and Péronne from 27 August to 4 September involved frequent moves forward by medical posts. Colonel Shepherd, in his report on the operations during the period in question, wrote: '[I]t might be borne in mind that for several days forward posts were constantly on the move and changed from hour to hour.'[72] The success of the arrangements was due to three main reasons. First, Ford cars were used as far forward as possible to evacuate casualties. Second, one tent subdivision of a field ambulance was held in reserve so that it could move forward when needed to establish a new ADS. Once the advance of other units was complete, the rear tent subdivision became the reserve unit, which would advance when next needed. Finally, the use of telephones between the ADS and the associated infantry brigade enhanced communication and coordination between medical and fighting units.[73] Colonel Shepherd reported that the 'system in practice was found to work admirably'.[74]

During the German Spring Offensive, between March and May 1918, it had become necessary to unwind some of the changes to the use of Australian field ambulances that had been made during stationary warfare. Subsequently, the mobility of the front during the fighting in late August and early September necessitated further changes, with a partial return to a more traditional structure for field ambulances. Colonel Shepherd wrote that, 'for such mobile operations', it was important to attach the ambulance bearer divisions to their respective infantry brigades.[75] The need for this change was echoed by Colonel Downey, ADMS 5th Australian Division, in his report on the action.[76] This was not a complete reversion to the original scheme used in early 1916 as the bearer and tent subdivisions of an Australian field ambulance were not linked. The tent subdivisions were used to staff various posts with one in reserve, as discussed above, and the bearer subdivision moved with its infantry brigade to evacuate casualties.

The medical arrangements for subsequent actions involving the Australian Corps in September and early October worked similarly to those in August. Colonel Barber, DDMS Australian Corps, recorded in his war diary on the days of the main offensives (18, 29/30 September and 5 October) that the casualty evacuation was smooth and the medical arrangements worked satisfactorily.[77] The Australian Corps was withdrawn from the line in the days following its final action on 5 October, and it did not return to active service in the First World War. The evacuation of casualties from the Australian divisional sectors was undertaken throughout the Hundred Days Offensive with minimal involvement from the imperial authorities. The processes were managed and refined by AAMC officers who were given the authority to make decisions as was appropriate to their rank and role in much the same way as RAMC officers made decisions within their divisions.

OPERATING IN FORWARD AREAS: THE DEVELOPMENT OF RESUSCITATION TEAMS

In the midst of these changes to the structures and processes that shaped the provision of medical care to Australian soldiers, the AAMC continued to refine medical treatments provided in the forward medical posts. While the focus remained on the efficient and prompt evacuation of casualties away from the front, members of the AAMC advocated for an 'operating centre' close to the front. On 18 May 1918 Colonel Downey, ADMS 5th Australian Division, wrote to the DDMS of the Australian Corps, Colonel Barber, to suggest the establishment of an 'Advanced (or Divisional) Operating Centre'.[78] The medical arrangements at the time required casualties to be evacuated a distance of 16 miles, and Downey was of the opinion that '[a] proportion of these cases would . . . materially benefit by early operation in the Divisional Area'.[79] He based this recommendation on a similar plan put in place during military operations before Bapaume in April 1917, and he also noted that there was provision for this in the *Field Service Regulations* and RAMC training. The recommendation was also based on the experience of the 14th Australian Field Ambulance (14AFA) in May 1918.

In the period 5–19 May 1918, 14AFA ran the 5th Australian Division's main dressing station. A report written by the Officer Commanding 14AFA, Lieutenant Colonel Thompson, outlined the operations performed at the MDS by a specialist team. In his report, Thompson demonstrated why these operating centres were necessary. He reported that in his opinion 'for every 1000 wounded evacuated there are not more than 20 cases which cannot be sent to the CCS', adding that 'in these 20 cases the long trip to CCS is almost always fatal, whereas an Advanced Operating Centre would save the lives of the majority of these'.[80]

Here Thompson highlighted one of the fundamental problems of military medicine in the First World War. The scale of casualties was such that efficient systems that provided the majority of cases with positive outcomes were needed; the system that had been developed, of minimal intervention in forward areas combined with rapid evacuation of casualties to well-equipped and staffed hospitals, fulfilled this need. Yet that system did not provide much more than palliative care for those whose wounds required immediate intervention. Thompson provided case notes for all seventeen operations conducted in the period, recording only one fatality with the rest being moved to a casualty clearing station in good condition. He reported: 'The experience gained at DAOURS [sic] indicates to me that there should be attached to each division, and placed at the disposal of the ADMS, an operative team.' He continued: '[T]his team should be placed at a distance of about 10 miles from the front line, and either attached to the Ambulance situated furthest back or placed in an isolated building or tentage in a location unlikely to be shelled.'[81]

As ADMS for the division, Downey was impressed by the work of the team operating at his main dressing station and wrote to Barber: 'I suggest therefore that under present conditions and during spring and summer when severe cases could, after operation, be sent immediately to CCS, that a surgeon be sent from a CCS to establish an Operating Centre at the Divisional Collecting Station.' He then highlighted further details that had facilitated the success of the experiment, reporting: 'In the case of this Division the CCS is situated in a very good house at Les Alencons [sic], containing electric light, and other conveniences.' He added: 'It happens also that the CO is an officer of considerable surgical experience, and at least one member of the unit is an Operating Theatre attendant of experience.'[82] Underlining his point that this suggestion was not intended to undermine or detract from the arrangements already existing, Downey concluded by writing: 'It is not suggested that the principle of "only urgent operations at a Field Ambulance" be departed from, except under the expert judgment of the surgeon in charge.'[83]

Colonel Barber forwarded the letter from Downey to Major General O'Keefe, the British Director of Medical Services for Fourth Army. Barber recommended to O'Keefe that Downey's proposal be adopted and that advance operating centres should be placed as far forward as possible. Barber wrote: 'If a patient is likely to die as the result of a long journey to CCS it would be better for him to remain close to the line and risk shell fire.' He thought these cases would not be common and suggested: 'Such cases are few in number and the accomodation [sic] should, I think, be limited to that for 30 cases.'[84] In Downey's opinion, a potentially life-saving operation conducted under the threat of shellfire, but with the possibility of survival, was preferable to a likely fatal journey to treatment.

O'Keefe's response was lukewarm: 'The principle of an Advanced Operating Centre is in some respects desirable, but the exigencies of the present warfare do not allow of it.'[85] O'Keefe then suggested that the time to carry a wounded soldier to a casualty clearing station would be under an hour. He showed enough interest in the proposed scheme to discuss it with Sir Anthony Bowlby, Consulting Surgeon to the BEF, but Bowlby was also sceptical of it. Informing Barber that he had discussed the plan with Bowlby and other consulting surgeons, O'Keefe told him they were all of the opinion that 'an extra hour on the road is more than compensated for by the advantage of getting a patient to a well-established hospital, where he can rest for ten or fifteen days [...] and escape the risk of shell gas and gun fire'.[86] O'Keefe and Bowlby therefore disagreed with the Australian medical officers on this point. O'Keefe finished his communication with Barber by criticising the location of the medical units for the 5th Australian Division, writing: 'I would remind you that at my recent inspection I pointed out that your MDS at DAOURS would more suitably be located at "LES ALLENCONS" [sic]; the trouble in this case is that your MDS is too far forward.'[87]

The criticisms of the plan from members of the RAMC did not deter the AAMC medical officers from making changes, albeit slightly modified from those originally advocated. Colonel Barber forwarded O'Keefe's response to Colonel Downey, ADMS 5AD, writing: 'It will therefore be necessary to provide, when possible, accomodation [sic] at MDS for cases which are not likely to survive the journey. This could be done at "LES ALLENCONS" [sic].'[88] Colonel Downey, in turn, forwarded O'Keefe's reply along with a memorandum outlining the arrangements to the headquarters of his division for the attention of the Commanding Officer. Downey reported that arrangements had already been made for urgent operations to be undertaken at the divisional collecting station at Les Alençons and demonstrated to the CO that this was in line with regulations, stating: 'This will be in accordance with *Field Service Regulations*, and the Station will not be an "Advanced Operating Centre" in the strict interpretation of the term.'[89] This was a semantic distinction rather than an accession to the criticisms of O'Keefe and Bowlby.

In response to O'Keefe's criticisms of the location of the 5th Australian Division's main dressing station, Downey demonstrated the competence of Australian medical men by reassuring the divisional CO that the site had been approved by the Deputy Director of Medical Services of the Australian Corps, was 11 500 yards from the front line, enabled the prompt reinforcement of stretcher-bearers, and had been moved 2000 yards backwards, further behind the lines, since the Director of Medical Services of the Fourth Army had visited, and it was therefore not where he had thought.[90]

When the Australian Corps returned to the line for the Battle of Hamel in early July 1918, surgical work was undertaken at the 4th Australian Division's main dressing station against the advice of imperial authorities. In his report on the work of the AAMC during the battle, Lieutenant Colonel McGregor, Acting ADMS for the division, wrote: 'Special mention must be made of the most excellent work at MDS by Major A. Holmes à Court in doing a) urgent surgical operations, b) blood transfusions.'[91] Major Alan Worsley Holmes à Court had worked in private practice in Sydney and as assistant physician at Sydney Hospital before the war. He enlisted in the AIF in March 1915 and worked on board the *Karoola* as medical officer. He was posted to the 2nd Australian General Hospital, stationed in France, before he was promoted to major and moved to the 4th Australian Field Ambulance.[92] Of Holmes à Court's work at Hamel, McGregor reported:

> The surgical operations were done to arrest haemorrhage and to remove badly shattered limbs. The Blood transfusion was done to counteract shock. After this treatment cases were put in a special resuscitation room and after they had reacted (2–4 hours) were sent on to CCS. Seven cases were transfused and on enquiry at CCS we were informed that 6 of these cases were doing well and had undoubtedly been saved by this intervention.[93]

McGregor was convinced of the importance of surgical interventions at main dressing stations for those who would not otherwise make it to a casualty clearing station. He concluded: 'I am strongly of the opinion that there should be a special transfusion team with each Division and that this team should work at the MDS or if possible even at the ADS.'[94]

Similarly, in his war diary from 4 July 1918, Colonel Barber, DDMS Australian Corps, wrote: 'Three Blood Transfusions (citrated blood) done at MDS which probably saved the lives of these patients. Will endeavour to develope [*sic*] this as far forward as possible under varying circumstances.'[95] Major General O'Keefe's opposition to medical interventions in forward areas had seemingly failed to dampen Barber's enthusiasm. Two weeks later Barber recorded that he had visited the British No. 5 Casualty Clearing Station, which was the one to which casualties in the Australian sector were being evacuated, and he had discussed the transfusion of citrated blood at main dressing stations with Major Gordon Gordon-Taylor of the RAMC, Consulting Surgeon to Fourth Army.[96] These ideas were then developed further, and a blood transfusion team was formed for the Battle of Amiens in early August 1918. This team of four was led by Major Holmes à Court and was stationed behind the line at St Acheul. It was available on demand to the Officers Commanding Main Dressing Stations in the Australian Corps.[97]

Major Holmes à Court wrote a report on the work of the surgical resuscitation team at the Battle of Amiens. In it he advocated for a further expansion of the scheme. He reported that an examination of the work of this group 'renders it obvious that energetic resuscitation in the forward area accompanied where it is necessary by surgical interference ... as well as blood transfusion and the judicious use of Gum Arabic Solution, has been the direct means of saving many lives'.[98] During the Battle of Amiens, Holmes à Court's team treated 60 patients and maintained the doctrine that had developed through earlier iterations of the scheme. He reported that 'at all times' the cases treated included 'only the most seriously wounded and those considered unfit to evacuate immediately to the CCS and which would in all probability die being unable to withstand the further journey without receiving immediate treatment'.[99] He suggested that a surgical resuscitation team working within this framework of treating only those men who would not survive transport to the casualty clearing station (shattered limbs, haemorrhages, severe shock), and not impeding the evacuation of the vast majority of cases, could be stationed at a main or advanced dressing station and save many lives. When not needed for surgery or transfusions, the members of the team would assist in the general work of the medical post.

This medical intervention contrasted with other ideas around medicine forward of casualty clearing stations, which emphasised minimal intervention and rapid evacuation to treatment further down the line. However, it was formalised in the Australian Corps on 21 August 1918 when Colonel Barber wrote a memorandum on the 'Establishment and Equipment for Divisional Resuscitation Teams in the Australian Corps'. The memorandum was sent to Major General O'Keefe, Director of Medical Services (DMS) for Fourth Army, and Surgeon General Sir Neville Howse, DMS AIF, was also sent a copy.[100] In the cover note, Barber informed O'Keefe that one team was already established and a second would soon be in place. Barber outlined this new formation, known from this point as divisional resuscitation teams rather than the different names used previously. These teams included two medical officers – a major capable of doing the surgical work, blood transfusions and resuscitation, and a captain who could administer nitrous oxide and oxygen and classify blood donors – as well as other ranks, including one non-commissioned officer to work in the theatre. Barber outlined the equipment provided for each team, including a motor ambulance car to be provided as needed by the relevant division. Although only two teams existed or were in the process of being formed at this point (3rd and 4th Australian Divisions), Barber provided for five teams, one for each of the Australian divisions.[101]

When the Australian Corps was withdrawn from the line in October 1918, work began immediately to train further men for work in the resuscitation teams. On 14 October, Holmes à Court led a meeting of the Resuscitation Committee.[102] This committee included Holmes à Court and the RAMC's Consulting Surgeon to the Fourth Army, Major Gordon-Taylor, as joint presidents, as well as the medical officers from each Australian division who would work in the divisional resuscitation teams. Their report was distributed widely, including to the General Officer Commanding (GOC) AIF, GOC Australian Corps, Director General of Medical Services for the British Armies in France, DMS Fourth Army and DMS AIF. In the report, the committee outlined the principles upon which the scheme was based, the type of medical intervention carried out and the rates of success, including some case notes.[103]

Major Gordon-Taylor, the RAMC's Consulting Surgeon to the Fourth Army, furnished his own report on the work of the AAMC in this field. He stated: 'Several months experience in the Casualty Clearing Zone behind the Australian Corps has enabled me to form an estimate of the excellent work of the Resuscitation Teams of that Corps.' He reported that '[t]here can be no room for doubt that very many lives have been saved by the work of Major Holmes à Court and the members of the other Resuscitation teams' and that 'their results conclusively prove the value of these methods of resuscitation in the Field Ambulances'. He also opined that the experience of these units coincided with 'that of the Casualty Clearing Hospitals that in Blood transfusion we have the most remarkable and valuable means of treating severe cases of shock and haemorrhage'.[104]

The support of the Consulting Surgeon for the Fourth Army might have helped in the development of the resuscitation teams as the 1st, 2nd and 5th Australian Divisions each sent their resuscitation teams to a different British casualty clearing station for twenty-one days training from 1 November 1918, and the 3rd and 4th Division teams were due to undergo further training in January 1919; however, the end of the war made this redundant.[105] Major Holmes à Court was Mentioned in Despatches in December 1918 for his work on resuscitation in forward areas, and he was awarded the French *Médaille des Épidémies (en argent)*.[106]

Maintaining control: The AAMC in 1918

Unlike the years preceding it, 1918 was not a year of drastic change in the way the AAMC managed sick and wounded Australian troops. The most significant change was one of circumstance, from a form of stagnant trench warfare to open, mobile warfare. This difference required the medical services once again to alter the medical arrangements for Australian soldiers. As a result, the deputy and assistant directors of medical services in the Australian Corps had to unwind and undo many of the reforms that they had made in 1916 and 1917. They did this themselves and were able to make those decisions on the basis of the experience and knowledge built up over three years of war. The most innovative change made by the AAMC – the development of the divisional resuscitation teams – while valuable to the AIF, did not alter the fundamental structures of the medical services, nor did it change the way the vast majority of sick and wounded soldiers interacted with the AAMC.

The creation of an Australian Corps and the acceptance of civilian medical expertise at the highest levels of the British army helped to ensure that the Australian medical men were able to make decisions without interference from those outside the chain of command. By mid-June, all officers at division and corps level were men who had enlisted in the AIF, and the AAMC had established itself and consolidated its position as a competent service able to work for its corps and in cooperation with the broader Allied forces.

CHAPTER | 4

A PLEASANT DOSE OF MEDICINE?

THE PURPOSE, PLACE AND PRACTICE OF AUXILIARY HOSPITALS

In November 1914, an Australian couple living in Middlesex, England, offered their house for use as a convalescent home for sick and wounded Australian soldiers recovering from injury. The AAMC accepted Mr and Mrs Charles Billyard-Leake's offer, and their house and its grounds, Harefield Park, became a convalescent hospital before eventually becoming 1st Australian Auxiliary Hospital (1AAH) Harefield. The AAMC originally intended it to house fifty to a hundred patients plus staff but, eight months after opening, the accommodation had been increased to provide a thousand beds for convalescing soldiers. While at least one soldier mused that its purpose was to house those who were not 'fit to die in their own homes', its main function was to rehabilitate sick and wounded soldiers for a return to duty.[1] The hospital eventually included surgical, medical, X-ray, massage and electric therapy as well as recreation and study departments. Along with the other auxiliary hospitals in the Australian network – 2nd Australian Auxiliary Hospital (2AAH), Southall, and 3rd Australian Auxiliary Hospital (3AAH), Dartford – it formed an integral part of the medical services provided to Australian soldiers wounded in the First World War.

Each of the three Australian auxiliary hospitals developed specialty areas of medical care with 2AAH becoming the prime location for fitting soldiers for prosthetic limbs and their subsequent training and rehabilitation. The Dartford hospital, 3AAH, specialised in war neuroses, shell shock and 'nervous conditions' and, finally, 1AAH at Harefield specialised in eye, ear, nose and throat problems, as well as taking general cases

Figure 4.1 Harefield House during an outdoor concert for patients and staff, 3 July 1915 (AWM P12670.015.001)

in need of further medical care. These three auxiliary hospitals provided for the vast majority of Australian cases.

The first three chapters of this book examined the provision of medical care to Australian soldiers between the front line and casualty clearing stations. This chapter shifts well behind the battlefront to evaluate the rehabilitation of Australian soldiers in auxiliary hospitals. Previously, historians have tended to consider the rehabilitation of Australian soldiers as an after-war issue. Stephen Garton and Marina Larsson paired discussions of rehabilitation with those of repatriation, pensions and the treatment of disabled ex-servicemen rather than with the provision of medical care to sick and wounded soldiers during the war.[2] The historiography of the rehabilitation and medical care of wounded British soldiers away from the battlefront demonstrates similar framing and lines of enquiry.[3] Given the lasting impact of the war on both the men who fought and the countries that sent them, this framing of the discussion has significant merit. For many men, their wounding was the first event in the process of casualty evacuation, treatment, rehabilitation, removal to Australia and return to civilian life – a life often supported by family, charitable organisations and war pensions provided by their government. However, for large numbers of sick and wounded soldiers, their stay in an auxiliary hospital assisted in their recovery before their return to the front or, if deemed unfit for active service, to a support or administrative role. In the First World War, a soldier's wounding did not necessarily signify the beginning of the end of his military service. David Noonan found that, on average, each Australian soldier was admitted to hospital 2.3 times.[4] For that to be the case, each soldier would have been rehabilitated and returned to duty twice. Auxiliary hospitals were integral to that process.

Some cultural historians of the First World War have sought to locate the study of rehabilitation within its wartime context, highlighting the voices of both the carers and the cared for. Jeffrey Reznick argues that the culture of caregiving shaped the wartime experience of both soldiers and civilians. For soldiers, this enabled a 'comradeship of healing' that was in addition to the comradeship developed in the trenches. He suggests that this made soldiers' separation from the rest of society more prominent, despite the ability of civilian society to participate in and contribute to caregiving. For civilians, participating in caregiving 'served as a means to express appreciation of Tommy despite the existence of a true gulf in experience'.[5] Ana Carden-Coyne discusses power dynamics in the rehabilitation process and links the Foucauldian concept of the 'biopower' of military medicine (i.e. how 'medicine and its institutions discipline bodies') to the patients' experience of war wounds.[6] In doing so, she articulates the need for analyses of the interactions between the patients' experience of wounding and the social and political networks of military medicine within hospitals and medical spaces.[7] This chapter examines those networks, including the civilian women who participated in caring for Australian soldiers, and their influence on the care provided to wounded servicemen.

At the same time as heeding Roy Porter's call for historians to place patient perspectives at the centre of medical histories, cultural historians have renewed their focus on discussions of power in the First World War.[8] These trends, combined with an emphasis on the British experience of rehabilitation, have resulted in a number of analyses of British patient masculinities in war.[9] Applying similar methodologies to the providers of care and analysing the nature of the work in hospitals can yield interesting results.[10] Owing to the structure of the Australian medical provision, this is particularly so in the Australian context.

In contrast to the British experience in rehabilitation hospitals, the gendered nature of the work is particularly prominent in the three Australian auxiliary hospitals. British auxiliary hospitals were associated with military hospitals in Britain and were under the control of the military, but their day-to-day management was the responsibility of charities, including the Red Cross and the YMCA. While the base of Australian operations remained in Australia, the auxiliary hospitals were set up in Britain to keep soldiers closer to the front. Consequently, the Australian auxiliary hospitals were under the authority and general management of the Australian Army Medical Corps (AAMC). The militarisation of this space placed Australian medical men in charge of medical care while the 'women's work' of nursing, social and domestic care was done by women through the Australian Army Nursing Service (AANS), members of the Voluntary Aid Detachment (VADs), charities, 'lady volunteers' and paid staff from the Women's Auxiliary Army Corps (WAAC). I suggest that the Australian model, which had a greater degree of military involvement in the quotidian experience of the hospital's community, increased military authority in this civilian-influenced medical space and harnessed the labour of women within boundaries that were tightly defined and reinforced.

This chapter analyses the purpose, place and practice of Australian auxiliary hospitals. It focuses on 1AAH Harefield, although it is informed by events in the rest of the Australian auxiliary hospital network. Beginning with a discussion of the medical boarding process, it then evaluates auxiliary hospitals as liminal spaces between home and war – spaces in which conflicting ideas about responsibility for medicine and participation in caregiving were played out. These spaces were primarily military hospitals, with the insatiable quest for efficiency resulting in discussions of economies of labour, yet the presence of women in a variety of roles and the hospital's location in a private home created an environment in which domesticity and gender difference were routinely and openly discussed. Finally, I survey the practice of rehabilitation in these hybrid spaces, establishing the effect the place of care had on the practice of care and the degree to which women were accepted as actors with expertise. This evaluation of why, where and how rehabilitative medicine was practised by the AAMC highlights the pursuit of efficiency in a military-controlled, civilian-influenced medical space, which in turn reveals the controlled participation of women; that is, it shows us who was allowed to care and in what circumstances.

EFFICIENCY: THE PURPOSE OF AUXILIARY HOSPITALS

Initially, 1AAH Harefield was intended to be a convalescent depot that would be a 'rest home' for officers, warrant officers, NCOs and rank-and-file soldiers to recuperate after illness or injury. Its secondary purpose was to act as a depot for collecting invalids for return to Australia. In February 1915, the plan was for the depot to hold 150 patients in summer and sixty in winter. On 31 May 1915 and in the aftermath of the failed landings on Gallipoli, Surgeon General William 'Mo' Williams, Director of Medical Services for the AIF in England, informed the British War Office that he had arranged to extend the depot to at least 500 beds, and it was then referred to as an 'auxiliary hospital' from that point.[11]

Australia's relatively small population, combined with the voluntary nature of military service, heightened the importance of efficiency in the deployment of its resources. An indication of the increasing need for efficiency can be found in the changing approach to medical boarding. In this process, a sick or wounded soldier would be paraded in front of a panel of doctors (the medical board), who would seek to classify him according to a set of criteria, estimate his recovery time, and predict the extent to which he would recover. Initially, at Harefield, soldiers were classified as fit for general service or either temporarily or permanently unfit for general service, but by February 1918 this had developed into the eight-part system, as shown in table 4.1. This classification dictated where soldiers went after they had recovered enough to leave hospital, with all discharged patients being sent to one of the four Australian command depots (ACDs). Three ACDs were located in Wiltshire with one in Sutton Veny and two in Hurdcott, and the fourth was in Weymouth, Dorset.

This classification of the utility of men's bodies was echoed in their post-war treatment as well. There were distinct similarities between the processes of return to duty during the war and the assessment of injury and the determination of pension entitlements after the war.[12] Economy – of men in the case of medical boarding and of money in the case of war pensions – was the underlying factor in both processes. The soldier's body was under surveillance from the moment he tried to enlist, and the need for more 'effective' troops (soldiers being classified as either effective or 'wastage') required the 'reconditioning' of invalids to be fit for some form of service. Thus, doctors became instruments of the State and were integral to maintaining the efficiency of the army through rehabilitation and assessments of fitness for duty.[13]

Table 4.1 Classification and disposal of patients from 1AAH Harefield

Class	General service	Home service	Disposal
A	Fit	–	1ACD, Sutton Veny
B1a	Temp. unfit < 6 months	Fit	1ACD, Sutton Veny; 4ACD, Hurdcott[a]
B1b	Temp. unfit < 6 months	Unfit	3ACD, Hurdcott
B2a	Temp. unfit > 6 months	Fit	2ACD, Weymouth
B2b	Temp. unfit > 6 months	Unfit	2ACD, Weymouth, then to Australia
C1	Permanently unfit	Fit	2ACD, Weymouth
C2	Permanently unfit	Temp. unfit	2ACD, Weymouth, then to Australia
C3	Permanently unfit	Perm. unfit	2ACD, Weymouth, then to Australia

[a] The less severe cases in this category were sent to Sutton Veny, the more severe cases to 4ACD, Hurdcott

Source: compiled from Surgeon General Neville Howse, 7 February 1918, war diary, Appendix 4, 1AAH, Harefield (AWM4 26/72/6)

As can be seen from table 4.1, the only soldiers who were repatriated to Australia were those who would be unfit for general service for more than six months, if not permanently so, and were also unfit for home service in that time. Soldiers who were fit for general service entered training to return to the fighting units at the front whereas those fit for home service undertook less physically taxing duties during their recovery, including working as orderlies in wards or in administrative roles.[14] The only patients to remain in England who could not be put to work in some capacity were those who would be able to return to front-line training in less than six months. In addition to the eight-part classification system shown in table 4.1, the B1a group was broken down into four further steps that then dictated how much 'graduated training and exercise' the recovering soldiers were expected to do. This ranged from general Swedish drill and special remedial exercises for those classified B2b, C2 and C3, through to walking four miles and running a hundred yards in both the morning and afternoon, as well as physical training, organised games and digging, and jumping of obstacles for those classified B1a4, the highest classification of those not currently fit for active service.[15]

When Australia entered the First World War, the decision was made to have the base of military operations for the AIF located in Australia. Given the distance from Europe to Australia, it was too inefficient to repatriate soldiers who could be rehabilitated relatively quickly. The process of returning soldiers to Australia took six weeks, only for recovered soldiers to have to reverse the journey a short time later, once an individual was fit for service once again. These voyages were uncomfortable for the wounded or sick soldier and could exacerbate their conditions. The alternative was for soldiers who would be able to return to some form of duty within six months to be housed in convalescent hospitals in England. Soldiers did not have to return to the same type of work as they had previously undertaken. Many returned as AAMC orderlies or as administrative staff if their condition was such that they could not return to their battalions. In keeping with the drive in the AAMC to provide effective medical care in an efficient manner, the purpose of auxiliary hospitals was therefore to take the 'wastage' of the AIF and rehabilitate those soldiers to a state of usefulness for the military and their country.

LOCATION AND SPACE: THE PLACE
OF AUXILIARY HOSPITALS

The place of auxiliary hospitals in the Australian system was different from the systems for other British Empire soldiers. British auxiliary hospitals were attached to military hospitals and, although under military control, they were managed by charitable organisations. Britain's provision extended to its Indian soldiers, whose invalids were cared for in Brighton, including in the famous Brighton Pavilion, as well as in Brockenhurst, Hampshire, and in Netley. The suggestion that King George V thought the wounded Indian soldiers should be housed in the Pavilion because 'they would feel more at home' in its oriental surrounds appears to be apocryphal, although Sir Walter Lawrence, who wrote a report on arrangements for sick and wounded Indian soldiers, thought the building and its surrounds particularly appropriate.[16]

Canadian and New Zealand soldiers, once they arrived in England from France, were distributed directly among their respective national hospital networks in Britain, although the Canadian soldiers were more easily despatched back to their homeland.[17] In contrast, once an Australian soldier was transported to a casualty clearing station in France or Belgium, the AAMC no longer had direct control over the medical care he received. Wounded Australian soldiers joined the British system of casualty treatment and proceeded through British hospitals in Britain for treatment and further surgery before being transported to an Australian auxiliary hospital. While the AAMC provided general hospitals and casualty clearing stations, they were not necessarily allocated to Australian sectors, nor were Australian patients automatically sent there. The Australian choice to maintain military control of a militarised domestic space away from its base of operations and separate from its major hospitals was unique.

Figure 4.2 A library and space for writing, I AAH Harefield. Owing to its setting in a family home, I AAH Harefield was a different environment from the medical units the soldiers would have experienced earlier in the casualty evacuation chain. (AWM H19078)

Harefield Park was in a convenient location for an auxiliary hospital, being only 20 miles from the centre of London and 2.5 miles from a railway station, making the transportation of patients to and from the hospital relatively simple. Yet the formation of a military hospital within a private home also posed problems for the AAMC, creating tension between the military and the homeowner. As mentioned previously, the house was donated by an Australian expatriate couple who lived in England. The agreement was nebulous, and it took less than six months for problems to be raised. In a report on the hospital, the Commanding Officer, Colonel Hayward, wrote: 'It was originally offered to the

Commonwealth as a Convalescent Hospital for from 50 to 100 patients – the formal agreement seems to have been loosely drawn, which has given rise to a good deal of difficulty.' He continued: 'It was converted, I am given to understand, into a 1000-bed Hospital without the consent of the owners.'[18] This conversion required structural changes to the house as well as the construction of wards in the grounds surrounding the main house.

Colonel Hayward suggested that much of the tension between the military and the Billyard-Leake family was due to an unreasonable act by the Australian Minister for Defence. Reporting that the minister had 'practically given Mr Leake a commission which he interpreted as giving him a right to have a say in the management of the Hospital, and he has always taken up the position that the OC and Officers are his guests'. Noting that the military abdicating authority to civilians in a military hospital was an 'untenable' situation, Hayward reported: 'The Commonwealth may be under an obligation to him – the Officers are the servants of the Government and only responsible to the Army Authorities.' Finally, Hayward suggested that this agreement had caused problems in the hospital, writing: 'A great disadvantage has been owing to Mr & Mrs Leake living in such close proximity to the Hospital and so intimately mixing with the patients. While cheerfully admitting that their kind interest and attention to patients has been of value I feel that it has not tended to improve discipline.'[19]

The failure to delineate lines of responsibility properly meant that the owner of the house was in a position to undermine the authority of the AAMC staff in the hospital. In the eyes of the AAMC officers, and despite the fact that he owned the home in which the hospital was located, Billyard-Leake did not have licence to interfere with the running of the hospital. The AAMC respected medical expertise and recognised military and imperial authority unless subverting them could result in substantially greater efficiency and outcomes. Mr Billyard-Leake's donation did not buy him authority in this space, and, while the AAMC was happy to make use of his donation, the Australian medical men of 1AAH Harefield did not recognise his claim to 'a commission' from the Minister for Defence.

As a result of this problem, Hayward made recommendations for the structure of any future agreements between the military and private property owners, writing that he 'felt strongly' that should a government accept 'an offer such as was Mr Leake's it should be only on the definite understanding that during the period of occupation the owner should have no interest in it otherwise than according to a definite agreement as to structural concerns or upkeep'.[20] Thus, Colonel Hayward argued for the assertion and maintenance of military discipline and authority in this military–medical space.

It was not just the nature of the care provided and the location of his hospital in a domestic setting that made 1AAH Harefield different from those the AAMC controlled elsewhere. For the most part, men staffed Australian medical–military units in France and Belgium. While women were present in those spaces, some as far forward as the 2nd Australian Casualty Clearing Station at Trois Arbres, they were in small numbers. In contrast, at Harefield Park, the female staff was not a small subset of those working in the hospital. On 31 March 1918, there were 203 men (21 officers and 182 other ranks from the AAMC) working at 1AAH, Harefield, as well as 197 women (86 on the nursing staff and 111 general service VADs). That suggests that almost half of the staff were women. However, these figures do not take into account the hospital's all-female massage staff; therefore even more women were working at 1AAH than a cursory glance at the numbers would suggest.

In addition to the women with varying degrees of specialised medical training who worked at the hospital, the AAMC also took advantage of the willing work of civilian women at Harefield. In its attempts to create a more efficient medical service, it relied increasingly on the employment of women behind the lines in auxiliary hospitals. As more and more men were needed on the battlefield, much of the work of orderlies in the auxiliary hospitals was handed over to civilians, frequently to civilian women.

On 10 July 1917, Lieutenant Colonel Bertram Milne Sutherland, the Officer Commanding 3AAH in Dartford, recorded in the hospital's war diary that he had discussed with General Howse (DMS AIF) extending the scope of the employment of 'Woman Labour' in the hospital.[21] Howse instructed him to investigate the matter, and two days later Sutherland wrote back outlining his recommendations. Those recommendations were based on the findings of a conference he had convened to discuss the matter with the Registrar, Quartermaster, Acting Matron and Superintendent of the WAAC staff of the hospital. At this stage, the WAAC already provided cooks for the kitchens and housemaids for the nursing sisters' quarters. Sister Minhennett, Acting Matron, listed the duties the maids would need to undertake in the wards, and it was decided that two maids were required in a ward of forty-six beds. This number was sufficient for the maids to work the same number of hours as the members of the WAAC who were already employed in the hospital as well as enabling them to have regular time off. The conference members decided that the heavier work – scrubbing large wards and carrying baskets of soiled linen – would be carried out by fatigue parties from the AAMC.[22]

Figure 4.3 Ward 32, 1AAH Harefield (Libraries Tasmania: Hobart A 246 5 NS669/20/1/8)

Sutherland listed three potential outcomes upon which he based his recommendations. First, he saw the opportunity for substantial financial savings in the weekly cost of wages. The weekly wages and associated costs of employing one sergeant, two corporals and thirty-seven privates was £106 7s 6d, whereas the cost for one 'overseer', twenty-eight wardsmaids and two housemaids was £16 19s 4d per week. Employing thirty-one women to do the work of forty men would save the AAMC £89 8s 2d per week or a saving of around 84 per cent.[23] Sutherland's second reason for recommending this change to Howse was that it would allow the men to be redeployed elsewhere or returned to Australia, resulting in a more efficient distribution of labour. The final reason given by Sutherland for the recommended change was that 'the duties being largely of the nature of Women's work will be more efficiently performed by women than by a male staff'.[24] Sutherland proposed that the maids should work in the wards where sisters were in charge rather than in the convalescent wards, which were managed by orderlies at 3AAH. This structure ensured that the civilian women working in the military hospital were managed by women. They would be under the authority of the Superintendent of the WAAC staff at 3AAH, Miss Gibson, and their day-to-day work was to be completed under the watchful eyes of the nurses.[25] Sutherland's recommendations were therefore based on a three-pronged understanding of efficiency: monetary efficiency, efficiency of manpower and efficiency of work.

The response to Sutherland's plan for the more efficient use of resources came from Colonel Thomas Griffiths, Acting Commandant of the AIF's Administrative Headquarters in Horseferry Road, London. Griffiths had enlisted in the colonial military forces in Melbourne in 1890 as a military staff clerk and had more than two decades experience in army administration.[26] He agreed with Sutherland's recommendations and requested that the Assistant Quartermaster General make the arrangements. Impressed with the potential savings for the AIF, Griffiths replied: 'It is noted from your memorandum that when the scheme has been brought completely into operation, there will be a saving to the AIF of approximately £89 a week, and at the same time a probable increase in efficiency.' He saw considerable value in this scheme and continued: 'The experiment will be carefully watched, because if it is found to be successful, it will be valuable in other hospitals.'[27]

After three years of war, the cost in terms of men, money and materials was mounting. In the period between the two unsuccessful conscription plebiscites in Australia, redeploying forty men and saving £89 per week could alleviate substantial strains on the AIF, especially if the efficiencies could be generalised across other hospitals or military units. In praising Sutherland for striving for greater efficiency and innovation, Griffiths wrote: 'I am glad to note that you and your Officers are not blindly following the usual routine in the conduct of the affairs of the Hospital without first inquiring as to whether it is the best available under the circumstances.'[28] The willingness to depart from convention and to question the underlying assumptions of medical organisation and practice is reminiscent of the work of the AAMC in its development of new casualty evacuation procedures. In the forward areas, the innovations were not contained to one unit but were spread among the AAMC's officers, and this sharing of knowledge continued behind the lines as well.

Civilian women worked on the non-medical staff of auxiliary hospitals beyond 3AAH in Dartford. On 23 January 1917, the Officer Commanding 1AAH Harefield reported that Administrative Headquarters had agreed to the use of civilian labour in the kitchens instead of orderly staff.[29] A year later, 1AAH followed in the footsteps of 3AAH by bringing in women to staff the hospital. On 4 January 1918, Lieutenant Colonel Yeatman, Commanding Officer of 1AAH Harefield, wrote to Howse confirming that forty-two women were to replace forty AAMC orderlies as both ward orderlies and labour staff. He requested a further complement of seven WAACs to act as housemaids and staff at the two houses in Harefield that were rented to accommodate the female civilian staff.[30] Once the civilian women had commenced work in these roles, Lieutenant Colonel Yeatman forwarded a report on the results to Howse. Yeatman wrote: 'Under the substitution scheme of women for men, 69 VAD General Service numbers (including administrative and hostel Staffs) have displaced 52 men struck off strength.' Apparently happy with the success of the change, Yeatman continued: 'On the whole the scheme appears to me to be working satisfactorily and I have much pleasure in being able to say that never before have wards and annexes been so clean as at present.'[31]

Thus, the recruitment of female labour to undertake 'women's work' was viewed as a success. Yet, as this was a new role, the limits of the VAD ward orderlies still needed to be set. These duties were clarified in Routine Orders No. 151 for 1AAH, on 1 May 1918, and recorded in the 1AAH unit war diary the following month. These women were to be addressed as 'Orderly' and, when on duty in the wards, they were supervised, instructed and 'helped in every way possible to learn' by the sister in charge of the ward. The sister was permitted to call on the VAD ward orderly to assist in nursing serious bed cases, but the VAD was not expected to scrub floors, 'sponge helpless bed patients' or do surgical dressings.[32] Fatigue parties of AAMC men were responsible for the scrubbing of floors, and the latter two duties were nursing duties. Here, like at 3AAH, distinctions were maintained between those with medical training and those without, as well as between 'women's work' and the heavier labour to be undertaken by men.

Despite the new female labour force taking on the non-medical 'women's work' of the hospital, not all women who were employed in those roles were deemed fit to serve at 1AAH Harefield. In September 1918, Yeatman wrote to Howse regarding the situation, stating: 'I wish to bring before your notice the fact that several General Service VADs reporting for duty from Devonshire House, by reason of ill health, have been found to be unsuitable for employment here.'[33] Devonshire House was the London residence of the Duke of Devonshire and the Cavendish family, the ground floor of which was given over to the British Red Cross Society for the First World War. The British Red Cross Society had sent women with existing medical conditions that were exacerbated by work to serve at 1AAH. Those women were given initially six, then eight, weeks of sick leave. This placed a drain on the efficiency of 1AAH, and Yeatman recommended to Howse that as general service VADs reporting to Harefield had 'no previous experience of the work, a probationary period of one month should be observed, at the end of which time, if suitable as regards health and adaptability the member should be enrolled and receive the Uniform Grant'.[34] In the same way that some men were unfit for active service, some women were unfit for work in this militarised setting. This had the potential to cause problems for the women. Some might have sought employment as a way to earn their own money, but many needed to find work in order to support their families after the earning capacity of their male relatives was limited by war injury or death. As men's bodies were constantly reassessed based on their utility for the State, when engaging in paid labour in service of their country, women's bodies were also subject to this test.

Alongside engaging in paid labour in support of the war effort, philanthropy and volunteering were two further ways in which members of the British (and Australian) public could participate in and contribute to the war. Fundraising, advocacy and, as will be seen, involvement in the care and recreation work of auxiliary hospitals were all forms of voluntary war service in which women participated. Jeffrey Reznick has argued that, in the British context, this was a form of wartime commemoration in which 'sites of rest, recovery and rehabilitation played their own roles ... becoming foci of public interest in aiding and honouring the manhood of the nation'.[35]

The location of 1AAH Harefield in an English village resulted in a different form of involvement in the medical provision from the Mother Country. In this instance, it was not a military intrusion but a civilian one, born out of a desire to improve the care for the Australian soldiers and perhaps indicative of the social contract that had formed between the soldier and the State, supported by the public and extended to the dominions.[36] This is exemplified by the actions of some women from the area around Harefield who saw advocating for the hospital's patients as part of their role. 'Certain ladies' viewed the rationing and dietary provisions for patients as inadequate and complained. This complaint reached the Australian High Commissioner in London, Sir George Reid, and the War Office sent imperial authorities to investigate. The complaint was considered to be 'unfounded'.[37]

The presence of so many women altered the relationships that developed within the hospital and highlight the differences between the auxiliary hospitals and the medical units discussed in the first three chapters of this book. A number of patients were married from 1AAH, and their brides were often nurses (who could marry with the permission of their Commanding Officer), VADs or local women who volunteered at the hospital.[38] There were also marriages between doctors and the women in and around the hospital, suggesting that they also experienced something of domestic felicity in this militarised environment.

Marriages from 1AAH Harefield were fairly common and were reported in the *Harefield Park Boomerang*, the hospital magazine. In the August 1918 edition, in the regular 'Hospital-ities' column, Lance Corporal W. Anderson, writing under the pseudonym 'Lyon Taemer', reported: 'Yet another offensive. This time the marriage microbe has attacked the hospital, and the wedding bells have been having a good time!'[39] Lyon Taemer then continued, describing the wedding of Private J. Wickham of the Tunnellers Company, who was then attached to the AAMC, to Miss Ruby Beatrice Freestone of Harefield. Lyon Taemer also informed readers of the wedding of Private Stanley Biggins of the Australian Field Ambulance to Miss Kate Lofty of High Street, Harefield. At that wedding, the hospital chaplain, Major Terry, officiated, the best man was Lance Corporal B. Sergeant and the bridesmaids were Miss Doris Lofty, sister of the bride, and a Miss Dowling, who were both VADs on the staff of 1AAH Harefield. The description includes details of the bride's and bridesmaids' attire, the flowers and the post-ceremony celebrations. In the same issue of the *Boomerang*, the engagement of Lieutenant Edward Whaley Billyard-Leake, son of the owner of Harefield Park, to Miss Leila Violet Douglas of Midlothian was announced. There was also a wedding in August 1917 between Driver L. Kirkley and Miss L.F. Essen, one of the VADs at Harefield. The story includes a photograph from outside the church, where local girls, with their weaving sticks, and the staff and patients of the hospital, with their walking sticks and crutches, formed an archway through which the happy couple proceeded to the cars.[40] Despite being at war and in a military hospital, for its patients and staff, the setting of the auxiliary hospital created space for intimacy and thoughts of domesticity.

Employing women changed the nature of the space and altered the relationship between the carer and the patient. Harefield's environment, in which marriage occurred relatively frequently, drew attention to the single women in the hospital and created a forum for a discussion of marriage. Many of these women were in paid positions with a measure of independence, occasioning Lyon Taemer to ask, in his 'Hospital-ities' column, why some women chose to remain single. He wrote: 'The question why so many women remain single is doubtless best known to themselves, and as men often rush in with their theories it is to women I look for a trustworthy explanation.' He continued: 'As we have a large number of female workers on the Staff, will some of them kindly forward me in writing their reasons "Why women remain single?"'[41]

Apparently disappointed with the number of responses, Lyon Taemer published three letters, one from a nursing sister and two from VADs at Harefield. The provenance of the letters is impossible to determine. It is possible they were not written by female members of the hospital's staff but were instead submitted by men in the hospital or, in fact, made up by the columnist himself. Assuming that they were written by a nurse and two VADs, they provide interesting insight into the willingness of the authors to discuss domestic gender roles in this military context.

In response to Lyon Taemer, one VAD quoted the words of Ethel Brunner in *The Elopement* stating that she wanted, ideally, a 'husband-companion' but was wary of letting into her life a 'husband-father', a 'husband-visitor', a 'husband-bully' or even a 'husband-gaoler'.[42] In what was perhaps the most forthright declaration of the three respondents, the sister stated why remaining single was more attractive than marrying the wrong man. She wrote:

> With the flower of the race gone over the seas, there only remain those who are running to seed. A concave-chested male biped, a small salary and a large family – does that sound alluring? To live contentedly on a crust of bread with the alter ego is an easier process in the pages of fiction than in flats in Paddington – but to share poverty in Pimlico with a Class 3 man, who is 'no class' when it comes to morals or ability, is a prospect too dreadful to contemplate with equanimity.[43]

Here she acknowledged the problems that faced women interested in marriage during and after the First World War. A large proportion of young men had been killed or seriously injured in the war, and many of those injuries would result in lifelong disability. The best men, in her estimation, the men of valour, had served their country in war. Those that remained were too old or not physically fit for service. She was aware that the life of a single woman who lived on a small salary in a London flat was challenging, but she preferred that prospect to spending her life with a man whom she considered unworthy of respect and lacking in moral courage or physical fitness. While the response of the sister is humorous, and perhaps demonstrates the use of hyperbole, it acknowledges that if she were to marry she might end up the full-time carer of a man unable to work, living in a society that did not look kindly upon married women working outside the home.

In this instance, the sister might have agreed with the second VAD who responded to Lyon Taemer. The VAD suggested that similar thoughts, when coupled with the behaviour of the Australian soldiers in the hospital, affected the way she interacted with her patients. She wrote that she enjoyed her 'bachelor girl's life too much to give it up', and that 'I have many good comrades amongst the men I know, and can enjoy their company extremely, but you Australians want too much, and expect me to fall in love with you, consequently I have to treat you with reserve, frankness, and friendliness'.[44]

These letters from female members of staff at 1AAH Harefield suggest that this hybrid military–domestic space created room for a relatively open discussion of gender roles and that the presence of significant numbers of women in the hospital altered the relationship between the carers and those for whom they cared. Civilians, especially women, were actively involved in daily activities at Harefield, unlike in the Australian-controlled medical units administering care for Australian soldiers on the Western Front. While women were present as far forward as casualty clearing stations, they worked in a limited variety of roles and did not have the same freedom to interact with soldiers in an environment of domesticity.

Figure 4.4 Snow! Nurses and patients participating in a snowball fight at 1AAH Harefield (AWM H16672)

Figure 4.5 Convalescing soldiers at 1AAH Harefield drawing a nurse on a sledge, with another patient in the background poised and ready to throw snowballs (AWM H18664)

By understanding place to be a combination of both the geographical location and the social and cultural life of the inhabitants, it is possible to view the organisation of 1AAH and its sister hospitals as spaces structured to reinforce gender norms. This environment required the AAMC to balance competing – and sometimes contradictory – demands. In contrast to the medical units between the front and the casualty clearing station, auxiliary hospitals were an environment in which civilian women undertook a variety of roles. From working-class roles such as housemaids, cooks and clerical work, to the more genteel middle-class assistance in letter-writing, socialising and needlework of the 'lady volunteers' (to be discussed further below), none of this work challenged society's existing ideas regarding types of work suitable for men and women. As will be seen below, the work of female physiotherapists went some way towards disrupting those gender roles; however, limitations and restrictions were placed on those women as well. It is clear from the marriages and discussions of women's choices to remain single that within this military-controlled environment, with numerous civilian women working in traditional female roles, a level of domestic relief from the war on the other side of the Channel was achieved. This domesticity, when aligned with and not hampering the purpose of the military unit, was permitted to flourish.

MEDICINE, MASSAGE AND FANCY WORK: PRACTISING CARE IN AUXILIARY HOSPITALS

Working in this hybrid military–domestic unit were the medical personnel of the AIF. At 1AAH Harefield, the medical and surgical departments undertook significant work, and the massage and electric therapy departments were kept fully occupied. These medical and allied health roles were supplemented by the Department for Recreation and Study, which provided entertainment, comforts and forms of vocational therapy to recovering soldiers. The primary concerns of AAMC officers was the medical care provided to Australian soldiers and the efficiency with which it was provided. While the social care and recreational activities provided by civilians were appreciated by the medical officers, their value was framed in terms of warding off idleness and boosting morale rather than because they possessed intrinsic value.

The Registrar of 1AAH Harefield, Major James A. Smeal of the AAMC, published a statistical report of the medical work undertaken in the hospital during 1916.[45] In the first five months of the year, the hospital received the last of the casualties from the Dardanelles campaign and then, from June, it started to receive casualties from France. The scale of the work increased during the year with 1548 admissions in the period from January to May and 8539 in the last seven months of the year. This reflects both the high rate of injury from the battlefields in France and the fact that the last major battle involving the Australians at Gallipoli was some time previously, in August 1915. Of the 9581 discharges from 1AAH in 1916, 3661 (or 38 per cent) were assessed as unfit for active service. However, of these, only 1072 were discharged directly to hospital ships and invalid transports bound for Australia. A similar number were discharged to work at headquarters or as staff for Harefield or other hospitals. The remainder were sent to the convalescent depot at Epsom, in Surrey, or one of the Australian command depots.[46]

Indicating the nature of the medical work at 1AAH, only ten soldiers died during the year. These ten deaths included multiple cases of tuberculosis, two of cancer, one of pneumonia and an instance with a shrapnel wound to the skull complicated by septic meningitis. A significant number of operations was performed during the year (863); however, the majority of them were secondary operations in cases where it was necessary to remove sequestra or foreign bodies from wounds or where amputations or reamputations of stumps were required. No soldier was evacuated directly from France to Harefield – they were first treated in British hospitals – so primary operations were less common but did include interventions owing

to appendicitis, hernia, varicocele and other similar illnesses and conditions that occur irrespective of the state of war.[47]

The condition of the patients as they arrived at 1AAH Harefield led the
medical officers there to question the standard of care provided by the
British hospitals that received Australian war casualties from France and
Belgium. In a letter to the DMS AIF, Neville Howse, Colonel Yeatman
wrote: 'In the opinion of the Senior Surgeon of this Hospital, who has
reported a number of specific cases to me, many cases admitted to this
Hospital on transfer from British Hospitals show evidence of not having
had the surgical care of and attention to their wounds which they should
have had from Medical Officers.'[48] Yeatman included a schedule of cases
that the Senior Surgeon suggested had received substandard care in British
hospitals and vouched for the factual accuracy of the details provided.
Yeatman viewed the rapidity of the improvement in patients' conditions
on arrival and treatment at Harefield as an indicator of the insufficiency of
previous medical interventions. He wrote to Howse: 'Faultiness of previous treatment is seen by the improvement which takes place in a few days
here; Sinuses which have been discharging pus for several weeks, due to
the presence of pieces of dead bone, clear up in a week or two after the
Sequestra are removed.' He continued: 'Fractures, improperly treated and
mal-united or in bad position, are corrected. In more than one case the
bone at the site of the fracture was found to be projecting through the
wound.' Finally, Yeatman suggested that the British hospitals had failed
to make many simple medical interventions, reporting: 'Drop-foot or
Drop-wrist, unsupported by splints, and unnecessary postural deform-
ities, are not unfrequently [sic] found to be present.'[49]

These problems with the care provision in British hospitals created
extra work for the surgical staff at Harefield. The situation was exacerbated by the fact that men transferred to Harefield from British hospitals
with lice-infected clothing, another problem to be rectified once they
arrived at 1AAH.[50] Yeatman did not frame his report as a complaint or
request that Howse investigate these issues further. He kept his superior
officer informed regarding issues of concern at 1AAH and left it to Howse
to decide whether they were problems that warranted further enquiry.
Yet, once October came, it was obvious that the problem of substandard
surgical care in British hospitals continued. Yeatman once again wrote to
Howse, this time on the condition of 'cot cases', and reported: '[T]here is
great room for improvement especially in the method of splinting of limb,
and in the treatment of septic bone injuries.' He informed Howse that a
'large proportion', after X-ray examination at Harefield, required

'immediate sequestrectomies performed with most striking results in the improvement of their wounds and general health. The better and more liberal diet they received here undoubtedly conduces largely to this end.'[51] As these latest cases arrived at Harefield little more than a month before the Armistice, any attempts to alter the condition of men on admission to Harefield did not have time to come into force before the hospital stopped receiving new cases in December 1918. It discharged its last patients in January 1919 and closed the following month.

While these cases of inadequate medical care caused pain and distress to patients, they might have provided part of the impetus for commencing 'Clinical Meetings of the Medical Staff'. These began in February 1918, and at the first of them the Senior Surgeon, Lieutenant Colonel Shaw, held a discussion on 'surgical diseases of the knee joint with special reference to displaced cartilages and treatment by appropriate splinting, illustrated by cases' from within the hospital.[52] Given Yeatman's statements regarding the inappropriate nature of the splints accompanying some of the new admissions from British hospitals, it is possible that this discussion was devised as a corrective so that the medical staff had a better understanding of the problems. These meetings were held weekly for the last ten months of the war. Subsequent weeks included sessions on 'Massage, Ionization and Electrical treatment generally' by Lieutenant Colonel Dennis, head of the Massage and Electrical Departments, followed by a discussion of shell shock and war neuroses led by Major Adams, Officer Commanding the 'Shellies'.[53]

Physiotherapists, then commonly known as masseurs (male) or masseuses (female), became integral to the rehabilitation of sick and wounded soldiers in Australian auxiliary hospitals during the First World War. They were responsible for more than massage, also providing other therapies including Swedish remedial exercises, hydrotherapy, and thermal and electrical treatments.[54] These professionals were university-educated men and women who had undertaken a two-year diploma at the Universities of Sydney, Melbourne or Adelaide. They shared some theory-based biomedical science subjects with medical students, then undertook specialist practical subjects and placements in hospitals and the community. As the war progressed, and the value of physiotherapy to the process of rehabilitating soldiers was increasingly understood, the universities offered short courses to interested recruits so that they could serve in the Army Massage Corps.[55] These recruits were then required either to cease practice at the end of the war or to complete the remainder of the full course. This mirrors some of the changes made during the war to the education of doctors who were able to have their degrees fast-tracked to enable them to serve the AIF as qualified doctors earlier than would otherwise have been possible.[56] Major Smeal, Registrar of 1AAH Harefield, saw value in the work of the massage corps. In 1916, the electrical treatment and massage department of the hospital completed 21 582 individual treatments on Australian soldiers, with 16 832 being hot air and massage and 4750 being electrical therapies. Of the work, Smeal wrote: 'The amount of work offering for this department has always been, until recently, more than the available staff could cope with, but splendid results have been obtained.'[57]

The Army Massage Corps initially included significant proportions of both men and women, creating difficulties regarding rank and status. Nurses were given the rank of honorary officers, and as the masseuses were classified as staff nurses, they too were treated as honorary officers. In the case of the masseurs, one man in each military district was made a lieutenant and the rest were designated as staff sergeants.[58] In effect, this meant that the female physiotherapists technically outranked most of their male colleagues. In response, the *Age* newspaper argued for commissioned officer posts for masseurs as thirty-three dentists had all been commissioned as lieutenants.[59] In a further indication of gender divisions among the staff at 1AAH Harefield, Yeatman wrote to Howse: '[It] is a good principle to keep [an exclusively] female massage staff at this Hospital. Masseurs do not work well or happily where the sexes are mixed.'[60] Sergeants were paid 10 shillings per day and lieutenants 15 per day while nurses, and therefore masseuses, were paid 7 shillings per day. Given the penchant of the Officers Commanding 1AAH for saving money by employing women instead of men, it is likely that cost was an added consideration in the decision to keep an all-female massage staff at Harefield.

In order to provide the level of care desired during a peak period, the medical officers of the AAMC decided to train unqualified orderlies to try to lessen the burden on the masseuses. This was deemed preferable to engaging qualified staff from elsewhere, potentially owing to the time for new staff to arrive, the cost of employing qualified practitioners, or a desire to maintain the harmony of an entirely female massage staff. Although male physiotherapists might not have worked happily when the sexes were mixed, male orderlies began to be trained in massage treatments, and they were trained by the female staff who were also treating between sixteen and twenty (and occasionally more) patients per masseuse per day. Lieutenant Colonel Dennis, Director of the Massage Department, reported to Lieutenant Colonel Yeatman: 'Extra work too has been thrown on the Staff in instructing orderlies in the elements of the work. These men have shewn keenness in their work, but owing to the amount of work to be done it is impossible to give time to them individually.' Dennis made particular note of the limitations of using these men as massage therapists, given that they had 'at the best, the most elementary knowledge of anatomy and physiology'. Dennis reassured Yeatman that 'Special attention is paid to instructing them as to the harm that can be done by wrong methods'.[61]

The idea of using orderlies as masseurs in Australian hospitals originally belonged to the Australian Director General of Army Medical Services, Surgeon General Richard Fetherston. This proposal 'angered both medical officers and physiotherapists', in part owing to the undermining of professional training and prestige.[62] Similar schemes were used in other medical services, particularly using men blinded in the war as they were thought to have a heightened sense of touch. Despite untrained workers being used in other contexts, the blurring of the boundaries between medical professions and between trained and untrained professional or civilian roles was a matter of contention for many medical services throughout the First World War.[63] As a result of these decisions, Harefield Park saw women with specialist knowledge placed in positions of authority and power over eager men, keen to learn a new professional skill. In addition to this authority over men in the hierarchy of staff, Ana Carden-Coyne has argued that the masseuse also had authority and power over the male body. Her hands had the capacity and authority to give pleasure, alleviate discomfort and inflict pain.[64]

Masseuses used their previous professional experience to improve outcomes for patients and broaden the education of some doctors. Mary Jennings, a trained physiotherapist with some nine years of pre-war professional experience, was an assistant in the Electrical and Massage Departments at 1 AAH Harefield.[65] She introduced a splint to assist patients with facial paralysis.[66] The splint minimised the significance of motor nerve injuries, which had an extended recovery time. Without assistance, these injuries hampered the range and power of motion to the muscles on the other side of the face. Lieutenant Colonel Dennis wrote that the 'simple yet effective appliance has been invented and brought to my notice by Miss Jennings'. He reported that Jennings used the splint before the war and it had 'been in use at Harefield for over two years. It consists of a piece of malleable German Silver Wire bent so as to hook over the ear of the affected side and into the corner of the mouth.'[67] The splint had a range of benefits including being light, unobtrusive and easy to make; it improved recovery times and was 'greatly appreciated by the Patients, who state they feel more comfortable and can masticate much better'.[68]

As has already been described, doctors shared information and formed medical societies for the instruction and discussion of problem cases or new treatments. This splint is an instance of knowledge being shared between a female physiotherapist and a male doctor. Even though Miss Jennings had been using the splint at 1AAH for two years before she showed it to Lieutenant Colonel Dennis, it was not until he wrote about it and discussed it among doctors (while giving due credit to Miss Jennings) that her innovation was recorded in the war diary of 1AAH.

At 1AAH, Harefield, medical care was not the only form of care practised by those in the hospital. Much of the activity at Harefield would be more accurately described as social care. The Recreation and Canteen Department managed the program of activities, which was extensive, with a large proportion of funding for the program coming from the Australian branch of the British Red Cross Society. These activities were enabled by the AAMC, funded by charities and staffed by volunteers from the surrounding areas. The department came under the authority of the Commanding Officer of the hospital and was managed by a Red Cross employee who was on loan to the hospital.

In the period from 1 June to 31 December 1917, the Recreation and Canteen Department reported that on average 130 men per week visited 'various places of amusement', generally theatres and other cultural attractions in London and the areas around the hospital. Also, small parties were often invited to tea with local ladies and gentlemen who sent their cars to chauffeur the wounded soldiers between the hospital and their houses.[69]

Figure 4.6 A local resident with her dog, car and a group of Australian soldiers at 1AAH Harefield (AWM P00162.008)

Entertainment was provided every evening in the hospital in the form of concerts, plays, lectures and cinema. Here the hospital was indebted to the Soldiers' Entertainment Fund, which sent a concert party every Thursday, the Victoria League, which provided 'Lantern Lectures' each Wednesday, and the Australian Red Cross, which sent a concert party or a dramatic party on alternate Tuesday evenings. The remaining nights were paid for by the profits generated from the patients' canteen, mostly through sales of cigarettes, tobacco and 'useful articles for the patients'. Recovering soldiers who were too ill to leave their beds had a special 'Cot Cinema Tea' provided every Monday, with cigarettes, tea and cakes available 'thanks to the generosity of the Medical officers, the Lady Canteen Workers and others'. A billiard room, writing room, library and music room were also available to patients.[70]

'Fancy work' was one form of recreation provided to patients. This consisted of instruction in hand embroidery, and the intention was 'to occupy, amuse, and please the Australian sick and wounded soldiers at Harefield Park'.[71] Initially, when all materials were provided to patients, the participation rates were low, but they increased after patients were charged cost price for thread. Needles, transfers and canvas were provided by the Commanding Officer's quarterly allowance. Other forms of craft were also encouraged, with basket-making being a common choice and blind patients making string bags.

Figure 4.7 Patients in the canteen at 1AAH Harefield (State Library of Queensland: Negative number 164831)

Figure 4.8 Patients in the billiard room at 1AAH Harefield (State Library of Queensland: Negative number 164832)

Figure 4.9 'For England, home and beauty, Australia will be there.' Fancy work by Private A.S. Smart, a patient at 3AAH Dartford, who had shrapnel wounds to his right arm. (AWM REL30298; NAA: B2455/Smart, Alfred Samuel)

Gender historians have examined the care provided to recovering soldiers, with activities including 'fancy work', basket-weaving and other arts and crafts seen as 'infantilizing and feminizing' the male patients.[72] The Australian War Memorial holds a number of examples of 'fancy work' completed by recovering soldiers, and records of the prizes given for competitions exist in the *Boomerang*. These therapies were a defence against idleness, and Carden-Coyne highlights the difference between these therapies and vocational rehabilitation, which was more akin to retraining for civilian work. She states that the therapeutic value of handicrafts 'was largely framed in terms of occupying the mind, averting introspection, and was associated with the industriousness of the work ethic'.[73] In discussing the gendered nature of the therapies, Carden-Coyne writes: 'They were also regarded as psychologically healing, helping the weary and embattled to regain manhood through a transitional state of feminized becoming, beginning with the gentle, womanly arts.' Arguing that therapies were framed on gendered lines, she continues: 'Before regaining the masculine grip of bayonets or guns, the patients learned to hand-stitch delicate material and knit woollen items, practices that were associated with women, such as sock-knitting for soldiers.'[74]

I am, however, not convinced that the activities were either consciously or subconsciously designed to transition the wounded soldier from infantilised being through a feminised state to the masculine ideal.[75] Rather, I argue that the activities were an expression of the gendered nature of the work and workers in the auxiliary hospital rather than the patients. While acknowledging that many of the activities available to wounded men, whose movement and bodily autonomy had been curtailed, were those ordinarily in the feminine realm, the particular activities offered at Harefield were available because of who provided the service.

The recreation and study department at Harefield was reliant on the labour of its 'lady volunteers'. These women, from the middle and upper classes of the area around Harefield, contributed to the culture of caregiving in the hospital. They did so by offering activities and teaching soldiers skills that were within their realm of expertise. Fancy work was not the only activity on offer in this scheme. Soldiers could also learn French and to play piano from the lady volunteers, all skills that were common among wealthier women in early twentieth-century Britain and seen as indicators of feminine gentility and education.

Fancy work required coordination, movement and fine motor skills, and could assist those recovering from injury. It could also be used to develop their non-dominant side in consequence of injury to their preferred hand. Additionally, if the embroidery was set up on a frame, patients with one hand were able to participate. The activity received the assent of the medical staff; thus the hospital war diary recorded: 'Doctors and Sisters often find the work very beneficial to patients. It seems a pleasant dose of medicine to many of them, and a very cheap one for the authorities.'[76]

It was not, however, an integral part of the rehabilitative process but an activity to occupy soldiers and fill their time. Furthermore, rather than infantilising and feminising soldiers, fancy work provided a creative outlet through which men could articulate a martial masculinity. While some soldiers embroidered what might be termed 'feminine' motifs like flowers on their canvas, much more common was the embroidery of national flags, military insignia and imperial symbols. At 2AAH Southall, three soldiers who were double amputees made a costume for the volunteer staffing the hospital canteen to wear (see figure 4.10 and figure 4.11).

Figure 4.10 Front of tabard embroidered by patients of 2AAH Southall, complete with military 'ribbons' embroidered on the left chest (AWM REL/01748.002)

Figure 4.11 Mrs Rattigan wearing the outfit made for canteen workers with one of the men who made it, Private Frederick Trice (AWM P01441.001)

It included AIF unit colour patches embroidered on the skirt, and it came with a tabard. On the back of the tabard was the symbol of the AIF, the rising sun, along with the Blue Ensign and the Union Jack. On the front was the rising sun again, together with eighteen medal 'ribbons' over the left breast including ribbons representing the Victoria Cross, Distinguished Service Order, Military Cross, Distinguished Conduct Medal and Military Medal. Rather than infantilising and feminising the men who did the embroidery, this conferred a martial legitimacy on the volunteer service of the civilian women in the hospital.

As the patients paid for the materials, they kept their finished work, and many sent it home to family and friends. As a way of raising funds for other programs in the hospital, other hospitals with similar programs sold the work if the soldiers had been given the materials. 1AAH held competitions and exhibitions of work by patients, and visitors to the hospital were often keen to purchase the items on display, but the reports in the war diary of the hospital and in the hospital magazine, the *Boomerang*, indicate that patients rarely parted with their work for money. With most of the work sent home to family and friends, the organisers of the program speculated that it would cause 'no doubt, as great wonder to those over there, as it does to those who can see the work being done here in England, when one knows full well that buttons sewn on, holes pulled together in socks etc, is the only sort of needle work that most of the Boys have ever done'.[77] Patients also bought up stocks of materials to use when sailing back to Australia. It was a cheap and effective way, especially for bedridden 'cot cases', to pass the time on the six-week journey. The 'fancy work' program was well known, and 'Several Hospitals at Home and Abroad [...] consulted the 1st AAH fancy work managers on how to start this work'.[78]

AUXILIARY HOSPITALS AS SITES OF MEDICAL–MILITARY AUTHORITY

1st Australian Auxiliary Hospital at Harefield was a hybrid space. Primarily a military environment, it was controlled by the Commanding Officer and administered by the Australian Department of Defence in conjunction with AIF Headquarters at Horseferry Road, London. Yet its location in a private family home, in a genteel area of Middlesex, with routine civilian involvement and interaction, created an atmosphere of domesticity. This, combined with the relative stability of both staff and patients, who spent more time in rehabilitation than at earlier stages of the casualty evacuation chain, created a community unlike those found in Australian medical–military units in France and Belgium.

There was very little British military involvement at Harefield. Interactions between the British and Australian militaries were confined to the point at which Australian patients were handed over to the AAMC at Harefield after they had received care in British hospitals. The Australian Commanding Officer of the hospital thought the Australians did not receive adequate care from the RAMC medical units during peak times, and reported those thoughts to the DMS, but there were no interventions from the British forces into the Australian sphere of responsibility.

British and Australian women played important roles in the daily life of the hospital. Their work was in both paid and voluntary roles, and in roles that required professional medical knowledge as well as those that did not. However, other than the masseuses employed at the hospital, none of these roles disrupted gender norms and were happily agreed to by the commanding officers of 1AAH, in part because of the savings made by employing female labour instead of that of enlisted men. While masseuses had a degree of autonomy and authority, and their work was respected, it was still supervised by the male director of the department, and they were paid less than men with the same qualification. The initial employment of a mixed physiotherapy staff had placed the gender and military hierarchies in conflict with each other as female physiotherapists, considered honorary officers, technically outranked some of their male colleagues. Creating an all-female massage staff, then, succeeded in promoting unit cohesion, saving the AAMC money and reasserting the gender hierarchy by ensuring the masseuses did not have authority over men with the same skills. When the female physiotherapists were placed in positions of authority over unskilled men, their authority was restricted to their professional realm where their medical knowledge and experience was privileged.

This significant involvement of women in the auxiliary hospital setting, with half the staff and the majority of volunteers being women, created an environment unlike those found in medical posts of other types administered by the AAMC. Although Ana Carden-Coyne has argued that the introduction of handicrafts such as embroidery and basket-weaving were gendered, with the wounded soldier being required to pass through a transitory, rehabilitative feminised state between infantilised passive being and masculine warrior, I argue that it was the work that was gendered in this instance, not the patient.[79] The activities described, although welcomed by military authorities, were within the realm of 'women's work' and therefore remained under the authority of the recreation department at Harefield Park. Undertaking 'fancy work' was not compulsory and was valued more by those in command for its ability to ward off idleness than for its rehabilitative effects, which, although acknowledged, were not the primary reasons for embracing it. Therefore, at Harefield Park, medical care was provided by Australian military men, assisted by nurses and physiotherapists, and supported by volunteers providing care and recreation in the form of activities in which they had skills. Civilian involvement in the hospital was considerable, yet the military purpose and control of the hospital was maintained and, as a result, care and recreation at Harefield took on a feminine tone.

The 1st Australian Auxiliary Hospital, Harefield Park, was a medical space under military control with considerable civilian influence. It was a place in which Britons and Australians interacted in official, professional and personal relationships. The physical space in which they lived and worked had originally been a private home, and many of the domestic comforts were maintained despite Harefield Park being a military hospital. This hybrid medical, military and domestic space created an environment in which romantic relationships were able to develop far enough for there to be numerous weddings from the hospital during the war. The civilian influence at Harefield, when combined with the work of women providing care in varied forms being a matter of routine, created an environment for intimacy and thoughts of domesticity. In this way, British–Australian interactions in the hospital pushed beyond the official and the professional and entered the realm of the personal. While the highest-ranked members of the AAMC appeared wary of the quality of care provided by British hospitals, this attitude did not trickle down and affect the professional and personal relationships that developed in the hospital. There were therefore limits to Australians' distrust of British involvement in Australian medical care.

The British public participated in a 'culture of caregiving', providing care for wounded British soldiers.[80] But this was not limited to British soldiers, with the British public extending that caregiving to at least one of the dominions. The generosity of the local community at Harefield was gratefully accepted and embraced by the Australian military authorities so long as they maintained control. All of these strands were held in tension to deliver control of medical care for sick and wounded Australian soldiers to Australian medical men.

CHAPTER 5

THE MOST DIFFICULT PROBLEM

PREVENTING AND TREATING VENEREAL DISEASE

In 1915, four months after the first convoy of Australian soldiers disembarked in Egypt, venereal disease (VD) infected roughly 10 per cent of the Australian Imperial Force (AIF).[1] In the Official History, Butler described it as 'a startling outburst' that resulted in 3 per cent of the force being 'constantly sick'.[2] Given that a significant number of soldiers were not only incapacitated but also occupying hospital beds that would be needed once combat casualties started to arrive, VD had serious implications for the efficiency of the AIF and its medical services.

On 27 April 1915, two days after the first Australian troops landed at Gallipoli, and once it became clear that the MEF had failed to reach its objectives, the AIF decided to clear all remaining VD cases from Australian hospitals in Egypt. On 4 May, 261 soldiers with longstanding cases of VD were repatriated, along with a number of soldiers who were medically unfit for service and should not have been enlisted. By the time they arrived in Australia, many of the VD-infected soldiers had recovered.[3] After an inauspicious start, VD would continue to plague the AAMC and the AIF, with Butler describing the outbreak as one 'which brought serious and far-reaching consequences and introduced the medical service to its most difficult problem in the war'.[4]

Throughout the war the AIF had one of the highest rates of VD of any combatant army.[5] Peter Stanley estimated that 55 000 members of the Australian Imperial Force were treated for VD.[6] In his statistical analysis of the AIF, David Noonan questioned Stanley's estimate and methodology but similarly concluded that 55 000 men were hospitalised on 69 300 occasions – the same number of infected men at which Stanley arrived.[7] This equates to at least one in seven members of the AIF being treated for VD at some point during the First World War.[8]

Complicating the statistics is the problem of determining how many soldiers contracted VD before they embarked for war. It is also impossible to assess accurately how many soldiers contracted VD but did not seek treatment, thus concealing their disease, or who sought treatment privately. What is clear is that a significant proportion of Australian soldiers were infected with VD, the rate reported was among the highest of the Allied armies, and that it was perceived to be a threat to the efficient functioning of the AIF at war.

The prevalence of VD in the AIF has been attributed to a number of factors. Their British counterparts, when on leave from France, were able to go home to family and friends and rejoin domestic life for a time. Australian soldiers were much less likely to be able to do so, unless they had family in the United Kingdom. This dislocation and lack of the supposed moderating influence of their friends and family, combined with feelings of loneliness, have been seen as the biggest factors in the high VD rates among Australian soldiers.[9] This is also demonstrated by the statistics, which show that where Australians most commonly caught VD was on leave, whether it be in London, Paris or Cairo.[10]

These explanations for the AIF's VD rate do not take into account the opportunities that being further from home created for the medical services in enabling different treatment and prevention options. In an environment in which disease was associated with sin, the AIF's location half a world away from Australia ensured that the use of prophylactic treatments was far less visible to a vocal section of Australian society, which argued that anything other than a moralist approach advocated vice. This resulted in the diminished influence of Australian purity movements when compared to the influence of British equivalents, such as the National Council for the Combating of Venereal Disease (NCCVD), which exerted influence over the actions of Britain's RAMC and the British army generally.[11]

The AIF's response to VD changed during the war. It transitioned from a haphazard, unofficial, moralist approach, which cast the soldier as part of the problem, to a systematic, officially sanctioned, pragmatic approach in which the soldier played a significant role in the solution. This shift was gradual, and the army initially tried to change behaviour through punitive consequences before settling on the medical response, which remained largely unaltered from 1917. This chapter traces the discussions about sex, soldiering, citizenship and disease, which occurred in public and private, through official and unofficial channels, and involving combat and medical officers, as well as their civilian counterparts. Other individuals and purity groups, including the Australian-born New Zealand sexual health campaigner Ettie Rout, were also involved in the discussion.

The chapter outlines the changes in the AAMC's policy on the treatment of VD and assesses its success in lessening the burden of VD on the AIF. It demonstrates that the AAMC came to understand that the prevention and treatment of VD was a medical concern to a greater degree than it was a moral one. In turn, the AAMC minimised the role of religious actors, including army chaplains, and harnessed the personal responsibility of the soldier. This chapter suggests that the scale of the problem, and the military context in which it was tackled, created the environment for a systematic response, and I argue that the AAMC's pragmatic approach to soldiers' sexual health was possible because it did not transgress existing gender norms but reinforced them.

'WAR ALWAYS BRINGS IT ON': SEX, DISEASE AND WAR

Sex, disease and war are three phenomena that are intimately linked.[12] Moreover, the history of sex in the AIF is tied to the history of sexuality in Australia more broadly. In Australia in the early twentieth century, purity and chastity were increasingly becoming the ideal for both men and women, but attempts to regulate sexuality were gendered as men were not expected to uphold the ideal of chastity. Women were cast as responsible for the chastity of both men and women, and at fault if the expected standard was not maintained.[13] Additionally, in early twentieth-century Australia, a shift emerged that cast current and future wives and children as innocent victims of the diseased male body.[14] This change constructed the male body as a site of contagion and charged men as guilty along with the prostitutes and 'loose women' from whom they supposedly contracted the disease. Often motivated by a patriarchal Social Darwinist worldview that attempted to maintain the strength, virility and purity of White Australia, this paradigm shift cast men as protectors of women and responsible for sexual health rather than passive victims of disease. This distinction was exploited by the AAMC in its attempts to combat VD in the First World War.

Neither broad social histories nor feminist histories of sex and sexuality have sufficiently addressed VD within the AIF. Lisa Featherstone examines the history of Australian sexuality using a Foucauldian frame-work to analyse 'the accumulation of bio-political power around bodies, and the resistance to these authorities'.[15] Frank Bongiorno's *Sex Lives of Australians: A History* covers similar territory to Featherstone's work, and both Bongiorno and Featherstone highlight the significance of the VD problem for the AIF and the potential consequences for the female popu-lations where soldiers were stationed. Given the scope of the works as wide-ranging histories of sex and sexuality in Australia, neither author examines the military context of VD treatment in detail, nor uses army reports, instructions or handbooks from the vast collections of them held by the Australian War Memorial and the National Archives of Australia. When they do examine the military context, the discussion is framed around soldiers' experiences and military responses in Egypt. The military context is also on the fringes of a number of feminist histories of VD and Australian attempts to regulate it during the First World War, including works by Philippa Levine, Judith Smart and Julie Tisdale.[16] Although examining wartime, these histories do not assess the methods used to regulate the behaviour of white dominion troops. Instead they focus on attempts to control women and non-white colonial soldiers, often through legislation.

Historians have analysed the attempts to manage venereal disease in the Entente armies of the First World War.[17] These analyses refute the idea that relationships between soldiers and women were one-dimensional transactional relationships usually defined as 'prostitution'. Prostitutes were not the only source of disease, and soldiers also contracted VD from so-called amateurs (who, rather than deriving their income from sex, were young working women who did not earn enough for luxuries like jewel-lery or trips to the theatre and 'went with soldiers for a good time rather than for money'),[18] as well as women with whom they were – or thought they were – in a loving, monogamous relationship. In a similar vein to these histories, Mark Harrison examines the British army's approach to the problem of sexually transmitted diseases.[19] He analyses the three main approaches to VD advocated by the British army: sexual continence, medically regulated prostitution and the use of preventive technology. Harrison argues that the British army's approach to VD 'was symptom-atic of the ambivalence of its top brass towards technologies developed prior to, or during, the war', suggesting that their resistance to innovation prevented the early adoption of new VD treatments, including Salvar-san.[20] He concludes that the conflation of military virtue and sexual restraint was partly a result of the women's and purity movements at home and the history of the British army, which was 'intertwined with that of movements for moral reform'.[21]

With many of these authors describing Australia as having one of the worst, if not the worst, record regarding VD, it is then surprising that no systematic analysis of VD in the Australian army has been attempted. Peter Stanley's *Bad Characters: Sex, Crime, Mutiny, Murder and the Australian Imperial Force* examined many of the actions of Australian soldiers that undermine the idea of the virtuous digger. His analysis includes VD but focuses on the rates of infection and the situations in which soldiers were likely to contract disease rather than attempts to control it or minimise its effects. In the official history, Butler discusses VD as it related to military efficiency and also its potential effects on the current and future wives and children of the soldiers. A specialist in obstetrics and gynaecology before the war, Butler was well placed to comment on the problem.[22] He was fairly forthright in his discussion of VD; however, whether deliberately or incidentally, his account glossed over many of the punitive consequences of VD and, while it demonstrated to the reader that army policies helped to slow the rate of infection, it does so without significant analysis of why they worked or why they were allowed to be implemented. Stanley's work has since inspired Raden Dunbar to explore further the problem of VD in the AIF.[23] Framing this work around the stories of five soldiers infected with VD and a number of those tasked with curing them, Dunbar focuses on the Egyptian base in Abassia and on those shipped back to Australia on *Wiltshire* and interned at Langwarrin, a military camp on the outskirts of Melbourne.

In contrast, this chapter argues, in line with Harrison, that the issue of VD was increasingly medicalised during the war with the AAMC becoming responsible not only for curative medicine but also for the maintenance of sexual health, an area not necessarily under the purview of the medical corps. While sexual health and illness became the domains of the AAMC, its approach to treatment was systematised and became more regimented. The AAMC limited medical officers' ability to use initiative or try innovative treatments, signifying a secondary process of the militarisation of medical treatment. This chapter examines the presence of this dual process and highlights the surveillance, control and punishment of soldiers, extending Butler's work to argue that the policies were effective because of the emphasis placed on self-discipline, the removal of punitive consequences for soldiers who sought medical assistance, and the establishment of trust between soldier and medical officer. Secondary to this argument, and echoing the work of Lisa Featherstone, this chapter also proposes that the AIF was able to be the location for a pragmatic approach to VD because that approach did not transgress the dominant gender roles of the time but reinforced them.

THE EARLY DAYS: PROPHYLAXIS AND INDECISION

The first few months the AIF spent in Egypt were notorious for the rate of VD infection; however, it is likely that many men would have had VD before they disembarked. With the rate of infection in the civilian population of Melbourne thought to be between 12 and 15 per cent, some men in the AIF would have had VD before they left Australia.[24] Furthermore, others would have contracted it while the ships they were travelling on were docked in ports *en route* to war. When the Australians arrived in Egypt, they set up camp at Mena, including hospitals, with the AAMC establishing 2nd Australian Stationary Hospital (2ASH), under the command of Lieutenant Colonel White, on 26 January 1915.

One of the two hospital sections was under the leadership of Major Bernhard Zwar, and he gathered statistics through 'careful personal enquiries' of the 300 patients under his care.[25] Of those 300 patients, 139 had gonorrhoea, six had syphilis and 155 had genital sores, mostly on the *frenum praeputii*. Zwar was convinced that some of those with genital sores would develop further syphilitic symptoms. Of the 300 cases, 250 stated that it was the first time they had contracted VD, and the majority of those cases stated that 'they had not previously taken risk of infection, nor had they known the nature of the risk'.[26] The remaining fifty patients reported having contracted VD on between one and twelve previous occasions. Out of the 300 patients, 158 had been under the influence of alcohol when they were exposed to infection, and 265 of the soldiers used some form of preventive or prophylactic method. This suggests that the soldiers knew they were at risk of infection even if they did not understand the long-term consequences of their actions or the extended treatment time. It is clear that most of the soldiers realised that some risk was involved if all but thirty-five of them made some attempt at preventing infection. After that initial period, Butler reported that the younger soldiers were sufficiently scared of the disease and the 'incorrigibles' were already infected.[27]

Yet Butler's optimism was misplaced, and VD continued to be a problem. In early 1915, some individual members of the AAMC took upon themselves the responsibility of trying to prevent the spread of VD among Australian soldiers in Egypt. This included Major James Barrett,

Registrar of the 1st Australian General Hospital (1AGH), meeting subsequent Australian arrivals in Egypt as they disembarked. He demonstrated the basics of VD prevention to Australian soldiers, and they were warned of the dangers of the common diseases. Furthermore, a circular giving eleven brief pointers on staying well in Egypt was also distributed to soldiers. 'Hints on Health in Egypt' was a one-page memo written by New Zealand's Colonel Neville Manders, Deputy Director of Medical Services for the Australia and New Zealand Army Corps (DDMS, ANZAC), and it covered such topics as clothing, safe drinking water, alcohol consumption and the effects of sun exposure. On the topic of women, it stated: 'Men must be careful to avoid any attempts at familiarity with native women: because if they are respectable they will get into trouble, and if they are not, venereal desease [sic] will probably be contracted.'[28] This statement highlights the dual construction of women in the fight against VD, with the ANZAC soldier being advised to avoid respectable women for the woman's sake and to stay away from those who were not respectable for his own sake.[29] In this case the respectable woman is clean, innocent and in need of male protection; the profligate is diseased and dangerous.

The AAMC was not the only section of the military that recognised VD as a problem for the AIF and put in place policies to limit its effects. The commander of the corps wrote a 'manly and straightforward' letter to the troops in which 'the moral and patriotic aspects were forcefully put before the troops'.[30] Australian soldiers had been encouraged to spend their money in Cairo among local traders; however, in an attempt to curb the spending of money on prostitutes, the limit of what AIF soldiers could withdraw each day was reduced to two shillings. In addition to these measures, soldiers who were in hospital with VD were not paid for the period they were away from their units. This termination of pay also applied to the allowance made available to their next of kin back home. Thus, it became easier for the family of a soldier to discover his indiscretions while he was away. Once a soldier had been discharged from hospital, his full pay was sent to his next of kin until the arrears of his domestic contribution had been repaid, leaving a soldier with little money of his own for a significant period.

There is little evidence of soldiers' responses to this policy as most did not record their experience of VD in their diaries or letters home. One famous case has been discussed by Mark Harrison.[31] A major in the British Expeditionary Force discovered his wife had been informed that he had contracted VD. After he found out that his wife knew of his indiscretions, the officer killed himself, which prompted the British army to alter its stance on the notification of a soldier's VD status. Given that such information was readily shared between the empire's medical services, it is possible that this was a contributing factor in the Australian army's later decision to change its policy.

With the continual arrival of new troops and reinforcements, VD became an ongoing problem for the AAMC. In recognition of the problem, a conference of senior medical officers was held at the Palace Hotel, Heliopolis, on 17 February 1915 'to devise an efficient means of combating venereal diseases in the Australian Imperial Force'.[32] The attendees were the highest ranked officers of the AAMC in Egypt and included a number of veterans of the South African War. There were no specialists in dermatology or VD in the group, which mostly consisted of general medical practitioners and surgeons, with an ophthalmologist, the Permanent Head of Public Health for South Australia and a specialist in obstetrics and gynaecology also present. Each of these men would have had some professional experience in treating VD but, at that time, the AAMC did not count among its officers a specialist in the treatment and prevention of these diseases. At the conference, Surgeon General Williams estimated that around a thousand men in the 1st and 2nd Australian Divisions were infected with VD on any given day and that a large number were unable to work. Noting that the proportion of men sick in the AIF appeared to be higher than in other forces, Williams asked the medical officers present to provide him with more precise numbers of those under their command who had contracted syphilis, soft chancre and gonorrhoea.[33]

The attendees discussed ways to tackle the problem of VD, including military assistance, use of prophylaxis, treatment, establishment of convalescent depots, and the treatment location for men affected by chronic or intractable VD. There was broad agreement that convalescent depots should be established away from the military action to alleviate pressure on hospitals, provide infected soldiers with specialist treatment and rest while they were recovering, and minimise the use of resources by VD patients close to the fighting. Lieutenant Colonel Brady Nash noted that a similar process existed in civilian life in Australia where men with gonorrhoea were treated as outpatients or privately by their general practitioner rather than as admitted patients in hospitals.[34] The medical officers also agreed that those who could readily be returned to duty should remain in Egypt but that those with intractable illness or syphilis, which had an extended recovery time, should be repatriated.

On the topic of treatment, there appears to have been little discussion with the Surgeon General requesting contributions from the others present. The only recommendation on that topic was that gonorrhoea be treated at the acute stage and then men returned to duty. There was some disagreement about whether to include the military authorities in the medical officers' efforts to limit the effects of VD. Surgeon General Williams suggested that they seek assistance from the military authorities to place areas containing brothels out of bounds, attach junior medical officers to sections of the military police to restrict the movement of those with VD, and mete out punishment to those who risked infection. Colonel Ryan suspected that the brothels would simply be moved if the area in which they were located was placed out of bounds, and Colonel Howse, then the Assistant Director of Medical Services for the 1st Australian Division, suggested that there was little point in requesting help from the military authorities 'since they have made no efforts to keep Cairo clean in the past, and have no power under the English law to do so'.[35] Lieutenant Colonel Ramsay Smith pointed out to the group that it was an offence in the United States Navy not to report exposure to VD, although there is no indication in the minutes that the attendees discussed the application of this policy to the AIF at this time.[36] This conference was convened less than four months after the first Australian convoy arrived in Egypt, and already the medical services were discussing ways of integrating medical and provost sections of the army in the prevention of VD. This suggests that VD was viewed as both a medical and a disciplinary problem and that multiple discrete approaches would be insufficient.

The most contentious issue discussed at the conference was the use of prophylaxis. Prophylactic treatment, also referred to as 'early treatment', was any form of medical intervention, whether performed by a medical officer, orderly or the soldier himself, after sex but before any visible signs of infection or other symptoms were present. It was distinguished from preventive options, which were at the soldiers' disposal before sex, and abortive treatment, which was necessary after symptoms were visible. The conference discussion centred around two points: whether prophylactic depots would be useful and effective, and whether disseminating information about the risks and effects of contracting VD would have any effect on the behaviour of soldiers. Prophylactic depots, often termed 'early treatment depots' and later 'Blue Light Depots' (as they were marked by a blue light), were usually tents within barracks, or rooms within army buildings, to which men were free to report for early treatment and examination. This consisted of an external antiseptic wash, the injection of a 10 per cent Argyrol solution into the urethra, smearing the genitals in calomel ointment and 'touching up' any abrasions with pure carbolic acid.[37]

Williams suggested that prophylactic depots could be established across Cairo and other centres where men spent time on leave. These would be staffed by a medical officer who was trained in administering prophylactic treatments, and made freely available for soldiers to use. Colonel Ryan was in favour of prophylaxis and thought that 'isolation tents' could be set up in regimental lines for soldiers to be treated upon their return from leave. Howse was sceptical of the suggestion, noting that a similar method of early treatment had been implemented on an *ad hoc* basis according to the initiative of the individual RMOs and had not been successful in curbing the rate of infection. Major Wilson suggested that despite Colonel Howse's objections he thought prophylactic depots would be successful if men could be persuaded to use them properly. Major Barrett was in favour of the use of prophylactic depots because brothels in Cairo had 'no conveniences for obtaining personal cleanliness', which was believed to help in the prevention of VD.[38]

There was little discussion of disseminating educational material to the troops. Williams invited the group to discuss whether 'circulars couched in plain and sensible language might be issued to the troops conveying to them a knowledge of the risk they run, and the fact that if infected they will take back to Australia a disease which would reduce their value as citizens'.[39] The only reference to discussion on this topic is from Howse, who suggested that there was little point in this approach, given that instructions about taking precautions had been delivered by RMOs to the men of the 1st Australian Division and it appeared that the men had not heeded their RMO's advice and taken preventive action. He also pointed out that, as already mentioned, Major Barrett had distributed circulars on the topic when the 2nd Australian Division arrived in Port Said, and the rate of infection in that division was higher than in the 1st Australian Division. Despite a general consensus that something had to be done to curb the impact of VD, aside from agreement on the medical treatment of VD once symptoms were visible, there was no unified position among the senior officers of the AAMC on preventive and prophylactic methods of limiting the effects of VD.

Compounding this lack of consensus, Howse's contributions to the conference discussion were obstructive. He was recorded as offering no suggestions and only stating when an idea had been tried before or when he thought it would not work. Butler credits him with setting up the

Australian response to VD, but this idea is untenable and is more a symptom of the hagiographic tendencies of the official medical historian where Howse was concerned. In contrast, historian Kate Blackmore notes: 'Neville Howse made clear his abstemious values regarding alcohol and venereal disease repeatedly in both official and unofficial correspondence.'[40] Howse was not a supporter of practices he saw as condoning vice so it is significant that, from 1917, the AAMC eventually instituted those practices under his leadership.

PROTECTING THE FLOWER OF WHITE AUSTRALIA

With no specialist in dermatology or VD, and no agreement on the appropriate method to lower the rate of infection, a haphazard approach to VD developed that was largely reliant on the efforts of the individual RMOs. The rate of infection did slow in the months following the conference, then the initial 'startling outburst' of VD was superseded as an issue for the AAMC by the commencement of preparations for the Dardanelles campaign. The lack of official records on VD in the months between April and December 1915 suggests that other matters were at the forefront of medical minds in the AAMC.

Once the Dardanelles campaign ended and Australian troops were evacuated to Egypt, the issue of VD soon reached crisis point. By March 1916, Neville Howse, who had previously rejected the idea as untenable, requested that General Birdwood, commander of Australian and New Zealand forces, place Cairo out of bounds for Australian soldiers.[41] The problem was significant enough for Brigadier General Robert Murray McCheyne Anderson, Deputy Assistant Quartermaster General for the Base Depot, to write to the Prime Minister of Australia directly to draw his attention to the prevalence of VD in the AIF.[42] In March 1916, the fight against the effects of VD remained focused on controlling the men's access to alcohol and the provision of other 'wholesome' entertainment options, mostly through the Young Men's Christian Association (YMCA). The army was concerned by any inference that it condoned vice so it did not systematically enlist medical approaches to prevention and prophylaxis; instead it continued the moralist line, supplemented by the actions of individual RMOs, and considered controlling access to brothels.

Non-government figures attempted to influence the treatment of VD in the Australian and New Zealand armies. Ettie Rout, head of the New Zealand Volunteer Sisterhood, spent considerable time working to limit the effects of VD on the armies of Australia and New Zealand during the First World War. She gained the confidence of senior government and army officials of both countries and wrote a letter to Colonel Rhodes on 12 March 1916 in which she described the Wasseh (Wazza) district, the area also known as 'Red Lane', where many brothels were located. Colonel Rhodes was a veteran of the South African War, Honorary Colonel of the 1st Mounted Rifles and a member of the New Zealand House of Representatives. During the First World War, he served as the New Zealand Government's Special Commissioner to Egypt and Galilee, where he reported on conditions for the troops. In 1916, while still a Member of Parliament, he was based in Europe as Commissioner of the New Zealand Red Cross. After touring the Wasseh district with a New Zealand gentleman and a guide between 6.30pm and 7.45pm on Saturday, 11 March 1916, Rout wrote to Colonel Rhodes:

> Outside notorious brothels long queues of soldiers waited their turn. One open door revealed a stairway with lines of soldiers going up and down – in and out. Soliciting and enticing was quite openly carried on. Bedizened and lustful women thronged the streets and doorways, many of them embraced by soldiers. Doors were open and soldiers could be seen inside the rooms sitting on women's laps or vice versa. Other open street doors revealed beds ready made, or a partition with the doorway inside curtained to hide the inmates temporarily. Our soldiers were in these places.[43]

Rout discussed the role of religious and other civilian groups working with the troops and the level of responsibility these groups should have for minimising VD infection rates. She wrote:

> From what I can gather I do not think the religious and other civilian persons working for the good of our troops ... would do anything to embarrass or hinder the military Medical Officers but the decision to sell prophylactics ... or to establish 'licensed houses' must rest with the military medical men. It is wise that measures for the control of sexual desire – such as the provision of wholesome recreation and amusements etc, and the general 'preventive work' of the YMCA – should be directed by such bodies as the YMCA; but measures taken for giving expression to sexual desire, or minimising the dangers of doing so, are no part whatever of YMCA work, though I think it is reasonable to hope they should refrain from any adverse criticism which would embarrass those already burdened with the onus of exceedingly unpleasant responsibility.[44]

British Headquarters in Cairo forwarded a copy of Rout's letter to Colonel Anderson at AIF Headquarters in Cairo along with the suggestion that Anderson should help to facilitate the development of alternative recreation opportunities for Australian troops, rather than having them visit the Wasseh district.[45] The majority of the Australian forces were soon moved to the Western Front. Consequently the AAMC and the AIF became less concerned with the availability of prostitutes and the lack of other, more suitable, forms of entertainment in Cairo.

The enlistment of a specialist in dermatology changed the AAMC's approach to VD. George Raffan enlisted in the AIF in November 1915 and was immediately attached to 1st Australian Dermatological Hospital (1ADH). He was a Fellow of the Royal College of Surgeons, Edinburgh, and held the position of Acting Honorary Physician at Royal Prince Alfred Hospital in Melbourne. He was a dermatologist and, at enlistment, he stated his specialty as 'syphilology', making him the logical choice to lead the AAMC's attempts at combating VD.[46] As well as becoming the Officer Commanding 1ADH, Raffan eventually became Principal Adviser on VD to the Director of Medical Services (DMS) for the AIF. He arrived in Egypt in early 1916 and, after a period of 'special duty to England', wrote a report on VD in the AIF for the DMS AIF, now Surgeon General Sir Neville Howse.

In that report, 'The Incidence of Venereal Disease in the AIF', Major Raffan outlined for Howse the scope of the problem and the need for reform, the methods used to try to lower the rate of infection and the results achieved.[47] Raffan's main reasons for reforming VD treatment included military efficiency and the sheer magnitude of the problem. He stated that 2300 men were in the venereal hospital in Egypt and at least that many were being treated privately in Cairo. His 'moderate estimate' was that at least 5000 soldiers were being treated at any one time. Raffan also suggested that the approach to VD be reformed in light of his view that each instance of 'irregular sexual intercourse in London is a probable source of infection' and because moral teaching had not 'induced men to remain continent from sexual relations'.[48] In addition to these reasons, Raffan also viewed VD as a threat to Australian masculinity and Australia's future prosperity. He wrote: 'The blood purity of the race is endangered owing to the ravages of uncontrolled venereal disease.' Betraying eugenicist ideas about the impact of VD, Raffan continued: 'The future of Australia is directly menaced because the flower of Australian manhood, the fathers of the next generation, is subjected to infection from syphilis and gonorrhoea.'[49] While Raffan acknowledged that men at war take risks and engage in behaviour they would avoid in their everyday lives, he constructed all non-marital sex as threatening to Australia's prosperity. This is in accordance with Lisa Featherstone's suggestion that 'discursively, sex was often imagined and understood as being about things other than pleasure: about nation, citizenship, reproduction, duty, disease, contagion, immorality and sin'.[50] As will be seen, linking sex to ideas of good citizenship and duty became a common theme in the information passed on to soldiers about VD.

In the same report to the DMS AIF, Major Raffan also outlined the methods that had been introduced to lower the rate of VD in the AIF. First, medical officers educated soldiers about the nature and consequences of VD. At a time when many thought that frequent sexual activity was needed to maintain strength and virility, Raffan stated: 'They are told that continence is not harmful, and are strongly advised to abstain from all forms of irregular sexual intercourse.'[51] The men were also told that if they decided to 'run the risk of infection' their best protection against VD was to use a 'French Letter' – a condom. Medical officers instructed soldiers in early treatment methods, and 'Nargol Outfits' were handed out to all soldiers going on leave, although soldiers could refuse them. These outfits, containing calomel ointment and Nargol jelly, were self-administered before and after intercourse, and men were informed that, if used, they would not guarantee safety but greatly reduce the risk of infection.[52]

It is doubtful that the discussion of the safety of sexual continence altered the behaviour of many soldiers. The early twentieth century saw increasing attempts to control and restrain male sexuality when doctors and scientists advocated continence in opposition to the commonly held belief that sexual activity was linked to health and vitality. Lisa Featherstone questioned the persuasiveness of the continence narrative, stating: 'Men often believed that they simply could not control their passions, their hydraulic sexual urges. Many believed women were there for the taking, to salve the "animal" part of man's nature.'[53] Here, popular opinion stood opposed to the increasing authority of medicine, with the male body as a site of conflict. Featherstone also noted the need to remind men continually of the importance of chastity, suggesting that the reminders were only necessary if the message had failed to change behaviour. Sexual continence was an oft-repeated theme in lectures and education materials until the end of the war, which, following Featherstone's reasoning, suggests that the soldiers were never entirely convinced; however, it is also possible that the AAMC believed this line of argument to be effective and therefore continued its use.

Raffan's final suggestion for reform at the time of the report was for soldiers to be treated in hospital for VD. No RMO was to treat a case of VD in the lines. Rather, his role was to evacuate all 'suspicious or actual' cases to a hospital as soon as possible for the medical officer there to assess and treat.[54] At this stage of the war, medical officers in the lines did not have the time – and most orderlies did not have the training – to treat VD adequately. Cases that reached a hospital within twelve hours of symptoms could be treated using the abortive 'sealing up' method, which often ensured that men could be returned to duty within a week. All cases where a definitive diagnosis of VD could be made were to be sent to the VD hospital.[55] This decision was later reversed with men being given prophylactic and abortive treatment in their units and evacuated to a VD hospital only if the abortive treatment failed to cure the disease. Orderlies were trained to provide the treatments and to staff early treatment depots in order to provide a better chance at success than a treatment self-administered by an untrained – and, in many cases, intoxicated – soldier.

In order to demonstrate the importance of early treatment, Raffan gave the example of a division where preventive methods were actively taught and Nargol Outfits and condoms were distributed to soldiers. In that division, 743 men had gone on leave between 10 July and 31 August 1916 and only one man contracted VD. In another instance, where preventive methods were not promoted with the same rigour, there were ninety-six cases in one training battalion. At the time of writing the report, there were 1200 cases in the VD hospital of which an estimated 300 were contracted in Australia, Egypt, France and Cape Town. In the period between 1 August and 18 October 1916, 80 000 Nargol Outfits and 17 000 condoms had been issued to soldiers with 8000 men passing through the Early Treatment Depot in London. Major Raffan concluded his report with the estimate that, had these reforms not been made, the 900 cases in the VD hospital would have numbered closer to 5000.[56]

1917: THE SHIFT TO A MEDICAL APPROACH

Following from his report on VD in the AIF, Raffan put forward a proposal to reform the way VD was treated by the AAMC. Based on these suggestions, in 1917, the AAMC made crucial changes to its procedures for treating and preventing VD in the AIF. New methods were implemented, extra bureaucracy was introduced to streamline the handling of VD cases, and at the Imperial Conference there was a discussion of the temptations encountered by soldiers and actions that could be taken to curtail them. Many of the changes stemmed from Major Raffan's report 'Suggested Reform in the Management of the Venereal Disease Problem'. Curiously, Raffan chose to communicate his suggested reforms directly with General Birdwood, GOC AIF, before he discussed them with Howse. Raffan wrote to Howse on 30 October 1916: 'Lieutenant General Sir W.R. Birdwood informed me that he was prepared to investigate a report on "Reform in the management of the Venereal Disease Problem", subject to such getting the approval of the DMS AIF. I respectfully beg to submit a report on this question for your consideration.'[57]

Assuming that Raffan accurately represented his correspondence with Birdwood, it demonstrates that Birdwood wanted to maintain the existing structures and leave medical care in the hands of medical officers. Birdwood was keen to have Raffan report his suggestions through the appropriate channels and not step outside the AAMC chain of command to communicate with the Corps Commander. Given that a number of the recommendations were ones to which Howse had previously expressed opposition, this might have been an attempt by Raffan to encourage Howse to re-examine his views with the weight of the Corps Commander behind them. If this was Raffan's strategy, he was partially successful as he was able to inform Howse that Birdwood was willing to engage with the problem further.

Raffan's attempts to improve his suggested reforms' chances of adoption did not end with trying to enlist Birdwood in his cause. Raffan did not send his report directly to Howse; he first sent it to Colonel Douglas Murray McWhae, Assistant Director of Medical Services for the AIF depots in the UK. Raffan might have been instructed to do so by Howse as McWhae was effectively Senior Medical Officer (SMO) of the largest number of Australian soldiers most likely to become infected with some form of VD. However, this role meant that McWhae had a particular interest in the problem of VD and might explain why Raffan thought McWhae would be eager to help change the way VD was treated, medically and in terms of discipline, in the AIF. Raffan wrote to McWhae: 'Would you please consider this recommendation and forward same to DMS with opinion & amendments suggested.'[58] This suggests that Raffan also tried to use McWhae's influence to get Howse to adopt the measures. McWhae forwarded Raffan's memorandum, along with his own views, to Howse soon after.[59]

In his memorandum, Raffan outlined the threat posed by VD, then articulated his criticisms of VD treatment up to that point. He wrote again of the dangers to the 'blood purity of the race' and his dismay at the 'flower of Australian manhood being subjected to infection from syphilis and gonorrhoea' and stated: 'Too large a percentage of the fighting force is rendered unfit for duty owing to infection from disease that is to a large extent preventable.'[60] Regarding the approach to VD taken by the AIF up to this time, Raffan stated: 'The penalties and consequences associated with the acquisition of venereal disease have not succeeded in preventing men from taking the risk of getting disease.' Suggesting that the penalties and consequences were unhelpful, he wrote: 'The only effect has been to induce men to conceal their disease, and when it is ultimately discovered or confessed the golden opportunity of effecting a speedy cure has been lost, and the disease has become chronic.'[61] The moralist and punitive approaches to VD up to this point had been shown to be ineffective, but those medical officers who, acting on their own initiative, had introduced some measure of preventive, prophylactic or non-punitive abortive treatment saw significantly lower rates of infection than those who did not use those methods. Based on '12 months close association with venereal disease as it affects the AIF', Raffan suggested that there were two ways in which VD could be prevented in the AIF. First, men could remain continent or take precautionary measures before they risked infection. Second, the AAMC could induce 'men to report to a Medical Officer [without fear of penalty] as soon as the first symptom of disease develops, so that early treatment can be instituted'.[62] The AAMC eventually used both of these suggestions in tandem.

Raffan believed there were three principal reasons why men did not come forward and report that they were infected with VD. First, shame and publicity were motivating factors. Raffan wrote: 'If a man enters a Venereal Hospital as a patient his relations and friends in Australia get to know of it [...] in consequence a man will do anything to avoid this publicity.'[63] In order to avoid his family and friends finding out, Raffan stated, 'He seeks advice and treatment from friends, chemists, and other "quacks", who are totally unfitted to cure the disease.' He continued: 'The thought of exposure drives him to conceal his disease from his Medical Officers, although it apparently does not stop him from taking the risk of acquiring disease.'[64] In order to remedy this situation, Raffan recommended that men who self-reported their disease to a medical officer at the first sign of disease should not have their names published as being sick in a venereal hospital. He wrote: 'With the fear of publicity removed, a certain number of men (in my opinion the large majority) will have no hesitation in reporting at once for examination and treatment.'[65]

Regarding the issue of shame, McWhae questioned the veracity of this suggestion in his recommendations to Howse. McWhae wrote: 'Are the names of men in Venereal Hospital published in any way so that it becomes known to friends, relatives or anybody that they are suffering from Venereal Disease? If not, then the paragraph in his report is inapplicable.'[66] There was evidently some confusion over whether names were recorded by the army and the level of disclosure to the soldier's next of kin. This is, however, partly explained by the second reason given by Raffan that he thought encouraged soldiers to conceal VD, namely that men incurred financial loss when they reported that they had contracted VD. A soldier with a wife and/or children was required to have a portion of his pay set aside for his family while he was away at war. Pay was stopped when a soldier was 'ineffective' because of his own actions, so when a relative went to withdraw money and there was none available, it was an indication that he was infected with VD (or another self-inflicted wound), was under arrest or had died. The pay office was, perhaps not surprisingly, one of the most efficient departments and was therefore one of the first indicators of illness or death for the next of kin.[67]

Along with having pay stopped once VD was contracted, soldiers also had to repay to the hospital system the cost of their treatment. According to Raffan, this meant that a soldier who was in hospital for six weeks could not draw pay for three months and a soldier in hospital for three months – quite a common occurrence with VD – would not receive any pay they could withdraw for close to six months. Upon discharge from hospital a soldier then faced leave restrictions and would not be eligible for leave for twelve months. Raffan suggested that these men 'lose heart' and become 'hardened and sullen law breakers'. Moreover, they 'lose all esprit de corps and their usefulness is greatly impaired, if they do not become utter wasters'.[68] To alleviate this problem Raffan suggested that soldiers should be ordered to report to their medical officer at the first sign of disease. If they failed to do so and were subsequently admitted to a VD hospital, soldiers would then be punished by having their pay withheld, for failing to follow an order rather than punished for contracting VD. Medical officers were able to tell whether VD was in its early stages or if it was chronic so many men could then receive the abortive sealing-up treatment and be fit to fight within a week. The goal of Raffan's suggestion was to 'sufficiently punish a man, without totally disheartening him'.[69]

Regarding financial loss, McWhae presented arguments both for and against accepting Raffan's recommendations. McWhae's first objection was that the government would be paying soldiers their full wage when they were in hospital and 'ineffective' owing to their own actions rather than to any injury as a result of military action. He also noted that this would be a significant expense. McWhae then questioned the ability of the medical officers to determine whether a soldier had reported at the first sign of disease and suggested that all men would say they sought medical attention at the first opportunity. Conversely, McWhae wrote that Raffan's suggestions would 'ensure that a large majority of men will report at once because they lose nothing by reporting sick'.[70]

Finally, Raffan argued that ignorance was a significant issue in attempts to prevent the spread of venereal disease. He wrote that the men were 'woefully ignorant' of the causes and consequences of VD, and he believed that a greater understanding of the issue would encourage them to avoid 'irregular' sexual intercourse altogether, or else take precautionary measures. His proposed solution was a scheme of education and suggested: 'Systematic instruction to Officers, Warrant Officers, NCO's [sic] and men regarding the facts of venereal disease, as well as the imparting of knowledge of the measures that should be adopted to reduce the incidence of disease.'[71] Although ambivalent towards Raffan's recommendations regarding financial loss, McWhae adopted in full Raffan's suggestions regarding the general level of ignorance among personnel in the AIF. McWhae did not make a recommendation to Howse on this matter; instead he simply wrote: 'Necessary action taken'.[72]

Raffan's continued work on VD drew his attention to the problem created by men going on furlough. On 30 March 1917, Raffan sent McWhae a report titled 'The incidence of Venereal Disease amongst men going on furlough from Australian Auxiliary and British Hospitals' and asked McWhae, once again, to pass it on to Howse with his comments, which McWhae did on 4 April 1917. In the report, Raffan described the size of the problem and outlined new procedures for VD. He reported: 'Considering that 60% of the total amount of Venereal Disease occurs amongst men on furlough from Hospitals, the machinery at present in operation to educate and instruct these men is in my opinion totally inadequate.'[73] Raffan recommended that a new system be implemented at Australian auxiliary hospitals (AAHs) and at Australian Headquarters at 130 Horseferry Road, London. Raffan suggested that a lecture should be given by a medical officer and a chaplain, who should be 'specially appointed to talk to men from the moral and social standpoint'.[74] This lecture was proposed for all men who were due to be discharged within a week, and Raffan reported that the combination of medical officer and chaplain had proved successful at No. 1 Australian Command Depot.

Raffan also recommended that all those discharged on furlough from an AAH be given an 'advice card' that provided information on where an Australian soldier could receive early treatment if necessary. Raffan advised that a medical officer see every man passing through headquarters in order to 'educate and instruct small groups of men at a time, in the room set apart for the purpose, on the dangers of irregular sexual inter-course and the methods available to prevent or abort venereal disease'.[75] He suggested that Nargol Outfits and French letters be issued free of charge and that a box of six French letters, for a man on fourteen days furlough, should be sufficient. In order to ensure that all soldiers proceed-ing on furlough received this advice, Raffan proposed that orders be issued stating: 'No furlough warrant shall be issued unless a man pro-duces a card of advice with the office stamp and date stamped thereon.'[76] For immediately after furlough, Raffan's suggestions included having a medical officer examine every soldier within twenty-four hours, instruct-ing those who had not used sanctioned preventive methods before inter-course to seek treatment immediately (irrespective of whether there were visible signs or symptoms), and advising those who had taken precautions that at the slightest indication of infection they should report to a medical officer with haste.[77]

One of the most significant changes made by the AAMC to curb the effect of VD was an administrative one. On 27 March 1917, Colonel McWhae wrote to the Senior Medical Officers (SMO) of Australian units in the UK regarding a new 'Weekly VD Return'. He informed them that each RMO under the SMO's authority was to return the form each Friday and that 'Each question is to be separately answered in detail and vague replies are not to be inserted'.[78] The sample McWhae discussed eventually became AIF Form 587.[79] The form was also known as Army Medical Corps (AMC) Form 4, and on it the medical officer for each unit was required to record a range of factors, including the number of soldiers who went on leave each week, the number who reported for prophylactic treatment, how many required abortive treatment, where they contracted the disease and whether each man had been inspected within twenty-four hours of his return to camp. Medical officers were also required to certify that they had given the monthly lecture on VD, had offered prophylactic kits to soldiers going on leave, the number accepted by soldiers and the number of condoms distributed.

McWhae wrote to medical officers who had particularly high rates of soldiers requiring abortive treatment or low rates of those accepting preventive or prophylactic treatment to question whether the medical officers in question were adequately carrying out their responsibilities. To the Officer Commanding the AAMC Training Depot, Parkhouse, McWhae wrote: 'Your attention is directed to the fact that the Early Treatment & Venereal Disease Returns for Parkhouse for the week ending 14th inst., are uniformly unsatisfactory.'[80] As examples of unsatisfactory numbers, McWhae included statistics from No. 1 Camp, which had seventy-three men on leave during the week concerned yet only four boxes of French letters and eighteen Nargol Outfits accepted and six soldiers evacuated to the VD hospital. No. 2 Camp only had two boxes of French letters and eight Nargol Outfits accepted by the forty-five soldiers going on leave. No men who returned from leave from No. 3 Camp were examined after their return, and No. 4 Camp had no French letters available. The Officer Commanding AAMC Training Depot was then asked to follow up these observations. McWhae wrote: 'Please carefully investigate personally the procedure adopted by the RMOs in each Camp in order to ensure that every man proceeding on any leave which necessitates the issuing of a leave pass is seen by the Medical Officer and advised regarding Early Treatment.' McWhae also wanted details of the procedures instituted, asking: 'Please also investigate the procedure by which he assures himself that all these men are again seen, examined and advised on their return from that leave. Please furnish a full report of the result of your investigation and steps taken by you to ensure satisfaction in future.'[81]

McWhae was not just interested in the number of preventive and prophylactic measures used; he also tried to ensure that lectures on VD happened in accordance with policy. He wrote to the OC AAMC Training Depot: 'You state that the routine monthly lecture has not been delivered, and do not answer the final question concerning advice to men who have taken the risk without proper precautions. Please furnish a report.'[82] Similar communications were sent by McWhae to the SMO, No. 1 Command Depot in June, when, for 187 men going on leave, there were no French letters available and only twenty Nargol Outfits were accepted. Thirty-seven men subsequently contracted VD after presumably using the prescribed abortive treatment. McWhae, somewhat ominously, told the SMO that 'Para. 1. of Circular Instructions No. 37 will be adhered to strictly in future'.[83]

These are just a handful of examples of the communications that helped establish the new procedures within the culture of the medical service. Through this administrative work, McWhae became one of Raffan's closest allies in the fight against VD. The introduction of Form 4 to the required paperwork was not just a bureaucratic response to a cultural problem; it was a way of making the medical officer of a unit personally accountable for the rate of VD infection among his troops, thereby transferring a measure of the surveillance previously applied to soldiers to their medical officers. Should the medical officer's efforts not be deemed satisfactory he was required to justify the work done. Thus, medical officers were required to institute the VD policies and procedures of the AAMC in their units irrespective of whether or not they agreed with the measures taken.

INSTRUCTIONS TO MEDICAL OFFICERS: THE IMPORTANCE OF THE WELL-TOILETED PENIS

Further contributing to 1917 as the landmark year in the prevention of venereal contagions was Major Raffan's distribution of instructions for medical officers on the treatment of venereal disease on 10 February 1917.[84] These instructions concerned information about the medical officers' responsibilities, the education of soldiers about VD and its effects, precautionary measures that should be adopted, the curiously named 'short-arm parades', and the disposal of VD cases. These instructions were subject to minor revisions over the remainder of the war, and are here compared to those issued on 16 September 1918 in order to highlight the changes made to the instructions.[85]

In the February 1917 instructions, Raffan outlined the idea underpinning the program, writing: 'Every irregular sexual intercourse must be regarded as a probable source of infection.'[86] He then attempted to persuade the non-medical hierarchy to support the work of the medical corps in limiting the effects of VD. Raffan wrote: 'All Officers must be duly instructed, and their cooperation sought in imparting certain broad facts regarding venereal disease, particularly as to the dangers run and the methods they should adopt to avoid disease.'[87]

This directive changed between February 1917 and September 1918. By the latter date, medical officers had been using Form 4 for months to report the number of soldiers availing themselves of various preventive and prophylactic methods and treatments. In September 1918 it was made clear to medical officers that they were responsible for the rate of VD infection within their units. Raffan, who in September 1917 had been promoted to lieutenant colonel,[88] told them: 'The success or failure of the campaign depends mainly upon the zeal and efficiency of the MO and the spirit in which he carries out instructions, comprised in the Return AIF Form 587. A mere perfunctory discharge of duty and filling up of forms will not suffice.'[89] The contrast between these statements, made around eighteen months apart, indicates the shift that occurred in the thinking around VD and demonstrates the change to it becoming a largely medical concern. Military hierarchies and authorities took a secondary role, only to be used if necessary to reinforce the medical message.

The second issue discussed by Major Raffan in the February 1917 instructions was that of 'precautionary methods to be adopted', which was discussed in three parts: French Letters, Nargol Outifts and Early Treatment. Regarding French letters, Raffan wrote: 'THE FRENCH LETTERS ARE THE ONLY COMPARATIVELY SAFE MEANS OF PREVENTING DISEASE. Those men who are accustomed to take the risk should be strongly advised to use French Letters. To make the procedure safer still, calomel ointment should be applied to the scrotum and skin surface adjoining the root of the penis.'[90] Raffan also suggested that each medical officer attempt to persuade the Commanding Officer of their unit to ensure that a supply of French letters was kept in the unit stores for men to purchase before going on leave. They cost two shillings each (around a third of a private's daily pay) and were also available at the Early Treatment Depot in Room 100A at AIF Headquarters, 130 Horseferry Road, London.[91] Lieutenant Colonel Raffan's September 1918 instructions regarding French letters did not differ substantially from the earlier ones, except that the responsibility for procurement shifted to the medical officer. Raffan wrote: 'Take care always to have an adequate supply on hand.'[92] This, once again, shifted the responsibility to the medical officer rather than the Commanding Officer of the unit.

Nargol Outfits, which included one tube of calomel ointment and one tube of Nargol jelly, were to be handed out to every man going on leave and the way to use them explained. Before sexual intercourse the soldier was supposed to smear his entire penis (glans, shaft, root, as well as scrotum and surrounding skin) with the calomel ointment as well as squeezing some into the meatus. After sex, soldiers were instructed to urinate, then wash thoroughly in soap, water and Lysol, if it was available. Half the Nargol was then to be inserted into the meatus within two hours – preferably within thirty minutes – of the act. Finally, the penis was again to be smeared in calomel ointment.[93]

By September 1918 the use of Nargol Oufits had been discontinued, and in their place was the 'Blue Label Outfit', which contained potassium

permanganate tablets, cotton wool, a 2-ounce bottle, three tubes of ointment and instructions. The ointment was a mix of calomel, camphor,
carbolic acid, lanolin and paraffin. This self-treatment kit was to be used
by the soldier both immediately before and after 'connection', and
detailed instructions were part of the monthly lectures to be delivered
to soldiers.[94]

Medical officers were advised in early 1917 to instruct soldiers who
had sex to report to the Early Treatment Depot at Horseferry Road, even
if the soldier had used a Nargol Outfit. Raffan urged the medical officers
to impress upon the soldiers the importance of haste in preventing infection. Informing them that the depot in London was always open, Raffan
wrote: 'There is always a man on duty day and night to attend to
applicants. A shilling or two spent on a taxi to get attention the same
evening would be very well spent.' He reinforced this message, informing
the medical officers: 'Early treatment at the London Depot lasting a few
minutes is preferable to late treatment at the Bulford Venereal Hospital
lasting a few weeks, or even months.'[95]

The instructions issued in September 1918 gave more information to
medical officers and subsequently soldiers regarding why prompt treatment was so important. Especially in the case of syphilis it was thought
that applying early treatment might be useless if the soldier waited more
than an hour from incurring the risk of infection. For gonorrhoea and
chancroid, attendance at a 'Blue Light Depot' within twelve hours of
connection virtually guaranteed that the soldier would remain healthy
and that it was still highly likely if early treatment was sought between
twelve and twenty-four hours after sex. After that point Raffan suggested
that the best course of action to prevent gonorrhoea and chancroid would
be to commence with the first day's treatment of the abortive method.[96]

The early treatment provided at the Blue Light Depot was invasive and
unpleasant, although it was relatively quick, only taking around thirty
minutes to administer. The first step was to get the soldier to urinate, and
if any discharge was present it was collected on a slide and examined
through a microscope. The penis and scrotum were then washed thoroughly in soap and water before being washed in a 1:2000 solution of
bichloride, biniodide or mercury. After this, a small, thin wooden appli-
cator (some versions of the same instructions suggest using a match) was
wrapped in cotton wool and dipped into a 10 per cent protosil solution
and inserted into the urethra for about half an inch and held there for
three minutes. Previous treatments involved injecting the solution via a
syringe, but that prevented some of the skin from coming into contact

with the solution as it was instead in contact with the needle. Once the cotton wool had been in place for three minutes, it was removed, then an orderly was to inject 1 drachm of 10 per cent protosil solution (or Argyrol if available), which was held inside the penis for five minutes by pinching it closed. A 30 per cent calomel ointment was then rubbed over the entire organ skin, around the root, frenum and prepuce for at least five minutes before it was wrapped in clean strips of linen.

Raffan argued that this method was far more useful than the previously sanctioned irrigation method, could be performed by an orderly and was more effective in all cases reporting more than twelve hours after connection. Raffan also pointed out that, as many men were under the influence of alcohol when they had sex, and they were encouraged to seek medical assistance as soon as possible afterwards, many were still drunk when they arrived at the Blue Light Depot. He wrote: 'It is not an easy thing for a man half intoxicated to irrigate himself with a bucket syphon apparatus.'[97]

The abortive treatment method in early 1917 followed similar principles to the early treatment method; however, from September 1918 onward it was far more invasive and involved. It lasted seven days, and on day 8 the soldier was either discharged to the lines as cured or, if he was not cured, evacuated to the venereal hospital. The treatment was effective, and Raffan wrote: 'It should be a regular result to cure at least 80% of all cases reporting for the Abortive Treatment. Anything below this standard shows that something is wrong, either in the organization or with the method of carrying out the treatment.'[98]

The method used was the result of the experience of the previous four years and was tailored to the supplies available to medical officers through the existing medical stores and chains of supply. Raffan informed medical officers: 'Experience has demonstrated that the "Massage-Plug" method is the best, and it will therefore be adopted to the exclusion of all other existing methods.' Limiting opportunities for MOs to use their own initiative in devising treatment methods, he continued: 'Any Medical Officer who desires to try a new method, or to modify the existing method in any particular, must receive the written authority of the DMS AIF, through the ADMS, AIF Tidworth, or the ADMS Division, before instituting any such method.'[99]

Raffan's September 1918 instructions also gave medical officers guidance on the apparatus to use based on the individual differences of the soldiers. There were two different methods for probing the penis, based on its size. The preferred method was to insert a large probe into the urethra 'to determine its general direction and whether there is any narrowing or other obstruction', before inserting, with a twirling rotary motion and while massaging the penis, another smaller probe dressed in cotton wool dipped in a 5 per cent Argyrol solution.[100] The cotton wool needed to go roughly 2.5–3 inches into the urethra but at least 1 inch beyond the tender area. The probe was then extracted by rotating it in the opposite direction, leaving the cotton wool inside the urethra as a plug. For a small meatus, the cotton wool strip was rolled up, dipped in the same Argyrol solution and pushed into place using a 'moderately large' probe.[101]

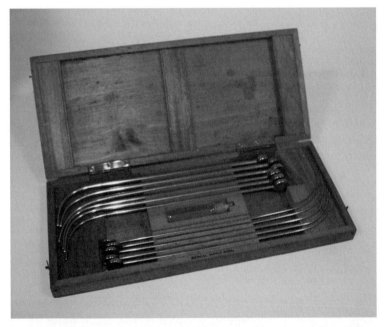

Figure 5.1 Urethral sounds. Used to determine the direction of the urethra and the location of any narrowing or obstruction. (Museums Victoria, HT34609)

Accordingly, the individual initiative used previously by medical officers in their efforts against VD was not completely stamped out but curtailed and placed within the medical–military hierarchy rather than being instituted on a divisional or corps basis. This systematisation of process was echoed in the systematisation of the supplies used. Given the number of men in combatant armies in Europe who were infected with VD, it is not surprising that there were shortages of particular supplies.

Raffan was aware of this and altered the instructions to medical officers accordingly: 'Argyrol has proved the most suitable; failing Argyrol, the next best is Protosil. Silver Nucleinate, although efficient, is more irritating, and is not recommended.'[102] Argyrol was in short supply during the war as it was the most effective solution in the treatment of VD.[103]

The introduction of 'short-arm parades' created a routine for the inspection of men's bodies. In these parades, soldiers presented their genitals for inspection by a medical officer. In February 1917, Raffan instructed that a parade should be held once a week and immediately after men returned from leave or arrived in camp for the first time. He also suggested that they were important both to prevent VD and to ensure the cleanliness of the foreskin. Regarding how they should be conducted, Raffan mandated that 'Short-arm Parades must be absolutely strict. No man should be allowed to escape them. If men know that their venereal disease is bound to be discovered sooner or later they will be induced to report early.' Underlining the importance of trust between patient and doctor, he suggested that '[t]he ideal system is for Medical Officers to gain the confidence of the men with regard to early reporting of suspected disease'.[104] This surveillance of the male body was intended to encourage men to report as early as possible for treatment.

By September 1918, the process of inspection through short-arm parades became more systematised. Raffan told MOs: 'These parades must be conducted under the control of a nominal roll. They tend to discourage concealment of disease, and very often a small sore is found which the man may regard as of no importance.'[105] This was a way of ensuring that minor problems did not turn into intractable diseases, thereby decreasing the efficacy of any future treatments. In the British and New Zealand armies these inspections were termed 'dangle parades', and in the British army a soldier could be asked at any time by an officer or NCO to drop his pants and present for a dangle parade, including in public areas of a camp.[106] In contrast, the AAMC's medical officers were routinely reminded that this could be a cause for embarrassment for a soldier and that short-arm parades should be conducted only one-on-one in a curtained-off area of a medical tent in order to engender trust between the soldier and the medical officer. Raffan was aware of this issue and told medical officers: 'Such examinations should be strictly private. It is unpleasant for men to be examined publicly, so let men come in to you singly. It is easy to shut off a portion of a hut, if not already done.'[107] These parades were systematic and ensured that men were paying adequate attention to hygiene as 'a well-toileted penis is less likely to become abraded than one under whose foreskin smedma [*sic*] and debris are allowed to gather and irritate the mucous membrane'.[108] These weekly parades were the strongest indicator of the willingness of the AAMC to surveil and attempt to control the bodies of the men it served.

'FOR THE SAKE OF AUSTRALIA'S WOMANHOOD': LECTURING AUSTRALIAN SOLDIERS

By 1917, all members of the AIF in the UK were supposed to have monthly lectures on the prevention, consequences and early treatment of venereal disease, and each base had to report back to headquarters to acknowledge whether or not this lecture had taken place. The lectures demonstrate the thinking behind the strategies implemented in the fight against venereal disease and covered a range of issues that influenced soldiers' decision-making with regard to their sexual health. The model lecture was included as an appendix in the instructions to medical officers in early 1917 and September 1918 and was supposed to be delivered to every unit in Britain each month. The actual wording to be used was at the discretion of the individual medical officer, but it was to contain the content outlined by Raffan in the sample.

The sample lecture from February 1917 began with statements about the broad problem that VD posed to the efficiency of the army and the honour of Australia. Raffan instructed the medical officers to remind soldiers that abstinence from sex was not harmful to them, and attempted to invoke their national pride. The sample lecture stated:

> The honour of Australia lies in the hands of the men who left their
> homes to serve her. It is a serious responsibility, and every man who is
> worthy will endeavor to keep a clean record, so that at the end of the
> war we shall be able to proudly state that the percentage of venereal
> disease cases in the Australian Army was remarkably low. Think of the
> national disgrace if the opposite results, and we have to state that the
> percentage of venereal disease was regrettably high.[109]

This statement made a soldier's VD record an indicator of his national pride and devotion to duty.

Medical officers were then to inform soldiers that every 'unprotected connection' needed to be thought of as a likely source of infection, especially in the case of amateurs. The preventive measures available to soldiers were then to be outlined in detail before the medical officer was to articulate the problems with concealing disease from the medical staff.

Soldiers were to be told: 'The man who conceals his disease will get it firmly established in his system and it may be months – even years – before he is cured. Take advantage of these opportunities to keep fit. Play the game fairly and the loss to the fighting strength from preventable disease will be considerably reduced.'[110] This lecture framed the manpower economy of the AIF as the personal responsibility of each soldier. Not only did VD have serious and potentially long-term consequences for the individual soldier's health but also it was within his power to bolster the AIF's fighting strength.

The lecture from September 1918 covers much the same territory as the early 1917 version. It commenced with a discussion of the idea of sexual continence and argued against the ideas that continence was damaging or harmful to a man's health and that incontinence was a demonstration of 'manliness'. As mentioned already, these ideas were prevalent in Australian society as well as in British and other societies. Unlike in late twentieth-century sexual health campaigns regarding the prevention of HIV/AIDS, the soldiers were not given instruction in other methods of sexual activity such as masturbation.[111] Lisa Featherstone found that masturbation was generally regarded as a threat to the army; she argues that it was considered able to 'render men unfit for military service and procreation which were vital to contemporary ideals of masculine citizenship'. She also found that 'the male body was therefore envisioned as a body to be disciplined'.[112] The idea that a woman was a necessary part of this equation is supported by the suggestion that masturbation was believed to result in the withering of a man's virility. By this reasoning, man derived his virility and masculinity from congress with a woman. The lectures by medical officers were not the first time this idea was presented to the soldiers. It was one that the medical officers adopted from the purity movements in Britain. Their pamphlets on 'True Manliness' discuss the importance of abstinence as an act of self-discipline encouraging men to '[hold] fast to those things which are certain still, the grand, simple landmarks of morality'. They were to do so in order to 'hand down an unbroken constitution to [their] children, and those high traditions which will make them in their turn the pure sons and daughters of a pure father'.[113]

In the September 1918 lecture, the discussion of continence was followed by an analysis of the effects of alcohol on the rate of infection. The number of soldiers who reported having been under the influence of alcohol when they incurred the risk of infection led medical officers to believe that they could reduce the rate of infection by reducing the consumption of alcohol.[114] It was also far more difficult to self-administer prophylactic treatment while intoxicated. Medical officers believed that the soldiers were not administering the process effectively, resulting in a higher than expected VD rate for those who had attempted prophylactic treatment. This idea of the link between alcohol and VD was also explored by British purity organisations; medical officers used the same argument as moralists but with a more pragmatic bent.[115]

In the lecture, the diseases themselves were then discussed, providing soldiers with information about the symptoms, complications and possible consequences for any future offspring. This was done in some detail; medical officers were asked to inform soldiers of the damaging effects of VD and not withhold graphic descriptions of the diseases, the discomfort of the symptoms and the effects on their future wives and children. Here the medical officers differed somewhat from the purity movements in their approach to passing on medical information. Both groups attempted to change soldiers' behaviour through a discussion of the complications for the wives and children of the soldiers.[116] The medical officers were asked to outline for the soldiers the medical consequences on the 'innocent' victims of the diseases. They were given a straightforward assessment of the potential for pain, miscarriage, death and illness. In contrast, the purity movement, exemplified by the White Cross League, issued pamphlets attempting to harness the masculine honour of the soldier as the protector of woman and cast him as a potential hero.[117] The AAMC also provided information to soldiers about the consequences of contracting VD for their own health whereas the White Cross League simply cast infected soldiers as delinquent and guilty rather than giving any information about the disease.

After this description of the disease, the soldiers were then informed of the need for prophylaxis and early treatment, and the problems posed by concealing the disease from their medical officer or using remedies from an unsanctioned source. Medical officers were required to tell soldiers that, if prophylactic treatment was sought and properly administered, the risk of infection was extremely low. Soldiers were also given statistics on the efficacy of the abortive treatment. They were informed that if they presented for the abortive treatment method, and it was too many hours after connection for the prophylactic treatment to be effective, they could still be cured of VD in 80 per cent of cases. This is where the attempts by the AAMC and the purity movements to prevent VD diverged markedly. The purity movements viewed the presentation of anything other than sexual continence as the promotion of vice so they did not advocate the use of prophylactics and actively worked against the implementation of a similar system for the British army.[118]

The methods of prophylaxis and early treatment used at Blue Light Depots were then outlined for soldiers. This was done so that soldiers knew what to expect from the treatment, and it was made clear to them that the longer they left seeking treatment, the more invasive and protracted the treatment was. The preventive measures at their disposal took five minutes; the prophylactic treatment, if administered within twenty-four hours of connection, took around thirty minutes; and the abortive treatment consisted of multiple treatments each day for a week. All of these were portrayed as preferable to needing to be hospitalised for an average of fifty-three days with regular treatments, oftentimes multiple invasive treatments per day.[119] Some parts of the army were concerned that the extended stay in hospital would be attractive to potential shirkers and wasters.[120] Viewing VD as a self-inflicted wound ensured that punitive consequences would be continued for those who were eventually admitted to hospital.[121]

The lecture was designed to end with an invocation to remain healthy for the sake of both military efficiency and the benefit of soldiers' country and empire. Medical officers were instructed to tell soldiers: 'At this critical period, the Empire can ill afford to lose a man from disease that is preventable. For the sake of Australia's womanhood and the welfare and happiness of the Commonwealth, keep your bodies and minds pure, for venereal disease is the great destroyer of national and individual happiness.'[122] The issue of VD was therefore framed in terms of national and imperial fidelity as well as one of masculine pride. This supports Featherstone's argument that the discourse about sex was rarely about pleasure. The pleasure of sex is not mentioned once in the lectures; sex was, however, framed in terms of patriotism, gender roles and health.

It is impossible to determine whether the lectures were effective in slowing the rate of disease because they were instituted at the same time and in conjunction with a range of other measures. What is significant is the way the problem of VD was framed and presented to the soldiers and how it differed from other messages regarding sexual health that were circulated at the time. While there were similarities in the approaches taken by the AAMC and the purity movements, such as the White Cross League and the National Council for Combating Venereal Disease, there were distinct differences. Both were trying to achieve the same goal: that of a reduction in the rate of venereal disease among soldiers. The purity movements attempted to do so by appealing to the soldier's sense of male pride and invoking the image of the protector.

The AAMC, in contrast, attempted to present evidence based on the medical understanding of the time and to promote a proactive approach to sexual health that acknowledged the reality that soldiers were willing to risk infection.

THE EFFICACY OF RAFFAN'S APPROACH TO VENEREAL DISEASE

Lieutenant Colonel Raffan wrote yet another report in 1918 outlining why treatment methods had worked and pinpointing the turning point in the prevention of disease. He stated that after Form 4 was added to the required paperwork of units and bases, the attempts to combat VD became more successful.[123] Raffan's statistics show that the rate of infection from VD decreased significantly during the war. From the initial 10 per cent of the relatively small contingent that initially landed in Egypt – a number that some analyses have suggested should be doubled[124] – the rate for the AIF depots in the UK decreased to 3.7 per cent in 1917 and further down to 2.34 per cent of men in 1918.[125] These rates include men from sections of the army who were not counted on the strength of the units in question (members of the Australian Flying Corps or those soldiers on leave from France), thereby inflating the percentage of men from AIF depots in the UK who had contracted VD. When these factors are allowed for, the rate of infection works out to just under 2 per cent of the force.

The weekly returns that were sent to headquarters on Form 4 in order to monitor the problem of venereal disease show that soldiers were willing to take the advice of the medical officers and proactively manage their sexual health. The number of advice cards accepted by soldiers was high, and Nargol Outfits were also routinely accepted by soldiers. As a general rule, fewer condoms than Nargol Outfits were taken by soldiers before they went on leave. This was to be expected, as condoms cost soldiers between two and three shillings each, whereas Nargol Outfits were free of charge to soldiers going on leave. The most startling information to be gleaned from the Form 4 statistics is the high rate of soldiers reporting for early treatment after returning from leave. Those statistics were compiled for the period 2 May 1918 to 2 January 1919 and, as can be seen in figure 5.2, when AIF units in the UK are considered together, the proportion of soldiers going on leave each week who returned and sought prophylactic, or early, treatment rarely dropped below 60 per cent. Over the same period, around 40 per cent of soldiers purchased French letters from their medical officer, and almost double that number accepted Blue Label Outfits. The number of soldiers requiring abortive treatment was also consistently low.

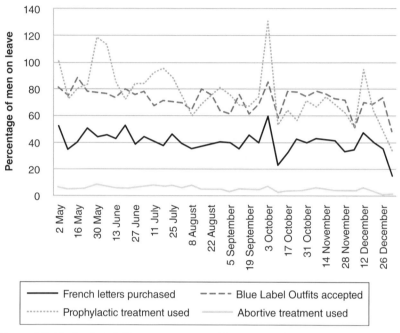

Figure 5.2 Methods in VD prevention used by men on leave in 1918 (AIF troops in the UK)
Source: compiled from 'Consolidated Prophylactic and Early Treatment Venereal Reports' (AWM27 376/189)

These statistics, especially for the percentage of men accepting Blue Label Outfits and purchasing French letters, are most likely inflated as some men would have taken more than one of each. They are also crude measures as they assume that the number of men going on leave was roughly equivalent to the number returning. This does not account for the different lengths of leave or battlefield developments that require the recall of large numbers from leave simultaneously. The spike in early October coincides with the withdrawal of the Australian Corps from the front lines and the issuing of leave passes to a large number of men. When read together, however, these statistics suggest that the Australian soldiers did heed the message from Lieutenant Colonel Raffan, conveyed through their regimental medical officers, that they were able to take personal responsibility for their sexual health.

Unlike in the British Army, where Joanna Bourke found that the majority of soldiers did not have 'irregular' sex throughout the First World War, the Form 4 statistics suggest that the majority of Australian soldiers did engage in casual sex, whether with prostitutes or with amateurs.[126] Furthermore, the statistics suggest that the majority of Australian soldiers also actively tried to avoid infection once the AAMC's scheme for the prevention and treatment of VD was in operation. As well as the widespread use of preventive techniques, during the period covered by these statistics, on average, more than 70 per cent of soldiers returning from leave reported for the invasive early treatment. AIF soldiers, when presented with detailed information about the threat posed by VD and informed of the various treatment options, took steps to minimise their risk of infection.

A further measure of the success of Raffan's VD prevention policies is the rate at which members of the AIF were admitted to the venereal disease hospital, 1ADH Bulford. As shown in figure 5.3, the proportion of those on leave each week who were sent to Bulford fluctuated wildly (for the same reasons mentioned above). When measured against the strength of the AIF in the UK, which averaged 27 283 during the period in question, however, the Bulford admissions average 0.28 per cent of the force and do not exceed 0.4 per cent. This was a substantial reduction in the rate of VD in the AIF from the beginning of the war, and the provision of abortive treatment in soldiers' units prevented many men being unnecessarily evacuated to Bulford.

WHY WAS PRAGMATISM POSSIBLE?

By early 1916, it was clear that the moralist and disorganised approach to VD that had prevailed in the AIF was not sufficient to combat the constant flow of VD cases into Australian military hospitals. Given the length of time taken to cure a man of VD once it had set in, it was far more efficient to prevent the infection or, if that was not possible, to treat it early. The role of the padre and organisations such as the YMCA as moral guardians and providers of wholesome diversions were never fully removed from the AIF. They played an important role in the prevention of disease and the entertainment of soldiers. But theirs were not the leading voices on VD for the AIF – that voice belonged to the AAMC. Once it became better organised and enlisted the expertise of a specialist dermatologist in George Raffan, the AAMC transformed the way VD was treated within the AIF. Raffan, in conjunction with other officers, particularly Douglas

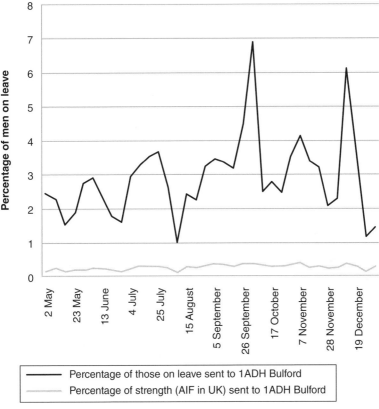

Figure 5.3 Percentage of AIF troops in the UK admitted to 1ADH Bulford in 1918
Source: compiled from 'Consolidated Prophylactic and Early Treatment
Venereal Reports' (AWM27 376/189)

McWhae and Bernhard Zwar, stepped away from the moralist approach previously dominant in the AIF and placed medical considerations at the forefront of the way the AAMC treated cases of VD. Even though Neville Howse was uncomfortable with these steps, he allowed them to become AAMC policy.

The realisation that men on leave were at a greater risk of contracting VD provided the evidence needed to change the way the AAMC treated VD. The months immediately preceding and following the Dardanelles campaign had high rates of infection and, after the majority of the AIF was relocated to France and England, the place most soldiers reported contracting VD was on leave in London. Once leave was acknowledged as a major factor in the army's attempts to combat VD and the punitive consequences put in place after the initial outbreak of VD were seen to have failed in their objectives, the army altered its approach once again to try to change the behaviour of its soldiers. It was clear to the army that fear of punishment was not sufficient to prevent soldiers from putting themselves at risk of contracting these diseases. The desire for sex, especially in a context where a soldier was routinely reminded of his mortality, was not outweighed by the fear of either disease or the punitive consequences of contracting it. Also, by turning the medical services into a force to be feared, the army had limited the AAMC's effectiveness in its attempts to combat the disease. Having the medical services mete out punishment as well as care further perpetuated an already serious problem.

The medicalisation of the treatment of VD in the AIF was evident in the increasing authority the AAMC had over issues of both sexual illness and health. Advocates of a medical response were able to point to isolated successes where an individual medical officer had implemented a strategy, then harnessed it on a larger scale for the AAMC. This wider dissemination of evidence-based medicine reinforced the AAMC as an appropriate custodian of military medicine. While there was continued involvement from organisations such as the NCCVD and White Cross League, this was usually in conjunction with the medical services. These groups did advocate a moralist approach to VD, which objected to any prevention methods that appeared to advocate vice, but their efforts were held in check by the pragmatic approach of the AAMC. Lisa Featherstone found that in the AAMC in the First World War 'the overwhelming push was towards medicalising, rather than moralising, venereal disease'.[127] Featherstone's conclusion is supported by the evidence presented in this chapter.

Michel Foucault, in *The History of Sexuality*, suggested that the confession had become an increasingly medicalised phenomenon. Sins were no longer confessed to priests in order to obtain absolution. He wrote:

> The confession is a ritual discourse in which the speaking subject is also the subject of the statement; it is also a ritual that unfolds within a power relationship, for one does not confess without the presence (or virtual presence) of a partner who is not simply the interlocutor but the authority who requires the confession, prescribes and appreciates it, and intervenes in order to judge, punish, forgive, console, and reconcile.[128]

Access to medical care required an act of confession, now anonymous, to be cleansed of disease.[129] The attempts to protect the anonymity of the soldiers were put in place to engender trust between the medical officer and the soldier-patient. The punitive consequences originally handed to soldiers upon their confession of having contracted VD acted as deterrents from seeking medical assistance within the army rather than as deterrents from having sex. By shifting this confession into the private space between doctor and patient rather than officer and soldier, the medical services were able to be of assistance to the soldier.

The pragmatic approach of the AAMC to VD could be implemented because it supported already entrenched gender roles. Lisa Featherstone's study of sex in pre-war Australia found that chastity was the expected norm for both men and women but that it was socially acceptable for men to contravene this norm. She also found that the role of women as sites of disease was changing. Prostitutes remained guilty of this charge; however, current and future wives were increasingly constructed as the innocent victims of male promiscuity rather than as harbingers of disease. By lecturing men that the only way to avoid infection was to remain chaste at the same time as providing preventive and prophylactic treatments should they 'slip', the AAMC attempted to reinforce the ideal of chastity while expecting and anticipating errant behaviour. As the lectures given to soldiers demonstrate, this was done not only to protect the efficiency of the army but also in the name of the women and future children of Australia. By maintaining disease as an external threat to the army, it was then possible to construct sexual incontinence as an offence against the soldiers' brothers-in-arms and therefore unpatriotic, rather than char-acterising it as merely scurrilous or incorrigible behaviour. This made contracting VD a crime against nation and wife; the soldier with VD was unpatriotic, and this was spelled out fairly explicitly to those in the AIF. It continues then that VD played a role in the development of soldiers' masculine and civic identities.

The AAMC adopted a pragmatic medically initiated and controlled approach to VD out of necessity and based on knowledge gained from civilian health care. The haphazard efforts of a few interested medical officers without any institutional support from the AAMC or the AIF resulted in VD becoming a significant problem for the AIF. This was not a surprise. VD had been associated with armies and navies for a long time, and the correlation between war and increased VD rates was well known among doctors and military officials of the time. The methods used in the prevention of VD by the AAMC in the first half of the First World War had simply failed. By continually preaching the importance of purity and chastity to soldiers and lecturing on the medical consequences of infection, yet simultaneously providing soldiers with prophylactic kits, early treatment depots and condoms, the AAMC reinforced the ideal of purity, the expectation that the ideal would be transgressed, and the medicalisation of the solution to the problem.

CONCLUSION

DEVELOPING AN AUSTRALIAN MEDICAL SERVICE

At the end of 1918, the Australian Army Medical Corps (AAMC) was a different organisation from the one that had existed when war was declared in 1914. Commencing the war with a regular staff of four officers, the AAMC rapidly expanded and developed. Almost entirely dependent on assistance from Britain and the Royal Army Medical Corps (RAMC) during the Gallipoli campaign in 1915, the AAMC, during the remaining years of the war, became more independent, developed its own practices and procedures, and asserted its expertise in order to have Australian medical control of Australian casualties.

The context and the structures of medical care in which the AAMC worked shaped the medical care it provided to the AIF. By analysing how, where and by whom medical care was provided to Australian soldiers in the First World War, this book has outlined the points at which imperial, military, medical and gender hierarchies competed for primacy in three forms of care: casualty clearance and evacuation in battle, rehabilitation after sickness or wounding, and the prevention and early treatment of venereal disease. These different forms of authority were under a constant process of renegotiation during the war, and this book argues that despite the different pressures and priorities at the three different sites of care, the AAMC was consistent in its desire to develop and maintain Australian medical control of AIF casualties.

Examining these structures of medical care reveals the link between events on the Gallipoli peninsula in 1915 and medical care later in the war on the Western Front. It demonstrates that Australia's medical services reformed the way they interacted with Britain after Gallipoli and that the success of the new arrangements at the Battle of Messines enabled Neville Howse a few days later to argue in front of the Dardanelles Commission that the AAMC was a capable provider of medical care during casualty evacuation.

Mapping the development of casualty clearance in the AAMC demonstrates how its internal negotiations and discussions informed the arrangements on the Western Front. These discussions indicate that concerns over the proximity of medical units to the front and anxieties about the distance between those units and the relevant casualty clearing station underpinned the various iterations of the medical arrangements. They also show that, in the changes to evacuation arrangements and the development of forward resuscitation teams, the AAMC was willing to depart from and work around British regulations.

Exploring the role of civilians in the AAMC demonstrates their considerable influence. From the work of civilian doctors in uniform fundamentally altering the way the corps approached its work and attempted to solve problems, to the influence of civilian women in auxiliary hospitals, the predominantly civilian nature of the AAMC was a distinctive feature of the corps. Its flexibility, adaptability and willingness to abandon or depart from doctrine were all substantially the results of civilian decision-making. The activities provided by female volunteers at Harefield Park, including fancy work, basket-weaving and painting, were not a threat to the masculinity of the recovering soldiers. Rather, middle-class women volunteering in the hospital used their expertise to provide recreation and entertainment to wounded soldiers – men whose bodies had been curtailed. Moreover, this emphasises the gendered nature of the work in medical–military contexts. As a general rule, men do medicine and women do care. There was a 'culture of caregiving' among British civilians, which was demonstrated in the way they cared for British soldiers.[1] As a result of research into the 1st Australian Auxiliary Hospital at Harefield Park, it is clear that the same culture of caregiving was extended to Australian soldiers as well.

Analysing the response to venereal disease demonstrates that Australian soldiers were not passive victims of VD, nor were they reckless in their attitudes to their sexual health. Medical officers for Australian units in the United Kingdom were required to report on the preventive methods used by men returning from leave. Collation of that data reveals that, throughout 1918, (1) more than 60 per cent of men going on leave accepted a preventive Blue Label Outfit; (2) around 40 per cent of men going on leave purchased French letters from the AIF; (3) more than 60 per cent of men returning from leave sought prophylactic treatment; and (4) less than 10 per cent of men returning from leave required abortive treatment. These statistics indicate that when provided with the relevant information and technology, and when the disclosure of sexual activity was met with medical assistance rather than punishment, Australian soldiers were proactive in managing their sexual health.

The First World War generally, and the Gallipoli campaign in particular, has been described as the moment in which the Australian nation was born. This view is problematic on many fronts, not least of which is that Australia was federated 14 years before the commencement of hostilities. Nevertheless, as far as the AAMC is concerned, Gallipoli was a turning point. The failure of the British military authorities to plan adequately for the evacuation of casualties during the initial landings and the August Offensive prompted the reorganisation and expansion of the Australian medical services.

Adherence to the traditional imperial hierarchy was detrimental to the evacuation of Australian casualties from Gallipoli. When Sir Neville Howse, then Assistant Director of Medical Services for the 1st Australian Division, perceived problems with the structure of the medical arrangements and alerted his superiors in the chain of command, his concerns were dismissed. At that stage the most senior member of the AAMC attached to the AIF, Surgeon General Williams, had no authority to direct Australian troops under the command of the MEF. As Howse was the highest-ranked medical officer with the AAMC units deployed to Gallipoli, he had no recourse to appeal decisions made by the British General Staff or the RAMC.

When called before the Dardanelles Commission, which investigated the campaign, Howse was forthcoming with his criticism of those in command. His statements that the medical arrangements were such that they amounted to criminal negligence and that he would recommend that the Australian Government never again entrust the medical care of its soldiers to imperial authorities were bold suggestions. He was able to make them with confidence, speaking many months after the Gallipoli evacuation, because the AAMC had just performed admirably during the evacuation of casualties from the Battle of Messines. That the plans at Gallipoli were no better for the British soldiers was immaterial; Howse and the AAMC were responsible to Australia for Australian casualties. This required them to maintain appropriate relationships within the military hierarchy of the British forces at the same time as reorienting their priorities to Australia first and the empire second.

In the time between the conclusion of the Dardanelles campaign and the Battle of Messines, the AAMC had taken control of medical arrangements for Australian units between the trench and the casualty clearing station (CCS). There were still British officers involved – the Deputy Director of Medical Services at corps level was an officer of the RAMC – but at the Battle of Messines the AAMC officers discussed the arrangements between themselves, then communicated their decisions up the chain of command for approval rather than waiting for them to be handed down. These findings support the arguments previously made by historians Mark Harrison and Gary Sheffield, who have argued that the medical services were more integrated into military operations and that a more consultative command structure existed on the Western Front compared to that in the Gallipoli campaign.[2]

Howse's push to have Australian control of Australian casualties was not that of an ardent nationalist. He argued that the medical services were primarily responsible for Australian soldiers and would be held to account by the Australian public for the care they provided. Howse described himself as Englishman and 'merely an adopted Australian'.[3] If the Australian Government did not intend ever to rely on the British Government to make adequate arrangements for its wounded in any future conflict, Australia would need to be able to provide that service from its own resources. Howse saw the continued presence of unnecessary imperial officers as detrimental to morale and, in 1918, argued that the experience gained in more than three years of war was sufficient to counteract any perceived or actual deficiencies owing to civilian medical men not having received military training to develop that military frame of mind so valued by Sir Ian Hamilton during the Dardanelles campaign. Howse's suggestion that the AIF should have developed competent officers by that stage of the war and should be able to 'stand on our own bottom'[4] – i.e. be its own entity, responsible for its own governance – present the promotion of Australian medical men within the AAMC and the Australian Corps, and therefore the removal of replaceable imperial officers, as the next logical step in the development of the AIF.

As imperial authority was gradually pushed out of the AAMC, there was no corresponding movement to prevent British civilian involvement, with the proviso that military and medical authority were maintained. This is evident in the work of the AAMC at the 1st Australian Auxiliary Hospital at Harefield Park. At Harefield Park, military interactions between British and Australian units were restricted to the point at which Australian soldiers recovering from wounding were handed over from British hospitals, which had responsibility for primary care, to the auxiliary hospital – a place of rehabilitation and recovery. Despite the lack of British military involvement in the auxiliary hospital, British civilian involvement was a daily occurrence. British civilians, especially women, took on a variety of paid and volunteer roles at Harefield Park in nursing positions, ward and household staff, and providing social care to recovering soldiers. Although it was subordinated to military and medical concerns, this involvement was welcomed by the AAMC and the different activities provided for the hospital's patients by the local residents of Harefield were acknowledged as valuable and routinely recorded in the unit's war diaries, thereby conferring legitimacy upon them. The relative frequency of marriages between local female residents of Harefield who worked in the hospital and Australian doctors and patients suggests that the AAMC's distrust of British actions after Gallipoli did not shift from the institutional and affect personal relationships.

British involvement in attempts to lessen the impact of venereal disease on the efficiency of the AIF was also limited. The RAMC was not substantially involved in this aspect of military medicine in the AIF, and civilian efforts were restricted to those areas that supported the AAMC's efforts without undermining them. Australian soldiers were encouraged to take advantage of entertainment and activities provided by British charities, and the AAMC leveraged the work of organisations concerned about the prevalence of VD in Britain. However, neither of these British civilian activities undermined the medical or military authority of the AAMC in this field. Therefore, while the war did not see the wholesale rejection of British involvement in the care of wounded Australian soldiers, where it was possible to have full Australian medical–military control of Australian sick and wounded, then Australian authority was asserted and British intervention decreased.

During the First World War, there was a distinction between military and civilian frames of mind, which was problematic for the AAMC. While the RAMC had a substantial permanent staff, the AAMC did not, and the lack of a military mindset among doctors was one of the criticisms RAMC officers made of Neville Howse during the Dardanelles Commission. The privileging of full-time medical–military men was a factor the RAMC itself would have to contend with as the war progressed and civilian doctors donned military uniforms in greater numbers. Yet, despite this supposedly underdeveloped military thinking in the AAMC, it still possessed military authority over soldiers. Its officers decided how, when and where soldiers received medical care on the Western Front and used their military authority to create a system to reduce the impact of venereal disease. While initial attempts to do so using military discipline as a disincentive did not succeed, the altered plans in place after 1917 relied on the individual soldier taking responsibility for his own health while maintaining the threat of punishment if he did not adequately practise self-care. Although the vast majority of doctors in the AAMC were civilians in uniform who had enlisted after the commencement of the First World War, they were willing and able to use the authority bestowed on them by their military position to provide adequate medical care to Australian soldiers.

Owing to the nature of the AAMC, it is difficult to separate military and medical hierarchies as they were deliberately mapped onto each other; however, AAMC doctors did challenge the priorities of the army at various points. On the Western Front, the large number of casualties posed a problem for the AAMC. The drive for efficiency required that those who were only slightly wounded be kept closer to the front to enable a rapid return to duty; however, the scale of the casualties was such that the evacuation lines clogged up and bottlenecks occurred. In order to remedy this situation, throughout 1916 and 1917, the AAMC altered the structure of the medical services from the front to the CCS. This resulted in an evacuation chain that only practised first aid closer to the front and moved casualties, with as little intervention as possible, back to more established and better equipped medical posts.

In 1918, responding to the military situation, the AAMC retreated from some of its changes, reinstating aspects of the previous doctrine. Yet it kept pushing to improve the care provided to wounded soldiers. The development of resuscitation teams in forward areas went against the prevailing wisdom on the level of treatment to be provided before evacuation. The AAMC officers concerned developed the plan and requested approval from RAMC officers to make the necessary alterations. This approval was not forthcoming, but the AAMC officers proceeded anyway. They slightly altered their plans so that they adhered to the letter of the *Field Service Regulations*, not to the recommendation of the British Fourth Army's Director of Medical Services. The scheme was a success, and it won the support of the Consulting Surgeon to the relevant CCS before being expanded.

The AAMC had clearly developed an understanding of military strategy and doctrine by 1918, and this supports Neville Howse's view that any deficiencies existing early in the war had been overcome after three years of warfare. These civilian doctors had adapted to their military environment and learned to manipulate it in order to care for wounded Australian soldiers. The medical and military priorities were held in tension and, although the AAMC routinely prioritised medical concerns, it developed the ability to do so within the military restrictions in place, further cementing the blended medical–military hierarchy.

The changes to the way the AAMC evacuated casualties from the front lines suggest that a degree of departure from the 'imperial army project' occurred during the war.[5] At the beginning of the war, most units of the AAMC were interchangeable with their RAMC equivalent. By the end of the war the work done along the casualty evacuation chain differed enough for it to be more difficult to fit the pieces of the imperial puzzle together. While the AAMC adhered to the letter of the *Field Service Regulations* during its 1918 campaigns, it interpretation of those regulations differed from that of the RAMC. Consequently, the size of the unit needed to maintain interoperability was much larger. Early in the war an Australian field ambulance unit could have served with the RAMC fairly easily. By 1918, in order to ensure smooth functioning, substituting a unit smaller than a corps would have caused problems. The imperial armies could still work together after the First World War, just at a different scale from that of 1914.

Gender hierarchies were expressed differently across the different forms of care provided by the medical services. Competing masculinities were on display at Gallipoli, where Neville Howse's authority was undermined and his expertise diminished by British descriptions of him as simply a general practitioner from country New South Wales. This description was used despite his leadership of the AAMC in the Pacific, his service in the South African War (for which he was awarded a Victoria Cross) and his promotion to Director of Medical Services for the AIF. This wartime blending of military and gender hierarchies reinforced the difficulties faced by civilian doctors in uniform in the AAMC.

Once women were incorporated into the medical spaces, gender became a more pronounced issue. The initial employment of a mixed physiotherapy team at Harefield Park challenged the gender hierarchy as female physiotherapists were treated as honorary officers. Despite being paid less than their male counterparts, they then outranked some of the men as only a limited number were made officers; the rest were other ranks. The problem of these competing military and gender hierarchies was resolved by creating an all-female physiotherapy staff at the hospital.

Ostensibly to promote unit cohesion, it also saved the AAMC money and was similar to the reasons given for the employment of female domestic labour in the hospital, although this had the added benefit of enabling the male labour to be redeployed. The female physiotherapists were placed in charge of unskilled male labour, but this was to enable the more efficient functioning of the hospital in times of peak work. In these instances their medical knowledge was the source of their higher status.

In its attempts to combat venereal disease, the AAMC established competing narratives of masculinity. By the end of the war, the ideal soldier was chaste and demonstrated self-control by abstaining from sex. Yet the AAMC knew from experience that this ideal was frequently transgressed so it described the seeking of medical assistance and the use of preventive and prophylactic treatments before and after sex as more honourable than the disregard of sexual health. This did not contradict widely held beliefs about male sexuality. Therefore gender hierarchies were not only present but also actively harnessed in the AAMC's attempts to limit the effects of venereal disease on the AIF.

David Noonan's statistical analysis of the AIF called into question Butler's conclusions regarding the medical services in the First World War.[6] Although based on incorrect statistical data, Butler's conclusions were generally sound. However, he was too willing to give credit for the successes of the AAMC to Neville Howse. While Howse certainly led the AAMC well and was responsible for the form of the medical services from 1916, he cannot be given credit for the success of the system of VD prevention. Howse was contrary and uncooperative in the initial discussions about VD prevention. He dismissed all suggestions made as either having been tried before or unlikely to work. Howse did eventually allow the pragmatic system to develop, but this occurred only after those below him in the hierarchy skillfully managed his abstemious views by building a consensus based on expertise and experience.

This book is necessarily constrained in scope. It has neither incorporated the work of the AAMC in Sinai and Palestine, nor the ANMEF's foray into the Pacific. The AIF's medical provisions in those campaigns, especially the former, would provide interesting cases for comparison with the provision on the Western Front and Gallipoli. The different landscapes and military contexts presented different problems for the medical corps, and future comparative analyses would enable a discussion of whether the findings of this book, regarding the structures that improved and impeded access to medical care, could be extended and applied to different theatres of war.

The AAMC had a significant presence behind the lines in France, where the medical units provided by Australia were a part of the broader British services. These broader responsibilities outside the AIF, between the casualty clearing station and the auxiliary hospital, draw the area outside the scope of this book. This international space is fertile ground for future studies of imperial cooperation and international medical networks. With the foundations already laid by Mark Harrison, there is space for further discussion of the role of formal and informal networks in the service of empire.[7]

As this book has fundamentally dealt with medical decision-making, and the examination of where responsibility for those decisions lay, I have not analysed the work of nurses in detail. In the AIF, nurses worked as far forward as casualty clearing stations so they are largely outside the scope of the first three chapters of this book. Their role within the auxiliary hospital was discussed in chapter 4 as they became responsible for managing aspects of civilian labour in the medical space, and their roles were contrasted with those of the female physiotherapists in the hospital. Scholarship on nursing in the First World War is creating an increasingly sophisticated historiography of the work of nurses and is interrogating the nature of the work and the professionalisation of nursing.[8]

It is impossible to completely tease apart the four hierarchies or forms of authority under consideration as they did not begin to interact at the commencement of the First World War. However, their relationships with each other were in a state of flux throughout the war and altered on the basis of the particular needs of the situations in which the AAMC worked. The debacle that was the medical arrangements for the Dardanelles campaign was an important moment for the AAMC. That was the point at which it became apparent to Neville Howse and other members of the corps that Australia could not afford to rely on British plans. Until at least the Dardanelles Commission hearings in 1917, if not for the rest of the First World War, the AAMC worked in Gallipoli's shadow. Locating that battle within the broader context of the First World War demonstrates one way in which Gallipoli was significant in Australian military history. It was the stimulus that precipitated the transformation of the AAMC into a more independent unit with medical and military expertise of its own. As a result, the AAMC asserted its authority and consolidated its control over sick, wounded and recovering Australian soldiers.

NOTES

Introduction: More than a man and his donkey

1 Johnston, *Stretcher-bearers*, p. 43.
2 Ibid., p. 43; Wilson, *Dust, Donkeys and Delusions*.
3 Buley, *Glorious Deeds of Australasians in the Great War*, p. 3.
4 For a systematic critique of every Simpson myth, see Wilson, *Dust, Donkeys and Delusions*.
5 Ibid., p. iii.
6 Holbrook, *Anzac, the Unauthorised Biography*, p. 1.
7 RSPCA Purple Cross Award, 19 May 1997, AWM REL25365. Murphy was the name most commonly used for Simpson's donkey, although it was sometimes used for Simpson himself. Other names for the donkey(s) include Abdul, Queen Elizabeth, Duffy No. 1 and Duffy No. 2.
8 Benson, *The Man with the Donkey*; Cochrane, *Simpson and the Donkey*; Curran, *Across the Bar*; Small, *Simpson and Duffy*; Curran, *Not Only a Hero*; Greenwood, *Simpson and His Donkey*; French, *The Donkey Who Carried the Wounded*; Stanley, *Simpson's Donkey*.
9 Butler, *The Western Front*, p. 605.
10 Noonan, *Those We Forget*.
11 Ibid., pp. 62, 135.
12 Ibid., p. 135.
13 Although women did serve as nurses and masseuses in the AAMS, no women were permitted to serve in the AAMC as doctors. In spite of this gender bar, female Australian doctors served with other national and charitable medical units in the First World War. For further details, see Sheard and Lee, *Women to the Front*; Neuhaus and Mascall-Dare, *Not for Glory*.
14 For a discussion of the work of stretcher-bearers in the AIF, see Johnston, *Stretcher-bearers*; for analysis of RAMC other ranks, see Meyer, *An Equal Burden*; and for a comparative look at stretcher-bearers across the British imperial forces, see Markovich, "'No time for tears for the dying'".
15 As will be shown, this was not always the case, and there were instances when AFAs were brought into service to reinforce the work of other brigades.
16 For an analysis of the development of CCSs, see Harrison, *The Medical War*, especially pp. 32–43.
17 For detailed descriptions of the evacuation chain, see ibid., pp. 65–91; Reid, *Medicine in First World War Europe*, pp. 27–70; Meyer, *An Equal Burden*, pp. 124–51.

18 Delaney, *The Imperial Army Project*, p. 5.
19 Ibid., pp. 297–8.
20 Ibid., p. 301.
21 Butler, *Problems and Services*, p. 546.
22 Harrison, *The Medical War*, p. 172.
23 Holbrook, *Anzac, the Unauthorised Biography*, p. 46.
24 Butler, *Gallipoli, Palestine and New Guinea*, p. v.
25 Ibid., p. v.
26 Ibid., p. vii.
27 Ibid., p. 479.
28 As an example, see ibid., p. 152.
29 Harrison, *The Medical War*, p. 172.
30 Tyquin, *Gallipoli: The Medical War*; Tyquin, *Gallipoli: An Australian Medical Perspective*.
31 Braga, *ANZAC Doctor*; Tyquin, *Neville Howse*; Murdoch, *Neville Howse VC*.
32 Harrison, *The Medical War*, p. 203.
33 Harrison, 'Medicine and the management of modern warfare', pp. 3–4.
34 Ibid., p. 4.
35 Cooter and Sturdy, 'Of war, medicine and modernity', p. 12.
36 Schock, 'Healing the patient, serving the State', p. 9.
37 Carden-Coyne, *The Politics of Wounds*, p. 3.
38 Ibid., p. 338.
39 Ibid., p. 338.
40 Bourke, *Dismembering the Male*, p. 172.
41 Smith, 'Medical inspection of state schoolchildren in Australia, c. 1905–14', pp. 5–20.
42 Carden-Coyne, *The Politics of Wounds*, p. 9.
43 Ibid., p. 266.
44 Condé, 'Imagining a collection', p. 28.
45 Ibid., p. 28.
46 *Harefield Park Boomerang* (hereafter *Boomerang*) 1, no. 1, 1916; 2, no. 11, 1918, AWM081392 TROOPSHIP SERIAL/The Harefield Park Boomerang.
47 Reznick, *Healing the Nation*, p. 68.
48 Ibid., p. 65.
49 Carden-Coyne, *The Politics of Wounds*, p. 12.

Chapter 1   Gallipoli: A case of criminal negligence?

1 Surgeon General Sir N.R. Howse, Evidence to Dardanelles Commission (hereafter DC), q. 27667, The National Archives, UK (henceforth TNA): CAB 19/33.
2 Ibid., q. 27675.
3 Butler, *Gallipoli, Palestine and New Guinea*, p. 87.
4 Ibid., p. 87.
5 'Force Order No. 1', General Staff, GHQ, MEF, war diary, 13 April 1915, AWM4 1/4/1 Part 2.
6 Lieutenant Colonel A.E.C. Keble, Statement to DC, TNA: CAB 19/29.

7 Brigadier General E.M. Woodward to CGS & QMG, General Staff, GHQ, MEF, war diary, 18 April 1915, AWM4 1/4/1 Part 2.

8 Brigadier General E.M. Woodward to CGS, General Staff, GHQ, MEF, war diary, 19 April 1915, AWM4 1/4/1 Part 2.

9 Surgeon General W.G. Birrell, DMS MEF, war diary, 1–24 April 1915, AWM4 26/3/1. Accounts differ as to whether Birrell was unwell, attending to his duties regarding the organisation of hospitals in Egypt, or some combination of the two.

10 Lieutenant Colonel A.E.C. Keble, Statement to DC, TNA: CAB 19/29.

11 Ibid.

12 Surgeon General Sir N.R. Howse, Evidence to DC, q. 27664, TNA: CAB 19/33.

13 Ibid.

14 Butler, *Gallipoli, Palestine and New Guinea*, p. 102.

15 Connor, *Anzac and Empire*, p. 60.

16 Ibid., p. 73. Barrett's perspective on the events at 1AGH can be found in Barrett, *A Vision of the Possible*; Barrett and Deane, *The Australian Army Medical Corps in Egypt during the First World War*.

17 Connor, *Anzac and Empire*, p. 74.

18 Colonel N.R. Howse, ADMS 1st Australian Division, war diary, 22 April 1915, AWM4 26/18/5.

19 Ibid., 23 April 1915.

20 Ibid., 25 April 1915.

21 For further information about the operational aspects of the campaign, see Prior, *Gallipoli*; Crawley and LoCicero, *Gallipoli*.

22 For details of the Ottoman defence of Gallipoli, see Uyar, *The Ottoman Defence Against the Anzac Landing*.

23 For further details on the operational aspects of the landings from a medical viewpoint, see Harrison, *The Medical War*; Tyquin, *Gallipoli: The Medical War*; Butler, *Gallipoli, Palestine and New Guinea*; Sheffield, 'Shaping British and Anzac soldiers' experience of Gallipoli'.

24 Colonel N.R. Howse, ADMS 1st Australian Division, war diary, 25 April 1915, AWM4 26/18/5.

25 Surgeon General Sir N.R. Howse, Evidence to DC, q. 27675, TNA: CAB 19/33.

26 Lieutenant Colonel J. Corbin, Evidence to DC, q. 28610, TNA: CAB 19/33.

27 Dardanelles Commission, *Final Report of the Dardanelles Commission*, para. 164.

28 Lieutenant Colonel C. Ryan, Evidence to DC, q. 28697, TNA: CAB 19/33.

29 Ibid., q. 28702.

30 Ibid., q. 28696.

31 Dardanelles Commission, *Final Report of the Dardanelles Commission*, para. 168.

32 For a comprehensive analysis of the August Offensive, see Crawley, *Climax at Gallipoli*.

33 Lieutenant Colonel A.E.C. Keble, Statement to DC, TNA: CAB 19/29.

34 DMS MEF, war diary, 1–11 July 1915, AWM4 26/3/1.

35 Ibid., 12–31 July 1915.
36 Lieutenant Colonel A.E.C. Keble, Statement to DC, TNA: CAB 19/29.
37 DMS MEF, war diary, 12–31 July 1915, AWM4 26/3/1.
38 Lieutenant Colonel A.E.C. Keble, Statement to DC, TNA: CAB 19/29.
39 Ibid.
40 Ibid.
41 Lieutenant Colonel J. Corbin, Evidence to DC, q. 28599, TNA: CAB 19/33.
42 Ibid., q. 28600.
43 Macleod, *Gallipoli*, pp. 63–4.
44 Bean, *Two Men I Knew*, pp. 36–7.
45 Tyquin, 'Sir William "Mo" Williams', pp. 68–81.
46 For further information, see Wilson, *The Downfall of the Liberal Party 1914–1935*; Macleod, 'General Sir Ian Hamilton and the Dardanelles Commission', pp. 418–41.
47 Dardanelles Commission, *First Report of the Dardanelles Commission*, para. 1.
48 Harrison, *The Medical War*, p. 12.
49 For example see Dardanelles Commission, *Final Report of the Dardanelles Commission*, para. 170.
50 Macleod, 'General Sir Ian Hamilton and the Dardanelles Commission', p. 420.
51 Lee, *A Soldier's Life*.
52 See for example General Sir I. Hamilton to Surgeon General Sir A. Keogh, 20 February 1917, Liddell Hart Centre for Military Archives, King's College London (hereafter LHCMA): HAMILTON 8/1/37; General Sir I. Hamilton to Surgeon General W.G. Birrell, 1 March 1917, LHCMA: HAMILTON 8/1/12; General Sir I. Hamilton to Surgeon General W. Babtie, 22 January 1917, LHCMA: HAMILTON 8/1/7.
53 General Sir I. Hamilton to Surgeon General Sir A. Keogh, 20 February 1917, LHCMA: HAMILTON 8/1/37.
54 Surgeon General Sir A. Keogh to General Sir I. Hamilton, 21 February 1917, LHCMA: HAMILTON 8/1/37.
55 Lieutenant Colonel A.E.C. Keble to General Sir I. Hamilton, 1 September 1917, LHCMA: HAMILTON 8/1/36.
56 Brigadier General E.M. Woodward to General Sir I. Hamilton, 10 November 1916, LHCMA: HAMILTON 8/1/67.
57 General Sir I. Hamilton to Surgeon General W.G. Birrell, 11 August 1917, LHCMA: HAMILTON 8/1/12.
58 General Sir I. Hamilton to Surgeon General Sir A. Keogh, 31 August 1917, LHCMA: HAMILTON 8/1/37; Hamilton's emphasis and crossing out.
59 Surgeon General Sir N.R. Howse, Evidence to DC, q. 27663–4, TNA: CAB 19/33.
60 Lieutenant Colonel A.E.C. Keble, Statement to DC, TNA: CAB 19/29.
61 Connor, *Anzac and Empire*, p. 74.
62 Hamilton to Munro-Ferguson, 6 October 1915, LHCMA: HAMILTON 7/1/42.
63 Bridge and Fedorowich, *The British World*; Fedorowich and Thompson, *Empire, Migration and Identity in the British World*; Fedorowich, 'Restocking the British World', pp. 236–69.

64 Bright and Dilley, 'After the British World', p. 547.
65 Bridge and Fedorowich, 'Mapping the British World', p. 3.
66 Meaney, 'Britishness and Australia', pp. 121–35.
67 Ibid., p. 132.
68 Surgeon General Sir N.R. Howse, Evidence to DC, q. 27677, TNA: CAB 19/33.
69 Ibid., q. 27869.
70 Sir A. Fisher to Surgeon General Sir N.R. Howse, Evidence to DC, q. 27870, TNA: CAB 19/33.
71 Ibid., q. 27871.
72 Ibid., q. 27872.
73 Ibid., q. 27873.
74 Ibid., q. 27874.
75 Egan, '"Nobler than missionaries"'.
76 Tyquin, *Little by Little*, p. 100.
77 Blackmore, *The Dark Pocket of Time*, p. 87.
78 Tyquin, *Little by Little*, p. 100.
79 Lieutenant Colonel A.E.C. Keble, Statement to DC, TNA: CAB 19/29.
80 Surgeon General Sir N.R. Howse, Evidence to DC, q. 27676, TNA: CAB 19/33.
81 Butler, *Gallipoli, Palestine and New Guinea*, pp. 429–35.
82 Surgeon General Sir N.R. Howse, Evidence to DC, q. 27757, TNA: CAB 19/33.
83 Harrison, *The Medical War*, p. 203.
84 Prior, *Gallipoli*, p. 67.
85 Ibid., p. 82.
86 Harrison, 'Medicine and the management of modern warfare', p. 2.
87 Ibid., p. 2.
88 Harrison, 'The medicalization of war', pp. 267–76.
89 Harrison, 'Medicine and the management of modern warfare', p. 4.
90 Ibid., pp. 4–5.
91 Ibid., p. 5.
92 Ibid., pp. 4–6.

Chapter 2 Medicine in the lines: Stationary warfare on the Western Front, 1916–17

1 Butler, *The Western Front*, p. 160.
2 The 3rd Australian Division did not arrive in France until November 1916, after the Australian units had been withdrawn from the line.
3 Harrison, *The Medical War*, p. 203.
4 Ibid., p. 120.
5 Ibid., p. 120.
6 Ibid., p. 65.
7 Major General J.W. McCay to Headquarters XI Corps, 25 July 1916, war diary, Appendix E, Formation Headquarters, 5th Aust. Div., AWM4 1/50/5 Part 3.
8 Bean, *The Australian Imperial Force in France, 1916*, p. 331.
9 Colonel C.H.W. Hardy, war diary, 9–10 July 1916, ADMS 5th Aust. Div., AWM4 26/22/6 Part 1.
10 Ibid., 10–14 July 1916.
11 Ibid., 15 July 1916.

12 Bean, *The Australian Imperial Force in France, 1916*, p. 334; Colonel C.H.W. Hardy, war diary, 15 July 1916, ADMS 5th Aust. Div., AWM4 26/22/6 Part 1.

13 Sheffield, *The Chief*; Harrison, *The Medical War*.

14 Colonel C.H.W. Hardy, war diary, 15 July 1916, ADMS 5th Aust. Div., AWM4 26/22/6 Part 1.

15 Ibid.

16 Colonel C.H.W. Hardy, '5th Australian Divisional Medical Order No. 1', 16 July 1916, war diary, Appendix, ADMS 5th Aust. Div., AWM4 26/22/6 Part 1.

17 Ibid.

18 CO 8th Aust Field Ambulance AIF to ADMS 5th Division, 18 July 1916, war diary, Appendix 6, 8th Australian Field Ambulance, AWM4 26/51/6.

19 Lieutenant-Colonel A.H. Tebbutt, war diary, 18 July 1916, 14th Australian Field Ambulance, AWM4 26/57/6; Captain N. Bullen, war diary, 18 July 1916, 15th Australian Field Ambulance, AWM4 26/58/3.

20 Captain N. Bullen, 'Report on work done by ambulance during action of 19th, 20th, 21st July', war diary, Appendix 22, 15th Australian Field Ambulance, AWM4 26/58/3.

21 Colonel A.E. Shepherd, war diary, 21 July 1916, 8th Australian Field Ambulance, AWM4 26/51/6.

22 Compiled from 'Percentage table showing location of wounds of casualties admitted to field ambulances in action 19th/20th July', war diary, Appendix 35, ADMS 5th Aust. Div., AWM4 26/22/6 Part 1.

23 Captain N. Bullen, 'Report on work done by ambulance during action of 19th, 20th, 21st July', war diary, Appendix 22, 15th Australian Field Ambulance, AWM4 26/58/3.

24 Ibid.

25 Ibid.

26 Ibid.

27 Sheffield, *The Somme*, p. 94.

28 Prior and Wilson, *The Somme*, p. 175.

29 For a detailed analysis of the battle from an operational perspective, see Hampton, *Attack on the Somme*.

30 Prior and Wilson, *The Somme*, p. 176.

31 Ibid., pp. 178–9.

32 Colonel A.H. Sturdee, war diary, Appendix C, ADMS 1st Aust. Div., AWM4 26/18/20.

33 Colonel A.H. Sturdee, Attestation Papers, National Archives of Australia (hereafter NAA): B2455/STURDEE ALFRED HOBART/8095734.

34 Compiled from Lieutenant-Colonel H.N. Butler, war diary, 22–26 July 1916, 3rd Australian Field Ambulance, AWM4 26/46/19.

35 Colonel A.H. Sturdee, Appendix C, war diary, ADMS 1st Aust. Div., AWM4 26/18/20.

36 Harrison, *The Medical War*, p. 120.

37 Colonel A.H. Sturdee, Appendix C, war diary, ADMS 1st Aust. Div., AWM4 26/18/20.

38 Colonel A. Sutton to RMOs 2AD, 2 August 1916, war diary, Appendix A, ADMS 2nd Aust. Div., AWM4 26/19/12.

39 Ibid.
40 Colonel A. Sutton, 'Report on AAMC Operations in Attack on August 4th, 1916', war diary, Appendix G, ADMS 2nd Aust. Div., AWM4 26/19/12.
41 Prior and Wilson, *The Somme*, p. 184.
42 Ibid., p. 183.
43 Colonel A. Sturdee, war diary, Appendix B, ADMS 1st Aust. Div., AWM4 26/18/21; also Colonel Shaw, 'Report on operations from August 12th to August 21st 1916', war diary, Appendix 8, 1st Australian Field Ambulance, AWM4 26/44/17.
44 Colonel A. Sturdee, war diary, Appendix B, ADMS 1st Aust. Div., AWM4 26/18/21; punctuation corrected to improve readability.
45 Ibid.
46 Some of the Australian divisions spent the winter of 1916–17 on the Somme. There they faced significant medical problems such as trench foot, frostbite and influenza. See Butler, *The Western Front*, pp. 74–103.
47 For analysis of the planning for Messines, see Falls, *Military Operations*.
48 Sheffield, 'Finest hour?', p. 65; Fox, *Learning to Fight*; Fox-Godden, '"Putting knowledge in power"', p. 11.
49 Owing to what appear to be transcription errors, the DADMS 3AD during the Battle of Messines is variously listed as J.H., J.F., J.A. and J.M. Anderson in a range of sources. The DADMS 3AD at this time was John Hubback Anderson AAMC, NAA, B2455/ANDERSON J H/1977480.
50 'Memo by Liet.-Col. J.F. [*sic*] Anderson CMG on Messines operations', AWM41 40.
51 Butler, *Problems and Services*, p. 280.
52 Harrison, *The Medical War*, p. 101.
53 Ibid., p. 101.
54 'Memo by Liet.-Col. J.F. Anderson CMG on Messines operations', AWM41 40.
55 MO Circular No. 1, 'Scheme of evacuation of wounded during MAGNUM OPUS', 21 May 1917, war diary, Appendix 3, ADMS 3rd Aust. Div., AWM4 26/20/8.
56 'Memo by Liet.-Col. J.F. Anderson CMG on Messines operations', AWM41 40.
57 Ibid.
58 Ibid.
59 Ibid.
60 Ibid.
61 Surgeon General Sir N.R. Howse, Evidence to DC, q. 27667, TNA, CAB 19/33.
62 Report by Major General Keogh to the Administrative Heads of Medical Services of Dominions, 4 September 1917, AWM25 481/367.
63 Butler, *The Western Front*, p. 823.
64 Report by Major General Keogh to the Administrative Heads of Medical Services of Dominions, 4 September 1917, AWM25 481/367.
65 Ibid.
66 Ibid.

67 The response of the New Zealand and Australian representatives is included in the same archive file at the Australian War Memorial as the memorandum from Keogh; however, any Canadian response that might have been written has not been located.

68 Colonel Parkes, DDMS NZEF to Sir Alfred Keogh, DGAMS War Office, 14 September 1917, AWM25 481/367.

69 General Sir A. Godley, CO NZEF to Surgeon General Sir A. Keogh, DGAMS War Office, 17 September 1917, AWM25 481/367.

70 Surgeon General Sir N.R. Howse, DMS AIF to Surgeon General Sir A. Keogh, DGAMS War Office, 28 September 1917, AWM25 481/367.

71 Ibid.

72 Lieutenant A.H. Moseley, OC 6AFA to Colonel Shepherd, ADMS 2AD, 13 October 1917, war diary, Appendix A, ADMS 2nd Aust. Div., AWM4 26/19/22.

73 'Report on medical aspect of operations extending from 1st October to 18th October 1917', war diary, Appendix 25, DDMS II ANZAC, AWM4 26/16/19.

74 Lieutenant A.H. Moseley, OC 6AFA to Colonel Shepherd, ADMS 2AD, 13 October 1917, war diary, Appendix A, ADMS 2nd Aust. Div., AWM4 26/19/22.

75 Colonel R.B. Huxtable, ADMS 1AD to DDMS I ANZAC, 'Medical arrangements First Australian Division', 28 September 1917, war diary, Appendix 8, ADMS 1st Aust. Div., AWM4 26/18/34.

76 Ibid. Major E.L. Hutchinson, ADMS 2AD 'Forward evacuation of wounded (2nd Australian Divisional Area)', 13 October 1917, war diary, Appendix A, ADMS 2nd Aust. Div., AWM4 26/19/22; ADMS 3AD 'Report on evacuation of wounded from sector held by Third Australian Division during operations 11th to 21st October', 25 October 1917, war diary, Appendix 13, ADMS 3rd Aust. Div., AWM4 26/20/13; Colonel Barber, ADMS 4AD, 'Recommendations', 20 October 1917, war diary, Appendix 17, ADMS 4th Aust. Div., AWM4 26/21/17.

77 Prior and Wilson, *Passchendaele*, p. 195.

78 Major J.B. Metcalfe for Colonel DDMS I ANZAC to DMS Second Army, 23 September 1917, war diary, Appendix, DDMS I ANZAC, AWM4 26/15/21.

79 DMS Second Army to Officers Commanding British 10th and 17th and 2nd and 3rd Canadian Casualty Clearing Stations, 24 September 1917, war diary, Appendix, DDMS I ANZAC, AWM4 26/15/21.

80 Lieutenant Colonel Blanchard, OC 3rd Canadian CCS to DMS Second Army, 25 September 1917, war diary, Appendix, DDMS I ANZAC, AWM4 26/15/21.

81 Lieutenant Colonel Davey, OC 2nd Canadian CCS to DMS Second Army, war diary, Appendix, DDMS I ANZAC, AWM4 26/15/21.

82 Lieutenant Colonel Warmott RAMC, OC 10CCS to DMS Second Army, 25 September 1917, war diary, Appendix, DDMS I ANZAC, AWM4 26/15/21.

Chapter 3 The Western Front in 1918: The AAMC in mobile warfare

1 In April 1917, Harry Chauvel became the first Australian promoted to lieutenant general and the first to command a corps in the war when he was placed in charge of the Desert Mounted Corps in Palestine.

2 Butler, *The Western Front*, p. 604.

3 Harrison, *The Medical War*, p. 87.
4 Surgeon General Sir N.R. Howse to Major General C.B.B. White, 20 July 1917, AWM 2DRL/1351, Item 2.
5 Ibid.
6 Ibid.
7 Before the war, Manifold worked in the Indian Medical Service as Inspector-General, Civil Hospitals.
8 Surgeon General Sir N.R. Howse to Major General C.B.B. White, 20 July 1917, AWM 2DRL/1351, Item 2.
9 George Walter Barber, Attestation Papers, NAA, B2455/BARBER G W/3048743.
10 Colonel C.C. Manifold, war diary, 18 February 1918, DDMS Australian Corps, AWM4 26/17/2.
11 Ibid.
12 Colonel C.C. Manifold, war diary, 10–19 January 1918, DDMS Australian Corps, AWM4 26/17/1.
13 Major Borwick for Brigadier-General, General Staff, Australian Corps, 17 January 1918, war diary, Appendix 3, DDMS Australian Corps, AWM4 26/17/1. For ease of reading, punctuation in the quote has been corrected.
14 Syllabus for Corps School of MOs, No. 2, war diary, Appendix 3, DDMS Australian Corps, AWM4 26/17/1.
15 Colonel A.E. Shepherd, war diary, 21 May 1918, ADMS 2nd Aust. Div., AWM4 26/19/29 Part 1.
16 Colonel C.C. Manifold, war diary, 18 February 1918, DDMS Australian Corps, AWM4 26/17/2.
17 DMS Fifth Army, 'Evacuation from Advanced Dressing Stations', 7 February 1918, AWM27 370/249.
18 Colonel C.C. Manifold, 'Medical arrangements: Issued under Australian Corps Defence Scheme', 14 March 1918, war diary, Appendix 3, DDMS Australian Corps, AWM4 26/17/3.
19 Ibid.
20 Ibid.
21 Ibid.
22 For further discussion of chemical warfare, see Palazzo, *Seeking Victory on the Western Front*.
23 Colonel C.C. Manifold, war diary, 24 March 1918, DDMS Australian Corps, AWM4 26/17/3. For ease of reading, punctuation in the quote has been corrected.
24 Captain K. Rae, RMO 9th Bn, AIF to Adjutant, 9th Bn, AIF, 13 March 1918, war diary, Appendix 32, ADMS 1st Aust. Div., AWM4 26/18/40.
25 Major L. May, RMO 11th Bn, AIF to Colonel Huxtable, ADMS 1AD, 19 March 1918, war diary, Appendix 33, ADMS 1st Aust. Div., AWM4 26/18/40.
26 Ibid.
27 Colonel R.B. Huxtable, 'Scheme for evacuating wounded from 1st Divisional Front by trench tramway', war diary, Appendix 2, ADMS 1st Aust. Div., AWM4 26/18/40.
28 Colonel A.E. Shepherd, 'Defensive scheme of evacuation of sick and wounded for right divisional sector of corps front', war diary, Appendix B, ADMS 2nd Aust. Div., AWM4 26/19/27.

29 Colonel W.H. Downey, 'Medical arrangements in the event of major operations on the divisional front', war diary, Appendix 3, ADMS 5th Aust. Div., AWM4 26/22/26.

30 Colonel F.A. Maguire, war diary, 21 March 1918, ADMS 3rd Aust. Div., AWM4 26/20/18.

31 Field Marshal Sir Douglas Haig, 'Special Order of the Day', 23 March 1918, war diary, Appendix 3, ADMS 3rd Aust. Div., AWM4 26/20/18.

32 Colonel F.A. Maguire, war diary, 21–28 March 1918, ADMS 3rd Aust. Div., AWM4 26/20/18.

33 Colonel G.W. Barber, war diary, 26 March 1918, ADMS 4th Aust. Div., AWM4 26/21/22.

34 Ibid. For ease of reading, punctuation has been corrected.

35 Colonel F.A. Maguire, war diary, 26 March 1918, ADMS 3rd Aust. Div., AWM4 26/20/18.

36 Lieutenant General Sir A.T. Sloggett to DMS Third Army, 2 April 1918, war diary, Appendix 5, ADMS 3rd Aust. Div., AWM4 26/20/19.

37 Ibid.

38 Colonel G.W. Barber, war diary, Appendix 1, 10 April 1918, DDMS Australian Corps, AWM4 26/17/4.

39 Ibid.

40 Ibid.

41 Colonel A.E. Shepherd, 'Emergency measures in necessity of quick evacuation', war diary, Appendix G, ADMS 2nd Aust. Div., AWM4 26/19/28.

42 Colonel W.H. Downey, 'Work of the Main Dressing Station, Period 21.4.1918 to 30.4.1918', war diary, Appendix 54, ADMS 5th Aust. Div., AWM4 26/22/27.

43 Colonel A.E. Shepherd, 'Report concerning high incidence of sickness in battalions during the past fortnight', 11 May 1918, war diary, Appendix E, ADMS 2nd Aust. Div., AWM4 26/19/29 Part 1.

44 Ibid.

45 Colonel R.R. Huxtable, 'Influenza', 21 June 1918, war diary, Appendix 11, ADMS 1st Aust. Div., AWM4 26/18/43 Part 1.

46 Ibid.

47 Major General J.H. Thomson for DGMS British Armies in France, 25 June 1918, war diary, Appendix 15, ADMS 1st Aust. Div., AWM4 26/18/43 Part 1.

48 Ibid.

49 Colonel W.H. Downey, 'ADMS Circular No. 9', war diary, Appendix 22, ADMS 5th Aust. Div., AWM4 26/22/29.

50 Sheffield, *The Chief*, p. 143.

51 Sir Douglas Haig, 19 May 1918, Haig's Diary with supps, vol. XXIX, National Library of Scotland (hereafter NLS), Acc.3155/127.

52 Ibid., 22 May 1918.

53 Ibid., 24 May 1918.

54 Carden-Coyne, *The Politics of Wounds*, p. 92.

55 Ibid., p. 13.

56 Lieutenant Colonel W.E.L.H. Crowther, war diary, 4 July 1918, ADMS 2nd Aust. Div., AWM4 26/19/31 Part 1.

57 Ibid.
58 Lieutenant Colonel R.S. McGregor, 'AAMC narrative of operation of 4th July 1918', 7 July 1918, war diary, Appendix 11A, ADMS 4th Aust. Div., AWM4 26/21/26.
59 Colonel A.E. Shepherd, war diary, 8 August 1918, ADMS 2nd Aust. Div., AWM4 26/19/32 Part 1.
60 Ibid.
61 Ibid., 9 August 1918.
62 Ibid., 6 August 1918.
63 Ibid., 7 August 1918. For ease of reading, the punctuation has been corrected in the quote.
64 Colonel K. Smith, 'Medical Arrangements No. 1', 5 August 1918, war diary, Appendix 9, ADMS 4th Aust. Div., AWM4 26/21/27.
65 Ibid., 28 August 1918.
66 Ibid., 28 August 1918.
67 Colonel K. Smith, 'Medical arrangements 8th – 10th August 1918', 28 August 1918, war diary, Appendix 20, ADMS 4th Aust. Div., AWM4 26/21/27.
68 Colonel G.W. Barber, DDMS Australian Corps to ADsMS of Australian Divisions, 12 August 1918, war diary, Appendix 4, DDMS Australian Corps, AWM4 26/17/8.
69 See chapter 2.
70 Colonel W.H. Downey, ADMS 5AD to DDMS Australian Corps, 9 August 1918, war diary, Appendix 44, DDMS Australian Corps, AWM4 26/17/8.
71 Colonel G.W. Barber, DDMS Australian Corps to ADsMS of Australian Divisions, 12 August 1918, war diary, Appendix 4, DDMS Australian Corps, AWM4 26/17/8.
72 Colonel A.E. Shepherd, Memorandum to Divisional Headquarters, 5 September 1918, war diary, Appendix Z3, ADMS 2nd Aust. Div., AWM4 26/19/32 Part 2.
73 Ibid.
74 Ibid.
75 Ibid.
76 Colonel W.H. Downey, 'Report on medical arrangements for operation on 27, 28, 29 and 30 August 1918', 2 September 1918, war diary, Appendix 37, ADMS 5th Aust. Div., AWM4 26/22/31 Part 2.
77 Colonel G.W. Barber, war diary, 18, 29–30 September 1918, DDMS Australian Corps, AWM4 26/17/9; Colonel G.W. Barber, war diary, 4–6 October 1918, DDMS Australian Corps, AWM4 26/17/10.
78 Colonel W.H. Downey, ADMS 5AD to DDMS Australian Corps, 18 May 1918, war diary, Appendix 15, ADMS 5th Aust. Div., AWM4 26/22/28.
79 Ibid.
80 Lieutenant Colonel C.W. Thompson, CO 14AFA, 'Report on operative work performed at the 5th Australian Divisional Main Dressing Station in DAOURS for Period 5th May 1918 to 19th May 1918', 30 May 1918, war diary, Appendix 15, ADMS 5th Aust. Div., AWM4 26/22/28.
81 Ibid.

82 Colonel W.H. Downey, ADMS 5AD to Colonel G.W. Barber, DDMS Australian Corps, 18 May 1918, war diary, Appendix 15, ADMS 5th Aust. Div., AWM4 26/22/28.

83 Ibid.

84 Colonel G.W. Barber, DDMS Australian Corps to Major General W.W. O'Keefe, DMS Fourth Army, 21 May 1918, war diary, Appendix 15, ADMS 5th Aust. Div., AWM4 26/22/28.

85 Major General W.W. O'Keefe, DMS Fourth Army, to Colonel G.W. Barber, DDMS Australian Corps, 24 May 1918, war diary, Appendix 15, ADMS 5th Aust. Div., AWM4 26/22/28.

86 Ibid.

87 Ibid.

88 Colonel G.W. Barber, DDMS Australian Corps, to Colonel W.H. Downey, ADMS 5AD, 25 May 1918, war diary, Appendix 15, ADMS 5th Aust. Div., AWM4 26/22/28.

89 Colonel W.H. Downey, ADMS 5AD to Headquarters, 5AD, 27 May 1918, war diary, Appendix 15, ADMS 5th Aust. Div., AWM4 26/22/28.

90 Ibid.

91 Lieutenant Colonel R.S. McGregor, 'AAMC narrative of operation of 4th July 1918', 7 July 1918, war diary, Appendix 11A, ADMS 4th Aust. Div., AWM4 26/21/26.

92 Alan Worsley Holmes à Court, NAA, B2455/HOLMES-A-COURT AW MAJOR/5823194.

93 Lieutenant Colonel R.S. McGregor, 'AAMC narrative of operation of 4th July 1918', 7 July 1918, war diary, Appendix 11A, ADMS 4th Aust. Div., AWM4 26/21/26.

94 Ibid.

95 Colonel G.W. Barber, war diary, 4 July 1918, DDMS Australian Corps, AWM4 26/17/7.

96 Ibid., 17 July 1918.

97 Colonel K. Smith, '4th Australian Division Medical Arrangements No. 1', 5 August 1918, war diary, Appendix 9, ADMS 4AD, AWM4 26/21/27.

98 Major A.W. Holmes à Court, 'Report of Surgical Resuscitation Team', Appendix 6E, DDMS Australian Corps, AWM4 26/17/8.

99 Ibid.

100 Colonel G.W. Barber, DDMS Australian Corps to DMS Fourth Army, 21 August 1918, war diary, Appendix 6, DDMS Australian Corps, AWM4 26/17/8.

101 Colonel G.W. Barber, DDMS Australian Corps, 'Memo on establishment and equipment for Divisional Resuscitation Teams in Australian Corps', 21 August 1918, war diary, Appendix 6, DDMS Australian Corps, AWM4 26/17/8.

102 Colonel G.W. Barber, DDMS Australian Corps, war diary, 14 October 1918, DDMS Australian Corps, AWM4 26/17/10.

103 Resuscitation Teams Committee, 'Australian Corps: Divisional Resuscitation Teams', war diary, Appendix 2, DDMS Australian Corps, AWM4 26/17/10.

104 Major G. Gordon-Taylor, Consulting Surgeon Fourth Army, 'Report of Consulting Surgeon Fourth Army', war diary, Appendix 2, DDMS Australian Corps, AWM4 26/17/10.
105 Colonel G.W. Barber, DDMS Australian Corps, 'Australian Corps: Medical Instructions – Routine No. 17', 19 October 1918, war diary, Appendix 2, DDMS Australian Corps, AWM4 26/17/10.
106 Alan Worsley Holmes à Court, NAA, B2455/HOLMES-A-COURT AW MAJOR/5823194.

Chapter 4 A pleasant dose of medicine? The purpose, place and practice of auxiliary hospitals

1 'Hospital Rules', *Boomerang* 1, no. 8, 1917, p. 4.
2 Garton, *The Cost of War*; Larsson, 'Restoring the spirit', pp. 45–59; Larsson, 'Families and institutions for shell-shocked soldiers in Australia after the First World War', pp. 97–114; Larsson, 'Who picks up the pieces?', p. 25; Larsson, *Shattered ANZACs*.
3 Koven, 'Remembering and dismemberment', p. 1167; Bourke, *Dismembering the Male*; Kowalsky, '"This honourable obligation"', pp. 567–84; Anderson, *Soul of a Nation*.
4 Noonan, *Those We Forget*, p. 130.
5 Reznick, *Healing the Nation*, p. 137.
6 Carden-Coyne, *The Politics of Wounds*, p. 13.
7 Ibid., p. 13.
8 Ibid., p. 10; Porter, 'The patient's view', pp. 175–98.
9 Meyer, *Men of War*; Bourke, *Dismembering the Male*; Carden-Coyne, *The Politics of Wounds*; Gagen, 'Remastering the body, renegotiating gender', pp. 525–41.
10 Meyer, *An Equal Burden*.
11 War diary, 28 October 1917, 1AAH Harefield Park, AWM4 26/72/1.
12 Blackmore, *The Dark Pocket of Time*, p. 87.
13 Ibid., pp. 132–5. For a discussion of this tension regarding war neuroses, see Leed, *No Man's Land*.
14 For a discussion of the redeployment of rehabilitated soldiers as orderlies in the RAMC, see Meyer, *An Equal Burden*; for a discussion of the work and responsibilities of stretcher-bearers, see Johnston, *Stretcher-bearers*.
15 Surgeon General Neville Howse, 7 February 1918, war diary, Appendix 4, 1AAH, Harefield, AWM4 26/72/6.
16 Harrison, *The Medical War*, pp. 61–2.
17 Butler, *The Western Front*, p. 427.
18 Colonel W.T. Hayward, Report on 1AAH, Harefield Park, AWM16 4364/22/1.
19 Ibid.
20 Ibid.
21 War diary, 10 July 1917, 3AAH Dartford, AWM4 26/74/2.
22 Ibid.
23 Lieutenant Colonel Bertram Milne Sutherland, CO 3AAH, to General Sir Neville Howse, DMS AIF, 12 July 1917, war diary, Appendix 1, 3AAH, Dartford, AWM4 26/74/2.

24 Ibid.

25 Ibid.

26 Thomas Griffiths, NAA, B2455/GRIFFITHS T/4703497.

27 Colonel Thomas Griffiths to Lieutenant Colonel Bertram Milne Sutherland, 14 July 1917, war diary, Appendix 1, 3AAH, Dartford, AWM4 26/74/2.

28 Ibid.

29 Lieutenant Colonel Yeatman, war diary, Appendix, 23 January 1917, 1AAH, Harefield, AWM4 26/72/1.

30 Lieutenant Colonel Yeatman to Surgeon General Howse, 4 January 1918, war diary, Appendix 1, 1AAH, Harefield, AWM4 26/72/5.

31 Lieutenant Colonel Yeatman to Surgeon General Howse, 4 April 1918, war diary, Appendix 2, 1AAH, Harefield, AWM4 26/72/7.

32 'Extract from No. 1 AAH Routine Orders No. 151 of 1/5/18 – General instructions in respect to the duties of a VAD ward orderly', war diary, Appendix 2, 1AAH, Harefield, AWM4 26/72/10.

33 Lieutenant Colonel Yeatman to Surgeon General Howse, 30 September 1918, war diary, Appendix 10, 1AAH, Harefield, AWM4 26/72/13.

34 Ibid.

35 Reznick, *Healing the Nation*, p. 140.

36 Harrison, *The Medical War*, p. 12.

37 Colonel Yeatman, war diary, ../1/1916 [*sic*], 1AAH, Harefield, AWM4 26/72/1 [date as indicated in file].

38 For a discussion of the dual nature of these spaces and the role of romance and flirtation, see Carden-Coyne, *The Politics of Wounds*, pp. 11–12.

39 Lyon Taemer, 'Hospital-ities', *Boomerang* 2, no. 8, 1918, p. 149.

40 'A wedding', *Boomerang* 1, no. 15, 1917, p. 7.

41 Lyon Taemer, 'Hospital-ities', *Boomerang* 2, no. 6, 1918, p. 97.

42 VAD, 'Why women remain single', *Boomerang* 2, no. 7, 1918, p. 130.

43 Ibid., p. 130.

44 Ibid., p. 130.

45 Major J.A. Smeal, 'Statistical report of work carried on during 1916', 1 March 1917, war diary, Appendix 3, 1AAH, Harefield, AWM4 26/72/1.

46 Ibid.

47 Ibid.

48 Lieutenant Colonel Yeatman to Surgeon General Howse, 8 February 1918, war diary, Appendix 3, 1AAH, Harefield, AWM4 26/72/6.

49 Ibid.

50 Ibid., 4 February 1918.

51 Lieutenant Colonel Yeatman to Surgeon General Howse, 8 October 1918, war diary, Appendix 2, 1AAH, Harefield, AWM4 26/72/13.

52 'Clinical meetings of medical staff', 2 March 1918, war diary, Appendix 1, 1AAH, Harefield, AWM4 26/72/6.

53 Ibid. 'Shellies' was a term of endearment used in the *Boomerang* to refer to patients with shell shock. See for example 'Reminiscences and curiosities', *Boomerang* 2, no. 10, 1918, p. 185.

54 McMeeken, 'Australian physiotherapists in the First World War', p. 54.

55 Ibid., p. 56.

56 Egan, '"Nobler than missionaries"', p. 212.
57 Smeal, 'Statistical report of work carried on during 1916', 1 March 1917.
58 McMeeken, 'Australian physiotherapists in the First World War', p. 56.
59 Ibid., pp. 56–7.
60 Lieutenant Colonel Yeatman to Surgeon General Howse, 7 January 1918, war diary, Appendix 3, 1AAH, Harefield, AWM4 26/72/5.
61 Lieutenant Colonel Dennis to Lieutenant Colonel Yeatman, 2 September 1918, 'Monthly report – Massage Department', August 1918, war diary, 1AAH, Harefield, AWM4 26/72/12.
62 McMeeken, 'Australian physiotherapists in the First World War', p. 59.
63 Watson, 'Wars in the wards', pp. 484–510; Fell and Hallett, *First World War Nursing*; Tyquin, 'Doctors and nurses', pp. 26–43; Harris, *More than Bombs and Bandages*; Hallett, *Containing Trauma*.
64 Carden-Coyne, *The Politics of Wounds*, p. 12; Carden-Coyne, 'Painful bodies and brutal women', pp. 139–58.
65 NAA, B2455/JENNINGS MARY JOSEPHINE/7369487.
66 Lieutenant Colonel C.E. Dennis, 'A simple splint for facial paralysis', 3 July 1918, war diary, Appendix P1, 1AAH, Harefield, AWM4 26/72/10.
67 Ibid.
68 Ibid.
69 'Record of work done by the Recreation & Canteen Department, 1st AAH, Harefield, from 1st June to end of December 1917', war diary, enclosed reports, 1AAH, Harefield, AWM4 26/72/5.
70 Ibid.
71 'Fancy Work', war diary, enclosed reports, 1AAH, Harefield, AWM4 26/72/5.
72 Carden-Coyne, 'Ungrateful bodies', p. 548; Carden-Coyne, *The Politics of Wounds*, pp. 264–9.
73 Carden-Coyne, *The Politics of Wounds*, p. 265.
74 Ibid., pp. 265–6.
75 Carden-Coyne, 'Ungrateful bodies'; Carden-Coyne, 'Painful bodies and brutal women'.
76 'Fancy Work', war diary, enclosed reports, 1AAH, Harefield, AWM4 26/72/5.
77 Ibid.
78 Ibid.
79 Carden-Coyne, *The Politics of Wounds*.
80 Reznick, *Healing the Nation*.

Chapter 5 The most difficult problem: Preventing and treating venereal disease

1 Butler, *Gallipoli, Palestine and New Guinea*, pp. 34, 76.
2 Ibid., p. 77.
3 Ibid., p. 188.
4 Ibid., p. 74.
5 Walter H. Long, President, Local Government Board, to Governor-General of Australia, Sir Ronald Munro Ferguson, 19 October 1917, NAA, A11803 1917/89/1026. The overall rate of infection is disputed, however, as is whether Australia was the worst or merely one of the worst offenders.

6 Stanley, *Bad Characters*, p. 228.
7 Noonan, *Those We Forget*, pp. 64–5, 132.
8 Ibid., p. 132.
9 Ibid., p. 134.
10 Butler, *Problems and Services*, p. 156.
11 Harrison, *The Medical War*, p. 156.
12 Hall, '"War always brings it on"'.
13 Featherstone, *Let's Talk about Sex* , pp. 8–9.
14 Ibid., p. 95.
15 Ibid., p. 3.
16 See for example Levine, *Prostitution, Race, and Politics*; Levine, 'Battle colors', pp. 104–30; Smart, 'Sex, the State and the "scarlet scourge"', pp. 5–36; Tisdale, 'Venereal disease and the policing of the amateur in Melbourne during World War I', pp. 33–54.
17 Gibson, 'Sex and soldiering in France and Flanders', pp. 535–79; Beardsley, 'Allied against sin', pp. 189–202; Rhoades, 'Renegotiating French masculinity', pp. 293–327; Kampf, 'Controlling male sexuality', pp. 235–58.
18 Smart, 'Sex, the State and the "scarlet scourge"', p. 23.
19 Harrison, 'The British Army and the problem of venereal disease', pp. 133–58; Harrison, *The Medical War*.
20 Harrison, 'The British Army and the problem of venereal disease', p. 134.
21 Ibid., p. 156.
22 Gurner, 'Butler, Arthur Graham (1872–1949)'.
23 Dunbar, *The Secrets of the Anzacs*.
24 Stanley, *Bad Characters*, p. 36.
25 'Notes by Major B.T. Zwar (No. 2 Australian Stationary Hospital) upon Venereal Disease in Egypt', AWM25 267/26.
26 Ibid.
27 Butler, *Gallipoli, Palestine and New Guinea*, p. 77.
28 Colonel N. Manders, 'Hints on health in Egypt', 1915, AWM27 376/40.
29 Featherstone, *Let's Talk about Sex*, p. 95.
30 Butler, *Gallipoli, Palestine and New Guinea*, p. 77.
31 Harrison, *The Medical War*, p. 156.
32 Minutes from Conference of Medical Officers, 17 February 1915, AWM27 376/201.
33 Ibid.
34 Ibid.
35 Ibid.
36 Ibid.
37 Ibid.
38 Ibid.
39 Ibid.
40 Blackmore, *The Dark Pocket of Time*, p. 91.
41 Surgeon General N.R. Howse to Lieutenant General Sir W. Birdwood, 7 March 1916, NAA, CP359/2 17.
42 Colonel R.M.M. Anderson to Hon. W.M. Hughes, MP, 23 February 1916, NAA, CP359/2 17.

43 Miss E.A. Rout to Colonel Rhodes, 12 March 1916, NAA, CP359/2 17.
44 Ibid.
45 W.H. George to Colonel R.M.M. Anderson, 14 March 1916, NAA, CP359/2 17.
46 'Addenda to CM Form A22', NAA, B2455 RAFFAN GEORGE/8023997.
47 Major G. Raffan to Surgeon General Sir N.R. Howse, 'The incidence of venereal disease in the AIF', 18 October 1916, AWM27 376/170.
48 Ibid.
49 Ibid.
50 Featherstone, *Let's Talk about Sex*, p. 11.
51 Raffan, 'The incidence of venereal disease in the AIF'.
52 Ibid.
53 Featherstone, *Let's Talk about Sex*, p. 47.
54 Raffan, 'The incidence of venereal disease in the AIF'.
55 Ibid.
56 Ibid.
57 Major G. Raffan to Surgeon General Sir N.R. Howse, 30 October 1916, AWM15 14379/7.
58 Major G. Raffan to Colonel D.M. McWhae, 25 February 1917, AWM15 14379/7.
59 Colonel D.M. McWhae to Surgeon General Sir N.R. Howse, 27 February 1917, AWM15 14379/7.
60 Major G. Raffan, 'Suggested reform in the management of the venereal disease problem', 30 October 1916, AWM15 14379/7 (hereafter Raffan, 'Suggested reform').
61 Ibid. Emphasis in original.
62 Ibid.
63 Ibid. Emphasis in original.
64 Ibid. Emphasis in original.
65 Ibid. Emphasis in original.
66 Colonel D.M. McWhae to Surgeon General Sir N.R. Howse, 27 February 1917, AWM15 14379/7.
67 Stanley, *Bad Characters*.
68 Raffan, 'Suggested reform'.
69 Ibid.
70 Colonel D.M. McWhae to Surgeon General Sir N.R. Howse, 27 February 1917, AWM15 14379/7.
71 Raffan, 'Suggested reform'.
72 Colonel D.M. McWhae to Surgeon General Sir N.R. Howse, 27 February 1917, AWM15 14379/7.
73 Major G. Raffan, 'Incidence of venereal disease amongst men on furlough from Australian auxiliary and British hospitals', 30 March 1917, AWM15 14379/7.
74 Ibid.
75 Ibid. Punctuation has been altered for ease of reading.
76 Ibid.
77 Ibid.

78 Colonel D.M. McWhae to SMO Hurdcott, Codford, Lark Hill, No. 1, 2, 3, 4, Cmd Depots, Park House, 27 March 1917, AWM15 14379/7.

79 'Early treatment and VD report', AIF Form 587/AMC Form 4, AWM27 376/157 PART 2.

80 Colonel D.M. McWhae ADMS AIF, Tidworth to OC AAMC Training Depot, Parkhouse, 16 June 1917, AWM15 14379/7.

81 Ibid.

82 Ibid., 23 April 1917.

83 Colonel D.M. McWhae ADMS AIF, Tidworth to SMO No. 1 Command Depot, Parham Down, 16 June 1917, AWM15 14379/7.

84 Major G. Raffan, 'Instructions to medical officers', 10 February 1917, AWM27 376/193 (hereafter Raffan, 'Instructions to medical officers').

85 Lieutenant Colonel G. Raffan, 'Instructions to medical officers regarding the prevention of venereal disease', 16 September 1918, AWM27 376/157 PART 2 (hereafter Raffan, 'Prevention of venereal disease').

86 Raffan, 'Instructions to medical officers'.

87 Ibid.

88 George Raffan, NAA, B2455 RAFFAN GEORGE/8023997.

89 Raffan, 'Prevention of venereal disease'.

90 Raffan, 'Instructions to medical officers'. Emphasis in original.

91 Ibid.

92 Raffan, 'Prevention of venereal disease'.

93 Raffan, 'Instructions to medical officers'.

94 Raffan, 'Prevention of venereal disease'.

95 Raffan, 'Instructions to medical officers'.

96 Raffan, 'Prevention of venereal disease'.

97 Ibid.

98 Ibid.

99 Ibid.

100 Ibid.

101 Ibid.

102 Ibid.

103 Ibid.

104 Major G. Raffan, 'Instructions to medical officers', 10 February 1917, AWM27 376/193.

105 Raffan, 'Prevention of venereal disease'.

106 Harrison, The Medical War, p. 155; Kampf, 'Controlling male sexuality', p. 236.

107 Raffan, 'Prevention of venereal disease'.

108 Ibid.

109 Major G. Raffan, 'Lecture to be delivered by RMOs concerning the prevention of venereal disease', 10 February 1917, AWM27 376/193.

110 Ibid.

111 Sendziuk, Learning to Trust, p. 27.

112 Featherstone, Let's Talk about Sex, pp. 49, 50.

113 White Cross League, True Manliness, White Cross League, Westminster, 1913, p. 31, Wellcome Library (hereafter WL), SA/BSH/L.4, p. 32.

114 Lieutenant Colonel G. Raffan, 'Lecture to be delivered by medical officers concerning the prevention of venereal disease', 16 September 1918, AWM27 376/157 PART 2.

115 National Council for Combating Venereal Diseases (hereafter NCCVD), *The Speakers' Handbook: Compiled for the Use of Lecturers Representing the National Council for Combating Venereal Diseases*, NCCVD, London, 1917, p. 18, WL: SA/BSH/L.1.

116 NCCVD, *The Deadly Peril of Venereal Diseases*, NCCVD, London, 1917, p. 5, WL: SA/BSH/L.1.

117 White Cross League, *A Paper for Men*, White Cross League, Westminster, p. 7, WL SA/BSH/L.4.

118 Harrison, *The Medical War*, p. 169.

119 Raffan, 'Lecture to be delivered by medical officers concerning the prevention of venereal disease'.

120 Harrison, *The Medical War*, p. 158.

121 Blackmore, *The Dark Pocket of Time*, p. 145.

122 Raffan, 'Lecture to be delivered by medical officers concerning the prevention of venereal disease'.

123 Lieutenant Colonel G. Raffan, 'Table showing the percentage of venereal disease from 18/1/17 until 7/3/18', AWM27 376/157 PART2.

124 Stanley, *Bad Characters*.

125 Raffan, 'Table showing the percentage of venereal disease from 18/1/17 until 7/3/18'.

126 Bourke, *Dismembering the Male*, p. 156.

127 Featherstone, *Let's Talk about Sex*, p. 104.

128 Foucault, *The History of Sexuality*, vol. 1, pp. 61–2.

129 Ibid., p. 62.

Conclusion: Developing an Australian medical service

1 Reznick, *Healing the Nation*.

2 Harrison, *The Medical War*, p. 120; Sheffield, *The Chief*.

3 Surgeon General Sir N.R. Howse, Evidence to Dardanelles Commission, q. 27676, TNA, CAB 19/33.

4 Surgeon General Sir N.R. Howse to Major General C.B.B. White, 20 July 1917, AWM, 2DRL/1351, Item 2.

5 Delaney, *The Imperial Army Project*.

6 Noonan, *Those We Forget*; Butler, *Gallipoli, Palestine and New Guinea*; Butler, *The Western Front*; Butler, *Problems and Services*.

7 Harrison, *The Medical War*.

8 See for example Fell and Hallett, *First World War Nursing*; Hallett, *Veiled Warriors*; Hallett, *Containing Trauma*.

BIBLIOGRAPHY

PRIMARY SOURCES
Australian War Memorial, Canberra
War diaries
AWM4 1/4 MEF
AWM4 1/50 5AD
AWM4 26/3 DDMS MEF
AWM4 26/15 DDMS 1ANZAC
AWM4 26/17 DDMS Australian Corps
AWM4 26/18 ADMS 1AD
AWM4 26/19 ADMS 2AD
AWM4 26/20 ADMS 3AD
AWM4 26/21 ADMS 4AD
AWM4 26/22 ADMS 5AD
AWM4 26/44 1AFA
AWM4 26/46 3AFA
AWM4 26/51 8AFA
AWM4 26/57 14AFA
AWM4 26/58 15AFA
AWM4 26/72 1AAH Harefield
AWM4 26/74 3AAH Dartford

Official records
AWM15
AWM16
AWM25
AWM27
AWM41

Other records
2DRL/1351 Personal Papers of Neville Howse
AWM081392 TROOPSHIP SERIAL/The Harefield Park Boomerang
REL25365 RSPCA Purple Cross and certificate of award to Simpson's donkey, Murphy
REL30298 – Rehabilitation Embroidery: Private A.S. Smart, 19 Battalion, AIF

National Archives of Australia, Canberra
A11803 – Governor Generals correspondence relating to the war of 1914–1918
CP359 – Personal Papers of Prime Minister Hughes

Personnel files
B2455/ANDERSON J H/1977480
B2455/BARBER GW/3048743
B2455/GRIFFITHS T/4703497
B2455/HOLMES-A-COURT AW MAJOR/5823194
B2455/JENNINGS MARY JOSEPHINE/369487
B2455/RAFFAN GEORGE/8023997
B2455/SMART ALFRED SAMUEL/8086584
B2455/STURDEE ALFRED HOBART/8095724

The National Archives, UK
CAB 19 – Special Commissions to Enquire into the Operations of War in Meso-
potamia (Hamilton Commission) and in the Dardanelles (Cromer and Pickford
Commission): Records

Liddell Hart Centre for Military Archives, King's College London
Hamilton Papers

Wellcome Library, London
Papers of the British Social Hygiene Council

National Library of Scotland, Edinburgh
Haig Papers

SECONDARY SOURCES

Anderson, J., *Soul of a Nation: War, Disability and Rehabilitation in Britain*, Manchester University Press, Manchester, 2011
Barrett, J., *A Vision of the Possible: What the RAMC Might Become*, H.K. Lewis, London, 1919
Barrett, J., and P.E. Deane, *The Australian Army Medical Corps in Egypt during the First World War*, Leonaur, 2013
Bean, C.E.W., *The Official History of Australia in the War of 1914–1918*, vol. 3: *The Australian Imperial Force in France, 1916*, Angus & Robertson, Sydney, 12th edn, 1941
——*Two Men I Knew: William Bridges and Brudenell White, Founders of the AIF*, Angus & Robertson, Sydney, 1957
Beardsley, E.H., 'Allied against sin: American and British responses to venereal disease in World War I', *Medical History* 20, no. 2, 1976, pp. 189–202
Benson, C.I., *The Man with the Donkey: John Simpson Kirkpatrick, the Good Samaritan of Gallipoli*, Hodder & Stoughton, London, 1965
Blackmore, K., *The Dark Pocket of Time: War, Medicine and the Australian State, 1914–1935*, Lythrum Press, Adelaide, 2008

Bongiorno, F., *The Sex Lives of Australians: A History*, Black Inc., Melbourne, 2012

Bourke, J., *Dismembering the Male: Men's Bodies, Britain and the Great War*, Reaktion Books, London, 1996

Braga, S., *ANZAC Doctor: The Life of Sir Neville Howse, Australia's First VC*, Hale & Iremonger, Sydney, 2000

Bridge, C., and K. Fedorowich, *The British World: Diaspora, Culture, and Identity*, Frank Cass, London, 2003

——(eds), 'Mapping the British World', *Journal of Imperial and Commonwealth History* 31, no. 2, 2003, pp. 1–15. doi:10.1080/03086530310001705576

Bright, R.K., and A.R. Dilley, 'After the British World', *Historical Journal* 60, no. 2, 201, pp. 547–68. doi:10.1017/S0018246X16000510

Buley, E.C., *Glorious Deeds of Australasians in the Great War*, Andrew Melrose, London, 1916

Butler, A.G., *The Australian Army Medical Services in the War of 1914–1918: Gallipoli, Palestine and New Guinea*, vol. 1, Australian War Memorial, Melbourne, 2nd edn, 1938

——*The Australian Army Medical Services in the War of 1914–1918: The Western Front*, vol. 2, Australian War Memorial, Canberra, 1940

——*The Australian Army Medical Services in the War of 1914–1918: Problems and Services*, vol. 3, Australian War Memorial, Canberra, 1943

Carden-Coyne, A., 'Ungrateful bodies: Rehabilitation, resistance and disabled American veterans of the First World War', *European Review of History: Revue européenne d'histoire* 14, no. 4, 2007, pp. 543–65

——'Painful bodies and brutal women: Remedial massage, gender relations and cultural agency in military hospitals, 1914–18', *Journal of War and Culture Studies* 1, no. 2, 2008, pp. 139–58

——*The Politics of Wounds: Military Patients and Medical Power in the First World War*, Oxford University Press, Oxford, 2014

Cochrane, P., *Simpson and the Donkey: The Making of a Legend*, Melbourne University Press, Melbourne, 1992

Condé, A.-M., 'Imagining a collection: Creating Australia's records of war', *ReCollections: Journal of the National Museum of Australia* 2, no. 1, 2007, pp. 25–36

Connor, J., *Anzac and Empire: George Foster Pearce and the Foundations of Australian Defence*, Cambridge University Press, Melbourne, 2011

Cooter, R., and S. Sturdy, 'Of war, medicine and modernity: Introduction', in *War, Medicine and Modernity*, ed. R. Cooter, M. Harrison and S. Sturdy, Sutton, Stroud, 1999

Crawley, R., *Climax at Gallipoli: The Failure of the August Offensive*, University of Oklahoma Press, Norman, 2014

Crawley, R., and M. LoCicero, *Gallipoli: New Perspectives on the Mediterranean Expeditionary Force, 1915–16*, Helion, Warwick, 2018

Curran, T., *Across the Bar: The Story of 'Simpson', the Man with the Donkey: Australia and Tyneside's Great Military Hero*, Ogmios Publications, Brisbane, 1994

——*Not Only a Hero: An Illustrated Life of Simpson, the Man with the Donkey*, Anzac Day Commemoration Committee (Queensland), Brisbane, 1998

Dardanelles Commission, *First Report of the Dardanelles Commission*, London, 1918

———*Final Report of the Dardanelles Commission*, London, 1919

Delaney, D.E., *The Imperial Army Project: Britain and the Land Forces of the Dominions and India, 1902–1945*, Oxford University Press, Oxford, 2017

Dunbar, R., *The Secrets of the Anzacs: The Untold Story of Venereal Disease in the Australian Army, 1914–1919*, Scribe, Melbourne, 2014

Egan, B., '"Nobler than missionaries": Australian medical culture 1880–1930', PhD thesis, Monash University, 1988

Falls, C., *Military Operations, France and Belgium, 1917*, vol. 1, Macmillan, London, 1940

Featherstone, L., *Let's Talk about Sex: Histories of Sexuality in Australia from Federation to the Pill*, Cambridge Scholars Publishing, Newcastle upon Tyne, 2011

Fedorowich, K., 'Restocking the British world: Empire migration and Anglo-Canadian relations, 1919–30', *Britain and the World* 9, no. 2, 2016, pp. 236–69

Fedorowich, K., and A.S. Thompson (eds), *Empire, Migration and Identity in the British World*, Manchester University Press, Manchester, 2013

Fell, A.S., and C.E. Hallett (eds), *First World War Nursing: New Perspectives*, Routledge, New York, 2013

Foucault, M., *The History of Sexuality*, vol. 1, Penguin Books, Melbourne, 2008

Fox, A., *Learning to Fight: Military Innovation and Change in the British Army, 1914–1918*, Cambridge University Press, Cambridge, 2018

Fox-Godden, A., '"Putting knowledge in power": Learning and innovation in the British Army of the First World War', PhD thesis, University of Birmingham, 2015

French, J., *The Donkey Who Carried the Wounded*, HarperCollins Australia, Sydney, 2010

Gagen, W.J., 'Remastering the body, renegotiating gender: Physical disability and masculinity during the First World War, the case of J.B. Middlebrook', *European Review of History: Revue Européenne d'histoire* 14, no. 4, 2007, pp. 525–41. doi:10.1080/13507480701752169

Garton, S., *The Cost of War: Australians Return*, Oxford University Press, Melbourne, 1996

Gibson, K.C., 'Sex and soldiering in France and Flanders: The British Expeditionary Force along the Western Front, 1914–1919', *International History Review* 23, no. 3, 2001, pp. 535–79

Greenwood, M., *Simpson and His Donkey*, Walker Books, Sydney, 2008

Gurner, C.M., 'Butler, Arthur Graham (1872–1949)', *Australian Dictionary of Biography*, National Centre of Biography, Australian National University, Canberra (retrieved 7 July 2016), adb.anu.edu.au/biography/butler-arthur-graham-5444

Hall, L.A., '"War always brings it on": War, STDs, the military, and the civilian population in Britain, 1850–1950', in *Medicine and Modern Warfare*, ed. R. Cooter, M. Harrison and S. Sturdy, Editions Rodopi, Amsterdam, 1999

Hallett, C.E., *Containing Trauma: Nursing Work in the First World War*, Manchester University Press, Manchester, 2009

——*Veiled Warriors: Allied Nurses of the First World War*, Oxford University Press, Oxford, 2014

Hampton, M., *Attack on the Somme: 1st Anzac Corps and the Battle of Pozières Ridge, 1916*, Helion, Solihull, 2016

Harris, K., *More than Bombs and Bandages: Australian Army Nurses at Work in World War I*, Big Sky Publishing, Sydney, 2011

Harrison, M., 'The British Army and the problem of venereal disease in France and Egypt during the First World War', *Medical History* 39, no. 02, 1995, pp. 133–58

——'The medicalization of war – The militarization of medicine', *Social History of Medicine* 9, no. 2, 1996, pp. 267–76

——'Medicine and the management of modern warfare: An introduction', in *Medicine and Modern Warfare*, ed. R. Cooter, M. Harrison and S. Sturdy, Editions Rodopi, Atlanta, 2004

——*The Medical War: British Military Medicine in the First World War*, Oxford University Press, Oxford, 2010

Holbrook, C., *Anzac, the Unauthorised Biography*, NewSouth Publishing, Sydney, 2014

Johnston, M., *Stretcher-bearers: Saving Australians from Gallipoli to Kokoda*, Cambridge University Press, Melbourne, 2015

Kampf, A., 'Controlling male sexuality: Combating venereal disease in the New Zealand military during two world wars', *Journal of the History of Sexuality* 17, no. 2, 2008, pp. 235–58

Koven, S., 'Remembering and dismemberment: Crippled children, wounded soldiers, and the Great War in Great Britain', *American Historical Review* 99, no. 4, 1994, pp. 1167–1202

Kowalsky, M., '"This honourable obligation": The King's National Roll Scheme for Disabled Ex-Servicemen 1915–1944', *European Review of History: Revue européenne d'histoire* 14, no. 4, 2007, pp. 567–84

Larsson, M., 'Restoring the spirit: The rehabilitation of disabled soldiers in Australia after the Great War', *Health and History* 6, no. 2, 2004, pp. 45–59

——'Families and institutions for shell-shocked soldiers in Australia after the First World War', *Social History of Medicine* 22, no. 1, 2009, pp. 97–114

——*Shattered ANZACs: Living with the Scars of War*, UNSW Press, Sydney, 2009

——'Who picks up the pieces?', *Melbourne Historical Journal*, no. 37, 2009, pp. 25–32

Lee, J., *A Soldier's Life: General Sir Ian Hamilton 1853–1947*, Macmillan, Basingstoke, 2000

Leed, E.J., *No Man's Land: Combat and Identity in World War I*, Cambridge University Press, Cambridge, 1979

Levine, P., 'Battle colors: Race, sex, and colonial soldiery in World War I', *Journal of Women's History* 9, no. 4, 1998, pp. 104–30

——*Prostitution, Race, and Politics: Policing Venereal Disease in the British Empire*, Routledge, New York, 2003

Macleod, J., 'General Sir Ian Hamilton and the Dardanelles Commission', *War in History* 8, no. 4, 2001, pp. 418–41

——Gallipoli: Great Battles, Oxford University Press, Oxford, 2015

Markovich, L., '"No time for tears for the dying": Stretcher-bearers on the Western Front, 1914–1918', PhD thesis, UNSW Canberra, 2015

McMeeken, J., 'Australian physiotherapists in the First World War', Health and History 17, no. 2, 2015, pp. 52–75

Meaney, N., 'Britishness and Australia: Some reflections', Journal of Imperial and Commonwealth History 31, no. 2, 2003, pp. 121–35. doi:10.1080 /03086530310001705636

Meyer, J., Men of War: Masculinity and the First World War in Britain, Palgrave Macmillan, Basingstoke, 2011

——An Equal Burden: The Men of the Royal Army Medical Corps in the First World War, Oxford University Press, Oxford, 2019

Murdoch, W., Neville Howse VC: Soldier, Surgeon & Citizen: A Biography of Major-General Sir Neville Howse VC, KCB, KCMG, KStJ, Amphion Press, Brisbane, 1997

Neuhaus, S.J., and S. Mascall-Dare, Not for Glory: A Centenary of Service by Medical Women to the Australian Army and Its Allies, Boolarong Press, Brisbane, 2014

Noonan, D., Those We Forget: Recounting Australian Casualties of the First World War, Melbourne University Press, Melbourne, 2014

Palazzo, A., Seeking Victory on the Western Front: The British Army and Chemical Warfare in World War I, University of Nebraska Press, Lincoln, 2000

Porter, R., 'The patient's view: Doing medical history from below', Theory and Society, vol. 14, no. 2, 1985, pp. 175–98

Prior, R., Gallipoli: The End of the Myth, UNSW Press, Sydney, 2009

Prior, R., and T. Wilson, Passchendaele: The Untold Story, Scribe, Melbourne, 2002

——The Somme, Yale University Press, New Haven, 2006

Reid, F., Medicine in First World War Europe: Soldiers, Medics, Pacifists, Bloomsbury Academic, London, 2017

Reznick, J.S., Healing the Nation: Soldiers and the Culture of Caregiving in Britain during the Great War, Manchester University Press, Manchester, 2004

Rhoades, M.K., 'Renegotiating French masculinity: Medicine and venereal disease during the Great War', French Historical Studies 29, no. 2, 2006, pp. 293–327

Schock, M., 'Healing the patient, serving the State: Medical ethics and the British medical profession in the Great War', PhD thesis, University of California, Berkeley, 2000

Sendziuk, P., Learning to Trust: Australian Responses to AIDS, UNSW Press, Sydney, 2003

Sheard, H., and R. Lee, Women to the Front: The Extraordinary Australian Women Doctors of the Great War, Ebury Press, Sydney, 2019

Sheffield, G., The Somme, Cassell, London, 2003

——'Finest hour? British forces on the Western Front in 1918: An overview', in 1918 Year of Victory: The End of the Great War and the Shaping of Victory, ed. A. Ekins, Exisle Publishing, Wollombi, NSW, 2010, pp. 54–68

——The Chief: Douglas Haig and the British Army, Aurum, London, 2011

——'Shaping British and Anzac soldiers' experience of Gallipoli: Environmental and medical factors, and the development of trench warfare', *British Journal for Military History* 4, no. 1, 2017 (retrieved 12 May 2019), bjmh.org.uk /index.php/bjmh/article/view/193

Small, M., *Simpson and Duffy*, Harcourt Brace Jovanovich, Sydney, 1989

Smart, J., 'Sex, the State and the "scarlet scourge": Gender, citizenship and venereal disease regulation in Australia during the Great War', *Women's History Review* 7, no. 1, 1998, pp. 5–36

Smith, F.B., 'Medical inspection of state schoolchildren in Australia, c. 1905–14', *Health and History* 10, no. 1, 2008, pp. 5–20

Stanley, P., *Bad Characters: Sex, Crime, Mutiny, Murder and the Australian Imperial Force*, Murdoch Books, Sydney, 2010

——*Simpson's Donkey: A Wartime Journey to Gallipoli and Beyond*, Murdoch Books, Sydney, 2011

Tisdale, J., 'Venereal disease and the policing of the amateur in Melbourne during World War I', *Lilith: A Feminist History Journal*, no. 9, 1996, pp. 33–54

Tyquin, M.B., *Gallipoli: The Medical War: The Australian Army Medical Services in the Dardanelles Campaign of 1915*, NSW University Press, Sydney, 1993

——'Sir William "Mo" Williams, KCMG, CB, KStJ, creator of Australia's army medical services – maligned or misunderstood?', *Journal of the Royal Australian Historical Society* 84, no. 1, 1998, pp. 68–81

——*Neville Howse: Australia's First Victoria Cross Winner*, Oxford University Press, Melbourne, 1999

——*Little by Little: A Centenary History of the Royal Australian Army Medical Corps*, Australian Military History Publications, Sydney, 2003

——'Doctors and nurses: Gender relations, jealousy, and maladministration in wartime', *Health and History* 13, no. 1, 2011, pp. 26–43. doi:10.5401/ healthhist.13.1.0026

——*Gallipoli: An Australian Medical Perspective*, Big Sky Publishing, Sydney, 2012

Uyar, M., *The Ottoman Defence against the Anzac Landing, 25 April 1915*, Big Sky Publishing, Sydney, 2015

Watson, J.S.K., 'Wars in the wards: The social construction of medical work in First World War Britain', *Journal of British Studies* 41, no. 4, 2002, pp. 484–510. doi:10.1086/341439

Wilson, G., *Dust Donkeys and Delusions: The Myth of Simpson and His Donkey Exposed*, Big Sky Publishing, Sydney, 2012

Wilson, T., *The Downfall of the Liberal Party 1914–1935*, Collins, London, 1966

Index